CW00742852

Nathaniel Hawthorne (July 4, 1804 – May 19, 1864) was an American novelist, dark romantic, and short story writer. His works often focus on history, morality, and religion. He was born in 1804 in Salem, Massachusetts, to Nathaniel Hathorne and the former Elizabeth Clarke Manning. His ancestors include John Hathorne, the only judge involved in the Salem witch trials who never repented of his actions. He entered Bowdoin College in 1821, was elected to Phi Beta Kappa in 1824, and graduated in 1825. He published his first work in 1828, the novel Fanshawe; he later tried to suppress it, feeling that it was not equal to the standard of his later work. He published several short stories in periodicals, which he collected in 1837 as Twice-Told Tales. The next year, he became engaged to Sophia Peabody. He worked at the Boston Custom House and joined Brook Farm, a transcendentalist community, before marrying Peabody in 1842. The couple moved to The Old Manse in Concord, Massachusetts, later moving to Salem, the Berkshires, then to The Wayside in Concord. (Source: Wikipedia)

Literary works:
Fanshawe (published anonymously, 1828)
The New Adam and Eve (1843)
The Scarlet Letter (1850)
The House of the Seven Gables (1851)
The Blithedale Romance (1852)
The Marble Faun: Or, The Romance of Monte Beni (1860)
The Dolliver Romance (1863) (unfinished)
Septimius Felton; or, the Elixir of Life (unfinished)
Doctor Grimshawe's Secret: A Romance (unfinished, 1882)
Twice-Told Tales (1837)
Grandfather's Chair (1840)
Mosses from an Old Manse (1846)
A Wonder-Book for Girls and Boys (1851)
Tanglewood Tales (1853)

SKETCHES AND STUDIES

NATHANIEL HAWTHORNE

PRINCE CLASSICS

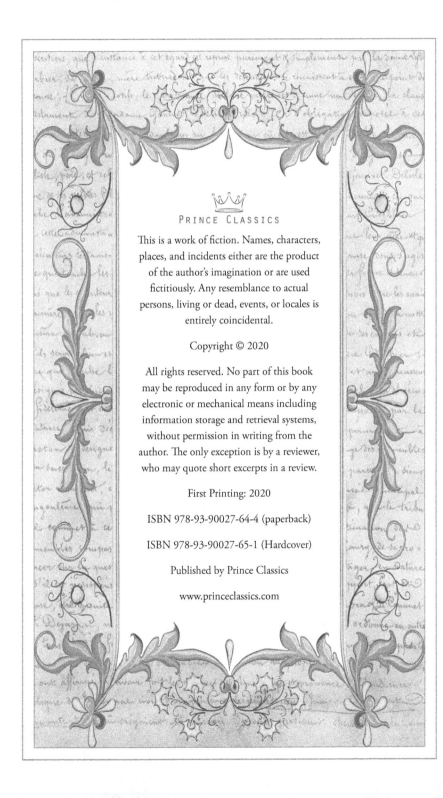

First Printing: 2020

ISBN 978-93-90027-64-4 (paperback)

ISBN 978-93-90027-65-1 (Hardcover)

Published by Prince Classics

www.princeclassics.com

Contents

SKETCHES AND STUDIES

LIFE OF FRANKLIN PIERCE.

PREFACE.

The author of this memoir—being so little of a politician that he scarcely feels entitled to call himself a member of any party—would not voluntarily have undertaken the work here offered to the public. Neither can he flatter himself that he has been remarkably successful in the performance of his task, viewing it in the light of a political biography, and as a representation of the principles and acts of a public man, intended to operate upon the minds of multitudes during a presidential canvass. This species of writing is too remote from his customary occupations—and, he may add, from his tastes— to be very satisfactorily done, without more time and practice than he would be willing to expend for such a purpose. If this little biography have any value, it is probably of another kind—as the narrative of one who knew the individual of whom he treats, at a period of life when character could be read with undoubting accuracy, and who, consequently, in judging of the motives of his subsequent conduct, has an advantage over much more competent observers, whose knowledge of the man may have commenced at a later date. Nor can it be considered improper (at least, the author will never feel it so, although some foolish delicacy be sacrificed in the undertaking) that when a friend, dear to him almost from boyish days, stands up before his country, misrepresented by indiscriminate abuse on the one hand, and by aimless praise on the other, he should be sketched by one who has had opportunities of knowing him well, and who is certainly inclined to tell the truth.

It is perhaps right to say, that while this biography is so far sanctioned by General Pierce, as it comprises a generally correct narrative of the principal events of his life, the author does not understand him as thereby necessarily indorsing all the sentiments put forth by himself in the progress of the work. These are the author's own speculations upon the facts before him, and may, or may not, be in accordance with the ideas of the individual whose life he writes. That individual's opinions, however,—so far as it is necessary to know them, —may be read, in his straightforward and consistent deeds, with more certainty than those of almost any other man now before the public.

The author, while collecting his materials, has received liberal aid from all manner of people—Whigs and Democrats, congressmen, astute lawyers, grim old generals of militia, and gallant young officers of the Mexican war—most of whom, however, he must needs say, have rather abounded in eulogy of General Pierce than in such anecdotical matter as is calculated for a biography. Among the gentlemen to whom he is substantially indebted, he would mention Hon. C. G. Atherton, Hon. S. H. Ayer, Hon. Joseph Hall, Chief Justice Gilchrist, Isaac O. Barnes, Esq., Col. T. J. Whipple, and Mr. C. J. Smith. He has likewise derived much assistance from an able and accurate sketch, that originally appeared in the "Boston Post," and was drawn up, as he believes, by the junior editor of that journal.

CONCORD, MASS., August 27, 1852.

CHAPTER I.

HIS PARENTAGE AND EARLY LIFE.

Franklin Pierce was born at Hillsborough, in the State of New Hampshire, on the 23d of November, 1804. His native county, at the period of his birth, covered a much more extensive territory than at present, and might reckon among its children many memorable men, and some illustrious ones. General Stark, the hero of Bennington, Daniel Webster, Levi Woodbury, Jeremiah Smith, the eminent jurist, and governor of the state, General James Miller, General McNeil, Senator Atherton, were natives of old Hillsborough County.

General Benjamin Pierce, the father of Franklin, was one of the earliest settlers in the town of Hillsborough, and contributed as much as any other man to the growth and prosperity of the county. He was born in 1757, at Chelmsford, now Lowell, in Massachusetts. Losing his parents early, he grew up under the care of an uncle, amid such circumstances of simple fare, hard labor, and scanty education, as usually fell to the lot of a New England yeoman's family some eighty or a hundred years ago. On the 19th of April, 1775, being then less than eighteen years of age, the stripling was at the plough, when tidings reached him of the bloodshed at Lexington and Concord. He immediately loosened the ox chain, left the plough in the furrow, took his uncle's gun and equipments, and set forth towards the scene of action. From that day, for more than seven years, he never saw his native place. He enlisted in the army, was present at the battle of Bunker Hill, and after serving through the whole Revolutionary War, and fighting his way upward from the lowest grade, returned, at last, a thorough soldier, and commander of a company. He was retained in the army as long as that body of veterans had a united existence; and, being finally disbanded, at West Point, in 1784, was left with no other reward, for nine years of toil and danger, than the nominal amount of his pay in the Continental currency—then so depreciated as to be almost worthless.

In 1780, being employed as agent to explore a tract of wild land, he purchased a lot of fifty acres in what is now the town of Hillsborough. In the spring of the succeeding year, he built himself a log hut, and began the clearing and cultivation of his tract. Another year beheld him married to his first wife, Elizabeth Andrews, who died within a twelvemonth after their union, leaving a daughter, the present widow of General John McNeil. In 1789, he married Anna Kendrick, with whom he lived about half a century, and who bore him eight children, of whom Franklin was the sixth.

Although the Revolutionary soldier had thus betaken himself to the wilderness for a subsistence, his professional merits were not forgotten by those who had witnessed his military career. As early as 1786, he was appointed brigade major of the militia of Hillsborough County, then first organized and formed into a brigade. And it was a still stronger testimonial to his character as a soldier, that, nearly fifteen years afterwards, during the presidency of John Adams, he was offered a high command in the northern division of the army which was proposed to be levied in anticipation of a war with the French republic. Inflexibly democratic in his political faith, however, Major Pierce refused to be implicated in a policy which he could not approve. "No, gentlemen," said he to the delegates who urged his acceptance of the commission, "poor as I am, and acceptable as would be the position under other circumstances, I would sooner go to yonder mountains, dig me a cave, and live on roast potatoes, than be instrumental in promoting the objects for which that army is to be raised!" This same fidelity to his principles marked every public, as well as private, action of his life.

In his own neighborhood, among those who knew him best he early gained an influence that was never lost nor diminished, but continued to spread wider during the whole of his long life. In 1789, he was elected to the state legislature and retained that position for thirteen successive years, until chosen a member of the council. During the same period he was active in his military duties, as a field officer, and finally general, of the militia of the county; and Miller, McNeil, and others learned of him, in this capacity, the soldier-like discipline which was afterwards displayed on the battle-fields of the northern frontier.

The history, character, and circumstances of General Benjamin Pierce, though here but briefly touched upon, are essential parts of the biography of his son, both as indicating some of the native traits which the latter has inherited, and as showing the influences amid which he grew up. At Franklin Pierce's birth, and for many years subsequent, his father was the most active and public-spirited man within his sphere; a most decided Democrat, and supporter of Jefferson and Madison; a practical farmer, moreover, not rich, but independent, exercising a liberal hospitality, and noted for the kindness and generosity of his character; a man of the people, but whose natural qualities inevitably made him a leader among them. From infancy upward, the boy had before his eyes, as the model on which he might instinctively form himself, one of the best specimens of sterling New England character, developed in a life of simple habits, yet of elevated action. Patriotism, such as it had been in Revolutionary days, was taught him by his father, as early as his mother taught him religion. He became early imbued, too, with the military spirit which the old soldier had retained from his long service, and which was kept active by the constant alarms and warlike preparations of the first twelve years of the present century. If any man is bound by birth and youthful training, to show himself a brave, faithful, and able citizen of his native country, it is the son of such a father.

At the commencement of the war of 1812, Franklin Pierce was a few months under eight years of age. The old general, his father, sent two of his sons into the army; and as his eldest daughter was soon afterwards married to Major McNeil, there were few families that had so large a personal stake in the war as that of General Benjamin Pierce. He himself, both in his public capacity as a member of the council, and by his great local influence in his own county, lent a strenuous support to the national administration. It is attributable to his sagacity and energy, that New Hampshire—then under a federal governor—was saved the disgrace of participation in the questionable, if not treasonable, projects of the Hartford Convention. He identified himself with the cause of the country, and was doubtless as thoroughly alive with patriotic zeal, at this eventful period, as in the old days of Bunker Hill, and Saratoga, and Yorktown. The general not only took a prominent part at all public meetings, but was ever ready for the informal discussion of political affairs at all places of casual resort, where—in accordance with the custom of the time and country—the minds of men were made to operate effectually upon each other. Franklin Pierce was a frequent auditor of these controversies. The intentness with which he watched the old general, and listened to his arguments, is still remembered; and, at this day, in his most earnest moods, there are gesticulations and movements that bring up the image of his father to those who recollect the latter on those occasions of the display of homely, native eloquence. No mode of education could be conceived, better adapted to imbue a youth with the principles and sentiment of democratic institutions; it brought him into the most familiar contact with the popular mind, and made his own mind a part of it.

Franklin's father had felt, through life, the disadvantages of a defective education; although, in his peculiar sphere of action, it might be doubted whether he did not gain more than he lost, by being thrown on his own resources, and compelled to study men and their actual affairs, rather than books. But he determined to afford his son all the opportunities of improvement which he himself had lacked. Franklin, accordingly, was early sent to the academy at Hancock, and afterwards to that of Francestown, where he was received into the family of General Pierce's old and steadfast friend, Peter Woodbury, father of the late eminent judge. It is scarcely more than a year ago, at the semi-centennial celebration of the academy, that Franklin Pierce, the mature and distinguished man, paid a beautiful tribute to the character of Madam Woodbury, in affectionate remembrance of the motherly kindness experienced at her hands by the school-boy.

The old people of his neighborhood give a very delightful picture of Franklin at this early age. They describe him as a beautiful boy, with blue eyes, light curling hair, and a sweet expression of face. The traits presented of him indicate moral symmetry, kindliness, and a delicate texture of sentiment, rather than marked prominences of character. His instructors testify to his propriety of conduct, his fellow-pupils to his sweetness of disposition and cordial sympathy. One of the latter, being older than most of his companions, and less advanced in his studies, found it difficult to keep up with his class; and he remembers how perseveringly, while the other boys were at play, Franklin spent the noon recess, for many weeks together, in aiding him in his lessons. These attributes, proper to a generous and affectionate nature, have remained with him through life. Lending their color to his deportment, and softening his manners, they are, perhaps, even now, the characteristics by which most of those who casually meet him would be inclined to identify the man. But there are other qualities, not then developed, but which have subsequently attained a firm and manly growth, and are recognized as his leading traits among those who really know him. Franklin Pierce's development, indeed, has always been the reverse of premature; the boy did not show the germ of all that was in the man, nor, perhaps, did the young man adequately foreshow the mature one.

In 1820, at the age of sixteen, he became a student of Bowdoin College, at Brunswick, Maine. It was in the autumn of the next year that the author of this memoir entered the class below him; but our college reminiscences, however interesting to the parties concerned, are not exactly the material for a biography. He was then a youth, with the boy and man in him, vivacious, mirthful, slender, of a fair complexion, with light hair that had a curl in it: his bright and cheerful aspect made a kind of sunshine, both as regarded its radiance and its warmth; insomuch that no shyness of disposition, in his associates, could well resist its influence. We soon became acquainted, and were more especially drawn together as members of the same college society. There were two of these institutions, dividing the college between them, and typifying, respectively, and with singular accuracy of feature, the respectable conservative, and the progressive or democratic parties. Pierce's native tendencies inevitably drew him to the latter.

His chum was Zenas Caldwell, several years older than himself, a member of the Methodist persuasion, a pure-minded, studious, devoutly religious character; endowed thus early in life with the authority of a grave and sagacious turn of mind. The friendship between Pierce and him appeared to be mutually strong, and was of itself a pledge of correct deportment in the former. His chief friend, I think, was a classmate named Little, a young man of most estimable qualities and high intellectual promise; one of those fortunate characters whom an early death so canonizes in the remembrance of their companions, that the perfect fulfilment of a long life would scarcely give them a higher place. Jonathan Cilley, of my own class,—whose untimely fate is still mournfully remembered,—a person of very marked ability and great social influence, was another of Pierce's friends. All these have long been dead. There are others, still alive, who would meet Franklin Pierce, at this day, with as warm a pressure of the hand, and the same confidence in his kindly feelings as when they parted from him nearly thirty years ago.

Pierce's class was small, but composed of individuals seriously intent on the duties and studies of their college life. They were not boys, but, for the most part, well advanced towards maturity; and, having wrought out their own means of education, were little inclined to neglect the opportunities that had been won at so much cost. They knew the value of time, and had a sense of the responsibilities of their position. Their first scholar—the present Professor Stowe—has long since established his rank among the first scholars of the country. It could have been no easy task to hold successful rivalry with students so much in earnest as these were. During the earlier part of his college course it may be doubted whether Pierce was distinguished for scholarship. But, for the last two years, he appeared to grow more intent on the business in hand, and, without losing any of his vivacious qualities as a companion, was evidently resolved to gain an honorable elevation in his class. His habits of attention and obedience to college discipline were of the strictest character; he rose progressively in scholarship, and took a highly creditable degree. [See note at close of this Life.]

The first civil office, I imagine, which Franklin Pierce ever held was that of chairman of the standing committee of the Athenaean Society, of which, as above hinted, we were both members; and, having myself held a place on the committee, I can bear testimony to his having discharged not only his own share of the duties, but that of his colleagues. I remember, likewise, that the only military service of my life was as a private soldier in a college company, of which Pierce was one of the officers. He entered into this latter business, or pastime, with an earnestness with which I could not pretend to compete, and at which, perhaps, he would now be inclined to smile. His slender and youthful figure rises before my mind's eye, at this moment, with the air and step of a veteran of the school of Steuben; as well became the son of a revolutionary hero, who had probably drilled under the old baron's orders. Indeed, at this time, and for some years afterwards, Pierce's ambition seemed to be of a military cast. Until reflection had tempered his first predilections, and other varieties of success had rewarded his efforts, he would have preferred, I believe, the honors of the battle-field to any laurels more peacefully won. And it was remarkable how, with all the invariable gentleness of his demeanor, he perfectly gave, nevertheless, the impression of a high and fearless spirit. His friends were as sure of his courage, while yet untried, as now, when it has been displayed so brilliantly in famous battles.

At this early period of his life, he was distinguished by the same fascination of manner that has since proved so magical in winning him an unbounded personal popularity. It is wronging him, however, to call this peculiarity a mere effect of manner; its source lies deep in the kindliness of his nature, and in the liberal, generous, catholic sympathy, that embraces all who are worthy of it. Few men possess any thing like it; so irresistible as it is, so sure to draw forth an undoubting confidence, and so true to the promise which it gives. This frankness, this democracy of good feeling, has not been chilled by the society of politicians, nor polished down into mere courtesy by his intercourse with the most refined men of the day. It belongs to him at this moment, and will never leave him. A little while ago, after his return from Mexico, he darted across the street to exchange a hearty gripe of the hand with a rough countryman upon his cart—a man who used to "live with his father," as the general explained the matter to his companions. Other men assume this manner, more or less skilfully; but with Frank Pierce it is an innate characteristic; nor will it ever lose its charm, unless his heart should grow narrower and colder—a misfortune not to be anticipated, even in the dangerous atmosphere of elevated rank, whither he seems destined to ascend.

There is little else that it is worth while to relate as regards his college course, unless it be that, during one of his winter vacations, Pierce taught a country school. So many of the statesmen of New England have performed their first public service in the character of pedagogue, that it seems almost a necessary step on the ladder of advancement.

CHAPTER II.

HIS SERVICES IN THE STATE AND NATIONAL LEGISLATURES.

After leaving college, in the year 1824, Franklin Pierce returned to Hillsborough. His father, now in a green old age, continued to take a prominent part in the affairs of the day, but likewise made his declining years rich and picturesque with recollections of the heroic times through which he had lived. On the 26th of December, 1825, it being his sixty-seventh birthday, General Benjamin Pierce prepared a festival for his comrades in arms, the survivors of the Revolution, eighteen of whom, all inhabitants of Hillsborough, assembled at his house. The ages of these veterans ranged from fifty-nine up to the patriarchal venerableness of nearly ninety. They spent the day in festivity, in calling up reminiscences of the great men whom they had known and the great deeds which they had helped to do, and in reviving the old sentiments of the era of 'seventy-six. At nightfall, after a manly and pathetic farewell from their host, they separated—"prepared," as the old general expressed it, "at the first tap of the shrouded drum, to move and join their beloved Washington, and the rest of their beloved comrades, who fought and bled at their sides." A scene like this must have been profitable for a young man to witness, as being likely to give him a stronger sense than most of us can attain of the value of that Union which these old heroes had risked so much to consolidate—of that common country which they had sacrificed everything to create; and patriotism must have been communicated from their hearts to his, with somewhat of the warmth and freshness of a new-born sentiment. No youth was ever more fortunate than Franklin Pierce, through the whole of his early life, in this most desirable species of moral education.

Having chosen the law as a profession, Franklin became a student in the office of Judge Woodbury, of Portsmouth. Allusion has already been made to the friendship between General Benjamin Pierce and Peter Woodbury, the father of the judge. The early progress of Levi Woodbury towards eminence had been facilitated by the powerful influence of his father's friend. It was a worthy and honorable kind of patronage, and bestowed only as the great abilities of the recipient vindicated his claim to it. Few young men have met with such early success in life, or have deserved it so eminently, as did Judge

18

Woodbury. At the age of twenty-seven, he was appointed to the bench of the Supreme Court of the state, on the earnest recommendation of old General Pierce. The opponents of the measure ridiculed him as the "baby judge;" but his conduct in that high office showed the prescient judgment of the friend who had known him from a child, and had seen in his young manhood already the wisdom of ripened age. It was some years afterwards when Franklin Pierce entered the office of Judge Woodbury as a student. In the interval, the judge had been elected governor, and, after a term of office that thoroughly tested the integrity of his democratic principles, had lost his second election, and returned to the profession of the law.

The last two years of Pierce's preparatory studies were spent at the law school of Northampton, in Massachusetts, and in the office of Judge Parker at Amherst. In 1827, being admitted to the bar, he began the practice of his profession at Hillsborough. It is an interesting fact, considered in reference to his subsequent splendid career as an advocate, that he did not, at the outset, give promise of distinguished success. His first case was a failure, and perhaps a somewhat marked one. But it is remembered that this defeat, however mortifying at the moment, did but serve to make him aware of the latent resources of his mind, the full command of which he was far from having yet attained. To a friend, an older practitioner, who addressed him with some expression of condolence and encouragement, Pierce replied,—and it was a kind of self-assertion which no triumph would have drawn oat,—"I do not need that. I will try nine hundred and ninety-nine cases, if clients will continue to trust me, and, if I fail just as I have today, will try the thousandth. I shall live to argue cases in this court house in a manner that will mortify neither myself nor my friends." It is in such moments of defeat that character and ability are mot fairly tested; they would irremediably crush a youth devoid of real energy, and, being neither more nor less than his just desert, would be accepted as such. But a failure of this kind serves an opposite purpose to a mind in which the strongest and richest qualities lie deep, and, from their very size and mass, cannot at once be rendered available. It provokes an innate self-confidence, while, at the same time, it sternly indicates the sedulous cultivation, the earnest effort, the toil, the agony, which are the conditions of ultimate success. It is, indeed, one of the best modes of discipline that experience can administer, and may reasonably be counted a fortunate event in the life of a young man vigorous enough to overcome the momentary depression.

Pierce's distinction at the bar, however, did not immediately follow; nor did he acquire what we may designate as positive eminence until some years after this period. The enticements of political life—so especially fascinating to a young lawyer, but so irregular in its tendencies, and so inimical to steady professional labor—had begun to operate upon him. His father's prominent position in the politics of the state made it almost impossible that the son should stand aloof. In 1827, the same year when Franklin began the practice of the law, General Benjamin Pierce had been elected governor of New Hampshire. He was defeated in the election of 1828, but was again successful in that of the subsequent year. During these years, the contest for the presidency had been fought with a fervor that drew almost everybody into it, on one side or the other, and had terminated in the triumph of Andrew Jackson. Franklin Pierce, in advance of his father's decision, though not in opposition to it, had declared himself for the illustrious man whose military renown was destined to be thrown into the shade by a civil administration, the most splendid and powerful that ever adorned the annals of our country, I love to record of the subject of this memoir that his first political faith was pledged to that great leader of the democracy.

I remember meeting Pierce about this period, and catching from him some faint reflection of the zeal with which he was now stepping into the political arena. My sympathies and opinions, it is true,—so far as I had any in public affairs,—had, from the first, been enlisted on the same side with his own. But I was now made strongly sensible of an increased development of my friend's mind, by means of which he possessed a vastly greater power than heretofore over the minds with which he came in contact. This progressive growth has continued to be one of his remarkable characteristics. Of most men you early know the mental gauge and measurement, and do not subsequently have much occasion to change it. Not so with Pierce: his tendency was not merely high, but towards a point which rose higher and higher as the aspirant tended upward. Since we parted, studious days had educated him; life, too, and his own exertions in it, and his native habit of close and accurate observation, had likewise begun to educate him.

The town of Hillsborough, in 1829, gave Franklin Pierce his first public honor, by electing him its representative in the legislature of the state. His whole service in that body comprised four years, in the two latter of which he was elected Speaker by a vote of one hundred and fifty-five against fifty-eight for other candidates. This overpowering majority evinced the confidence which his character inspired, and which, during his whole career, it has invariably commanded, in advance of what might be termed positive proof, although the result has never failed to justify it. I still recollect his description of the feelings with which he entered on his arduous duties—the feverish night that preceded his taking the chair—the doubt, the struggle with himself—all ending in perfect calmness, full self-possession, and free power of action when the crisis actually came.

He had all the natural gifts that adapted him for the post; courtesy, firmness, quickness and accuracy of judgment, and a clearness of mental perception that brought its own regularity into the scene of confused and entangled debate; and to these qualities he added whatever was to be attained by laborious study of parliamentary rules. His merit as a presiding officer was universally acknowledged. It is rare that a man combines so much impulse with so great a power of regulating the impulses of himself and others as Franklin Pierce. The faculty, here exercised and improved, of controlling an assembly while agitated by tumultuous controversy, was afterwards called into play upon a higher field; for, during his congressional service, Pierce was often summoned to preside in committee of the whole, when a turbulent debate was expected to demand peculiar energy in the chair.

He was elected a member of Congress in 1833, being young for the station, as he has always been for every public station that he has filled. A different kind of man—a man conscious that accident alone had elevated him, and therefore nervously anxious to prove himself equal to his fortunes—would thus have been impelled to spasmodic efforts. He would have thrust himself forward in debate, taking the word out of the mouths of renowned orators, and thereby winning notoriety, as at least the glittering counterfeit of true celebrity. Had Pierce, with his genuine ability, practised this course; had he possessed even an ordinary love of display, and had he acted upon it with his inherent tact and skill, taking advantage of fair occasions to prove the power and substance that were in him, it would greatly have facilitated the task of his biographer.

To aim at personal distinction, however, as an object independent of the public service, would have been contrary to all the foregone and subsequent manifestations of his life. He was never wanting to the occasion; but he waited for the occasion to bring him inevitably forward. When he spoke, it was not only because he was fully master of the subject, but because the exigency demanded him, and because no other and older man could perform the same duty as well as himself. Of the copious eloquence—and some of it, no doubt, of a high order—which Buncombe has called forth, not a paragraph, nor a period, is attributable to Franklin Pierce. He had no need of these devices to fortify his constituents in their high opinion of him; nor did he fail to perceive that such was not the method to acquire real weight in the body of which he was a member. In truth, he has no fluency of words, except when an earnest meaning and purpose supply their own expression. Every one of his speeches in Congress, and, we may say, in every other hall of oratory, or on any stump that he may have mounted, was drawn forth by the perception that it was needed, was directed to a full exposition of the subject, and (rarest of all) was limited by what he really had to say. Even the graces of the orator were never elaborated, never assumed for their own sake, but were legitimately derived from the force of his conceptions, and from the impulsive warmth which accompanies the glow of thought. Owing to these peculiarities,—for such, unfortunately, they may be termed, in reference to what are usually the characteristics of a legislative career,—his position before the country was less conspicuous than that of many men who could claim nothing like Pierce's actual influence in the national councils. His speeches, in their muscular texture and close grasp of their subject, resembled the brief but pregnant arguments and expositions of the sages of the Continental Congress, rather than the immeasurable harangues which are now the order of the day.

22

His congressional life, though it made comparatively so little show, was full of labor, directed to substantial objects. He was a member of the judiciary and other important committees; and the drudgery of the committee room, where so much of the real public business of the country is transacted, fell in large measure to his lot. Thus, even as a legislator, he may be said to have been a man of deeds, not words; and when he spoke upon any subject with which his duty, as chairman or member of a committee, had brought him in relation, his words had the weight of deeds, from the meaning, the directness, and the truth, that he conveyed into them. His merits made themselves known and felt in the sphere where they were exercised; and he was early appreciated by one who seldom erred in his estimate of men, whether in their moral or intellectual aspect. His intercourse with President Jackson was frequent and free, and marked by friendly regard on the part of the latter. In the stormiest periods of his administration, Pierce came frankly to his aid. The confidence then established was never lost; and when Jackson was on his death-bed, being visited by a gentleman from the North (himself formerly a democratic member of Congress), the old hero spoke with energy of Franklin Pierce's ability and patriotism, and remarked, as with prophetic foresight of his young friend's destiny, that "the interests of the country would be safe in such hands."

One of President Jackson's measures, which had Pierce's approval and support, was his veto of the Maysville Road Bill. This bill was part of a system of vast public works, principally railroads and canals, which it was proposed to undertake at the expense of the national treasury—a policy not then of recent origin, but which had been fostered by John Quincy Adams, and had attained a gigantic growth at the close of his Presidency. The estimate of works undertaken or projected, at the commencement of Jackson's administration, amounted to considerably more than a hundred millions of dollars. The expenditure of this enormous sum, and doubtless other incalculable amounts, in progressive increase, was to be for purposes often of unascertained utility, and was to pass through the agents and officers of the federal government—a means of political corruption not safely to be trusted even in the purest hands. The peril to the individuality of the states, from a system tending so directly to consolidate the powers of government towards a common centre, was obvious. The result might have been, with the lapse of time and the increased activity of the disease, to place the capital of our federative Union in a position resembling that of imperial Rome, where each once independent state was a subject province, and all the highways of the world were said to meet in her forum. It was against this system, so dangerous to liberty and to public and private integrity, that Jackson declared war, by the famous Maysville veto.

It would be an absurd interpretation of Pierce's course, in regard to this and similar measures, to suppose him hostile either to internal or coastwise improvements, so far as they may legitimately be the business of the general government. He was aware of the immense importance of our internal commerce, and was ever ready to vote such appropriations as might be necessary for promoting it, when asked for in an honest spirit, and at points where they were really needed. He doubted, indeed, the constitutional power of Congress to undertake, by building roads through the wilderness, or opening unfrequented rivers, to create commerce where it did not yet exist; but he never denied or questioned the right and duty to remove obstructions in the way of inland trade, and to afford it every facility, when the nature and necessity of things had brought it into genuine existence. And he agreed with the best and wisest statesmen in believing that this distinction involved the true principle on which legislation, for the purpose here discussed, should proceed.

While a member of the House of Representatives, he delivered a forcible speech against the bill authorizing appropriations for the Military Academy at West Point. He was decidedly opposed to that institution as then, and at present organized. We allude to the subject in illustration of the generous frankness with which, years afterwards, when the battle smoke of Mexico had baptized him also a soldier, he acknowledged himself in the wrong, and bore testimony to the brilliant services which the graduates of the Academy, trained to soldiership from boyhood, had rendered to their country. And if he has made no other such acknowledgment of past error, committed in his legislative capacity, it is but fair to believe that it is because his reason and conscience accuse him of no other wrong.

It was while in the lower house of Congress that Franklin Pierce took that stand on the slavery question from which he has never since swerved a hair's breadth. He fully recognized, by his votes and by his voice, the rights pledged to the South by the Constitution. This, at the period when he so declared himself, was comparatively an easy thing to do. But when it became more difficult, when the first imperceptible movement of agitation had grown to be almost a convulsion, his course was still the same. Nor did he ever shun the obloquy that sometimes threatened to pursue the northern man who dared to love that great and sacred reality— his whole, united, native country—better than the mistiness of a philanthropic theory.

He continued in the House of Representatives four years. If, at this period of his life, he rendered unobtrusive, though not unimportant, services to the public, it must also have been a time of vast intellectual advantage to himself. Amidst great national affairs, he was acquiring the best of all educations for future eminence and leadership. In the midst of statesmen, he grew to be a statesman. Studious, as all his speeches prove him to be, of history, he beheld it demonstrating itself before his eyes. As regards this sort of training, much of its good or ill effect depends on the natural force and depth of the man. Many, no doubt, by early mixture with politics, become the mere politicians of the moment,—a class of men sufficiently abundant among us,—acquiring only a knack and cunning, which guide them tolerably well through immediate difficulties, without instructing them in the great rules of higher policy. But when the actual observation of public measures goes hand in hand with study, when the mind is capable of comparing the present with its analogies in the past, and of grasping the principle that belongs to both, this is to have history for a living tutor. If the student be fit for such instruction, he will be seen to act afterwards with the elevation of a high ideal, and with the expediency, the sagacity, the instinct of what is fit and practicable, which make the advantage of the man of actual affairs over the mere theorist.

And it was another advantage of his being brought early into the sphere of national interests, and continuing there for a series of years, that it enabled him to overcome any narrow and sectional prejudices. Without loving New England less, he loved the broad area of the country more. He thus retained that equal sentiment of patriotism for the whole land with which his father had imbued him, and which is perhaps apt to be impaired in the hearts of those who come late to the national legislature, after long training in the narrower fields of the separate states. His sense of the value of the Union, which had been taught him at the fireside, from earliest infancy, by the stories of patriotic valor that he there heard, was now strengthened by friendly association with its representatives from every quarter. It is this youthful sentiment of Americanism, so happily developed by after circumstances, that we see operating through all his public life, and making him as tender of what he considers due to the South as of the rights of his own land of hills.

Franklin Pierce had scarcely reached the legal age for such elevation, when, in 1837, he was elected to the Senate of the United States. He took his seat at the commencement of the presidency of Mr. Van Buren. Never before nor since has the Senate been more venerable for the array of veteran and celebrated statesmen than at that time. Calhoun, Webster, and Clay had lost nothing of their intellectual might. Benton, Silas Wright, Woodbury, Buchanan, and Walker were members; and many even of the less eminent names were such as have gained historic place—men of powerful eloquence, and worthy to be leaders of the respective parties which they espoused. To this dignified body (composed of individuals some of whom were older in political experience than he in his mortal life) Pierce came as the youngest member of the Senate. With his usual tact and exquisite sense of propriety, he saw that it was not the time for him to step forward prominently on this highest theatre in the land. He beheld these great combatants doing battle before the eyes of the nation, and engrossing its whole regards. There was hardly an avenue to reputation save what was occupied by one or another of those gigantic figures.

Modes of public service remained, however, requiring high ability, but with which few men of competent endowments would have been content to occupy themselves. Pierce had already demonstrated the possibility of obtaining an enviable position among his associates, without the windy notoriety which a member of Congress may readily manufacture for himself by the lavish expenditure of breath that had been better spared. In the more elevated field of the Senate, he pursued the same course as while a representative, and with more than equal results.

Among other committees, he was a member of that upon revolutionary pensions. Of this subject he made himself thoroughly master, and was recognized by the Senate as an unquestionable authority. In 1840, in reference to several bills for the relief of claimants under the pension law, he delivered a speech which finely illustrates as well the sympathies as the justice of the man, showing how vividly he could feel, and, at the same time, how powerless were his feelings to turn him aside from the strict line of public integrity. The merits and sacrifices of the people of the Revolution have never been stated with more earnest gratitude than in the following passage:—

"I am not insensible, Mr. President, of the advantages with which claims of this character always come before Congress. They are supposed to be based on services for which no man entertains a higher estimate than myself—services beyond all praise, and above all price. But, while warm and glowing with the glorious recollections which a recurrence to that period of our history can never fail to awaken; while we cherish with emotions of pride, reverence, and affection the memory of those brave men who are no longer with us; while we provide, with a liberal hand, for such as survive, and for the widows of the deceased; while we would accord to the heirs, whether in the second or third generation, every dollar to which they can establish a just claim,—I trust we shall not, in the strong current of our sympathies, forget what becomes us as the descendants of such men. They would teach us to legislate upon our judgment, upon our sober sense of right, and not upon our impulses or our sympathies. No, sir; we may act in this way, if we choose, when dispensing our own means, but we are not at liberty to do it when dispensing the means of our constituents.

"If we were to legislate upon our sympathies—yet more I will admit—if we were to yield to that sense of just and grateful remuneration which presses itself upon every man's heart, there would be scarcely a limit for our bounty. The whole exchequer could not answer the demand. To the patriotism, the courage, and the sacrifices of the people of that day, we owe, under Providence, all that we now most highly prize, and what we shall transmit to our children as the richest legacy they can inherit. The War of the Revolution, it has been justly remarked, was not a war of armies merely—it was the war of nearly a whole people, and such a people as the world had never before seen, in a death struggle for liberty.

"The losses, sacrifices, and sufferings of that period were common to all classes and conditions of life. Those who remained at home suffered hardly less than those who entered upon the active strife. The aged father and another underwent not less than the son, who would have been the comfort and stay of their declining years, now called to perform a yet higher duty—to follow the standard of his bleeding country. The young mother, with her helpless children, excites not less deeply our sympathies, contending with want, and dragging out years of weary and toilsome days and anxious nights, than the husband in the field, following the fortunes of our arms without the proper habiliments to protect his person, or the requisite sustenance to support his strength. Sir, I never think of that patient, enduring, self-sacrificing army, which crossed the Delaware in December, 1777, marching barefooted upon frozen ground to encounter the foe, and leaving bloody footprints for miles behind then—I never think of their sufferings during that terrible winter without involuntarily inquiring, Where then were their families? Who lit up the cheerful fire upon their hearths at home? Who spoke the word of comfort and encouragement? Nay, sir, who furnished protection from the rigors of winter, and brought them the necessary means of subsistence?'

"The true and simple answer to these questions would disclose an amount of suffering and anguish, mental and physical, such as might not have been found in the ranks of the armies—not even in the severest trial of that fortitude which never faltered, and that power of endurance which seemed to know no limit. All this no man feels more deeply than I do. But they were common sacrifices in a common cause, ultimately crowned with the reward of liberty. They have an everlasting claim upon our gratitude, and are destined, as I trust, by their heroic example, to exert an abiding influence upon our latest posterity."

With this heartfelt recognition of the debt of gratitude due to those excellent men, the senator enters into an analysis of the claims presented, and proves them to be void of justice. The whole speech is a good exponent of his character; full of the truest sympathy, but, above all things, just, and not to be misled, on the public behalf, by those impulses that would be most apt to sway the private man. The mere pecuniary amount saved to the nation by his scrutiny into affairs of this kind, though great, was, after all, but a minor consideration. The danger lay in establishing a corrupt system, and placing a wrong precedent upon the statute book. Instances might be adduced, on the other hand, which show him not less scrupulous of the just rights of the claimants than careful of the public interests.

Another subject upon which he came forward was the military establishment and the natural defences of the country. In looking through the columns of the "Congressional Globe," we find abundant evidences of Senator Pierce's laborious and unostentatious discharge of his duties— reports of committees, brief remarks, and, here and there, a longer speech, always full of matter, and evincing a thoroughly-digested knowledge of the subject. Not having been written out by himself, however, these speeches are no fair specimens of his oratory, except as regards the train of argument and substantial thought; and adhering very closely to the business in hand, they seldom present passages that could be quoted, without tearing them forcibly, as it were, out of the context, and thus mangling the fragments which we might offer to the reader. As we have already remarked, he seems, as a debater, to revive the old type of the Revolutionary Congress, or to bring back the noble days of the Long Parliament of England, before eloquence had become what it is now, a knack, and a thing valued for itself. Like those strenuous orators, he speaks with the earnestness of honest conviction, and out of the fervor of his heart, and because the occasion and his deep sense of it constrain him.

By the defeat of Mr. Van Buren, in the presidential election of 1840, the administration of government was transferred, for the first time in twelve years, to the Whigs. An extra session of Congress was summoned to assemble in June, 1841, by President Harrison, who, however, died before it came together. At this extra session, it was the purpose of the whig party, under the leadership of Henry Clay, to overthrow all the great measures which the successive democratic administrations had established. The sub-treasury was to be demolished; a national bank was to be incorporated; a high tariff of duties was to be imposed, for purposes of protection and abundant revenue. The whig administration possessed a majority, both in the Senate and the House. It was a dark period for the Democracy, so long unaccustomed to defeat, and now beholding all that they had won for the cause of national progress, after the arduous struggle of so many years, apparently about to be swept away.

The sterling influence which Franklin Pierce now exercised is well described in the following remarks of the Hon. A. O. P. Nicholson:—

"The power of an organized minority was never more clearly exhibited than in this contest. The democratic senators acted in strict concert, meeting night after night for consultation, arranging their plan of battle, selecting their champions for the coming day, assigning to each man his proper duty, and looking carefully to the popular judgment for a final victory. In these consultations, no man's voice was heard with more profound respect than that of Franklin Pierce. His counsels were characterized by so thorough a knowledge of human nature, by so much solid common sense, by such devotion to democratic principles, that, although among the youngest of the senators, it was deemed important that all their conclusions should be submitted to his sanction.

"Although known to be ardent in his temperament, he was also known to act with prudence and caution. His impetuosity in debate was only the result of the deep convictions which controlled his mind. He enjoyed the unbounded confidence of Calhoun, Buchanan, Wright, Woodbury, Walker, King, Benton, and indeed of the entire democratic portion of the Senate. When he rose in the Senate or in the committee room, he was heard with the profoundest attention; and again and again was he greeted by these veteran Democrats as one of our ablest champions. His speeches, during this session, will compare with those of any other senator. If it be asked why he did not receive higher distinction, I answer, that such men as Calhoun, Wright, Buchanan, and Woodbury were the acknowledged leaders of the Democracy. The eyes of the nation were on them. The hopes of their party were reposed in them. The brightness of these luminaries was too great to allow the brilliancy of so young a man to attract especial attention. But ask any one of these veterans how Franklin Pierce ranked in the Senate, and he will tell you, that, to stand in the front rank for talents, eloquence, and statesmanship, he only lacked a few more years."

In the course of this session he made a very powerful speech in favor of Mr. Buchanan's resolution, calling on the President to furnish the names of persons removed from office since the 4th of March, 1841. The Whigs, in 1840, as in the subsequent canvass of 1848, had professed a purpose to abolish the system of official removals on account of political opinion, but, immediately on coming into power, had commenced a proscription infinitely beyond the example of the democratic party. This course, with an army of office-seekers besieging the departments, was unquestionably difficult to avoid, and perhaps, on the whole, not desirable to be avoided. But it was rendered astounding by the sturdy effrontery with which the gentlemen in power denied that their present practice had falsified any of their past professions. A few of the closing paragraphs of Senator Pierce's highly effective speech, being more easily separable than the rest, may here be cited.

"One word more, and I leave this subject,—a painful one to me, from the beginning to the end. The senator from North Carolina, in the course of his remarks the other day, asked, 'Do gentlemen expect that their friends are to be retained in office against the will of the nation? Are they so unreasonable as to expect what the circumstances and the necessity of the case forbid?' What our expectations were is not the question now; but what were your pledges and promises before the people. On a previous occasion, the distinguished senator from Kentucky made a similar remark: 'An ungracious task, but the nation demands it!' Sir, this demand of the nation,—this plea of STATE NECESSITY,—let me tell you, gentlemen, is as old as the history of wrong and oppression. It has been the standing plea, the never-failing resort of despotism.

"The great Julius found it a convenient plea when he restored the dignity of the Roman Senate, but destroyed its independence. It gave countenance to and justified all the atrocities of the Inquisition in Spain. It forced out the stifled groans that issued from the Black Hole of Calcutta. It was written in tears upon the Bridge of Sighs in Venice, and pointed to those dark recesses upon whose gloomy thresholds there was never seen a returning footprint.

"It was the plea of the austere and ambitious Strafford, in the days of Charles I. It filled the Bastile of France, and lent its sanction to the terrible atrocities perpetrated there. It was this plea that snatched the mild, eloquent, and patriotic Camillo Desmoulins from his young and beautiful wife, and hurried him to the guillotine with thousands of others equally unoffending and innocent. It was upon this plea that the greatest of generals, if not men,—you cannot mistake me,—I mean him, the presence of whose very ashes within the last few months sufficed to stir the hearts of a continent,— it was upon this plea that he abjured the noble wife who had thrown light and gladness around his humbler days, and, by her own lofty energies and high intellect, had encouraged his aspirations. It was upon this plea that he committed that worst and most fatal acts of his eventful life. Upon this, too, he drew around his person the imperial purple. It has in all times, and in every age, been the foe of liberty and the indispensable stay of usurpation.

"Where were the chains of despotism ever thrown around the freedom of speech and of the press but on this plea of STATE NECESSITY? Let the spirit of Charles X. and of his ministers answer.

"It is cold, selfish, heartless, and has always been regardless of age, sex, condition, services, or any of the incidents of life that appeal to patriotism or humanity. Wherever its authority has been acknowledged, it has assailed men who stood by their country when she needed strong arms and bold hearts, and has assailed them when, maimed and disabled in her service, they could no longer brandish a weapon in her defence. It has afflicted the feeble and dependent wife for the imaginary faults of the husband. It has stricken down Innocence in its beauty, Youth in its freshness, Manhood in its vigor, and Age in its feebleness and decrepitude. Whatever other plea or apology may be set up for the sweeping, ruthless exercise of this civil guillotine at the present day, in the name of LIBERTY let us be spared this fearful one of STATE NECESSITY, in this early age of the Republic, upon the floor of the American Senate, in the face of a people yet free!"

In June, 1842, he signified his purpose of retiring from the Senate.

It was now more than sixteen years since the author of this sketch had been accustomed to meet Frank Pierce (that familiar name, which the nation is adopting as one of its household words) in habits of daily intercourse. Our modes of life had since been as different as could well be imagined; our culture and labor were entirely unlike; there was hardly a single object or aspiration in common between us. Still we had occasionally met, and always on the old ground of friendly confidence. There were sympathies that had not been suffered to die out. Had we lived more constantly together, it is not impossible that the relation might have been changed by the various accidents and attritions of life; but having no mutual events, and few mutual interests, the tie of early friendship remained the same as when we parted. The modifications which I saw in his character were those of growth and development; new qualities came out, or displayed themselves more prominently, but always in harmony with those heretofore known. Always I was sensible of progress in him; a characteristic—as, I believe, has been said in the foregoing pages—more perceptible in Franklin Pierce than in any other person with whom I have been acquainted. He widened, deepened, rose to a higher point, and thus ever made himself equal to the ever-heightening occasion. This peculiarity of intellectual growth, continued beyond the ordinary period, has its analogy in his physical constitution—it being a fact that he continued to grow in stature between his twenty-first and twenty-fifth years.

He had not met with that misfortune, which, it is to be feared, befalls many men who throw their ardor into politics. The pursuit had taken nothing from the frankness of his nature; now, as ever, he used direct means to gain honorable ends; and his subtlety—for, after all, his heart and purpose were not such as he that runs may read—had the depth of wisdom, and never any quality of cunning. In great part, this undeteriorated manhood was due to his original nobility of nature. Yet it may not be unjust to attribute it, in some degree, to the singular good fortune of his life. He had never, in all his career, found it necessary to stoop. Office had sought him; he had not begged it, nor manoeuvred for it, nor crept towards it—arts which too frequently bring a man, morally bowed and degraded, to a position which should be one of dignity, but in which he will vainly essay to stand upright.

In our earlier meetings, after Pierce had begun to come forward in public life, I could discern that his ambition was aroused. He felt a young man's enjoyment of success, so early and so distinguished. But as years went on, such motives seemed to be less influential with him. He was cured of ambition, as, one after another, its objects came to him unsought. His domestic position, likewise, had contributed to direct his tastes and wishes towards the pursuits of private life. In 1834 he had married Jane Means, a daughter of the Rev. Dr. Appleton, a former president of Bowdoin College. Three sons, the first of whom died in early infancy, were born to him; and, having hitherto been kept poor by his public service, he no doubt became sensible of the expediency of making some provision for the future. Such, it may be presumed, were the considerations that induced his resignation of the senatorship, greatly to the regret of all parties. The senators gathered around him as he was about to quit the chamber; political opponents took leave of him as of a personal friend; and no departing member has ever retired from that dignified body amid warmer wishes for his happiness than those that attended Franklin Pierce.

His father had died three years before, in 1839, at the mansion which he built, after the original log-cabin grew too narrow for his rising family and fortunes. The mansion was spacious, as the liberal hospitality of the occupant required, and stood on a little eminence, surrounded by verdure and abundance, and a happy population, where, half a century before, the revolutionary soldier had come alone into the wilderness, and levelled the primeval forest trees. After being spared to behold the distinction of his son, he departed this life at the age of eighty-one years, in perfect peace, and, until within a few hours of his death, in the full possession of his intellectual powers. His last act was one of charity to a poor neighbor—a fitting close to a life that had abounded in such deeds. Governor Pierce was a man of admirable qualities—brave, active, public-spirited, endowed with natural authority, courteous yet simple in his manners; and in his son we may perceive these same attributes, modified and softened by a finer texture of character, illuminated by higher intellectual culture, and polished by a larger intercourse with the world, but as substantial and sterling as in the good old patriot.

34

Franklin Pierce had removed from Hillsborough in 1838, and taken up his residence at Concord, the capital of New Hampshire. On this occasion, the citizens of his native town invited him to a public dinner, in token of their affection and respect. In accordance with his usual taste, he gratefully accepted the kindly sentiment, but declined the public demonstration of it.

CHAPTER III.

HIS SUCCESS AT THE BAR.

Franklin Pierce's earliest effort at the bar, as we have already observed, was an unsuccessful one; but instead of discouraging him, the failure had only served to awaken the consciousness of latent power, and the resolution to bring it out. Since those days, he had indeed gained reputation as a lawyer. So much, however, was the tenor of his legal life broken up by the months of public service subtracted from each year, and such was the inevitable tendency of his thoughts towards political subjects, that he could but very partially avail himself of the opportunities of professional advancement. But on retiring from the Senate he appears to have started immediately into full practice. Though the people of New Hampshire already knew him well, yet his brilliant achievements as an advocate brought him more into their view, and into closer relations with them, than he had ever before been. He now met his countrymen, as represented in the jury box, face to face, and made them feel what manner of man he was. Their sentiment towards him soon grew to be nothing short of enthusiasm; love, pride, the sense of brotherhood, affectionate sympathy, and perfect trust, all mingled in it. It was the influence of a great heart pervading the general heart, and throbbing with it in the same pulsation.

It has never been the writer's good fortune to listen to one of Franklin Pierce's public speeches, whether at the bar or elsewhere; nor, by diligent inquiry, has he been able to gain a very definite idea of the mode in which he produces his effects. To me, therefore, his forensic displays are in the same category with those of Patrick Henry, or any other orator whose tongue, beyond the memory of man, has moulded into dust. His power results, no doubt, in great measure, from the earnestness with which he imbues himself with the conception of his client's cause; insomuch that he makes it entirely his own, and, never undertaking a case which he believes to be unjust, contends with his whole heart and conscience, as well as intellectual force, for victory. His labor in the preparation of his cases is said to be unremitting; and he throws himself with such energy into a trial of importance as wholly to exhaust his strength.

Few lawyers, probably, have been interested in a wider variety of business than he; its scope comprehends the great causes where immense pecuniary interests are concerned—from which, however, he is always ready to turn aside, to defend the humble rights of the poor man, or give his protection to one unjustly accused. As one of my correspondents observes, "When an applicant has interested him by a recital of fraud or wrong, General Pierce never investigates the man's estate before engaging in his business; neither does he calculate whose path he may cross. I have been privy to several instances of the noblest independence on his part, in pursuing, to the disrepute of those who stood well in the community, the weal of an obscure client with a good cause."

In the practice of the law, as Pierce pursued it, in one or another of the court houses of New Hampshire, the rumor of each successive struggle and success resounded over the rugged hills, and perished without a record. Those mighty efforts, into which he put all his strength, before a county court, and addressing a jury of yeomen, have necessarily been, as regards the evanescent memory of any particular trial, like the eloquence that is sometimes poured out in a dream. In other spheres of action, with no greater expenditure of mental energy, words have been spoken that endure from age to age—deeds done that harden into history. But this, perhaps the most earnest portion of Franklin Pierce's life, has left few materials from which it can be written. There is before me only one report of a case in which he was engaged— the defence of the Wentworths, at a preliminary examination, on a charge of murder. His speech occupied four hours in the delivery, and handles a confused medley of facts with masterly skill, bringing them to bear one upon another, and making the entire mass, as it were, transparent, so that the truth may be seen through it. The whole hangs together too closely to permit the quotation of passages.

The writer has been favored with communications from two individuals, who have enjoyed the best of opportunities to become acquainted with General Pierce's character as a lawyer. The following is the graceful and generous tribute of a gentleman, who, of late, more frequently than any other, has been opposed to him at the bar:—

"General Pierce cannot be said to have commenced his career at the bar in earnest until after his resignation of the office of senator, in 1842. And it is a convincing proof of his eminent powers that he at once placed himself in the very first rank at a bar so distinguished for ability as that of New Hampshire. It is confessed by all who have the means of knowledge and judgment on this subject, that in no state of the Union are causes tried with more industry of preparation, skill, perseverance, energy, or vehement effort to succeed.

"During much of this time, my practice in our courts was suspended; and it is only within three or four years that I have had opportunities of intimately knowing his powers as an advocate, by being associated with him at the bar; and, most of all, of appreciating and feeling that power, by being opposed to him in the trial of causes before juries. Far more than any other man, whom it has been my fortune to meet, he makes himself felt by one who tries a case against him. From the first, he impresses on his opponent a consciousness of the necessity of a deadly struggle, not only in order to win the victory, but to avoid defeat.

"His vigilance and perseverance, omitting nothing in the preparation and introduction of testimony, even to the minutest details, which can be useful to his clients; his watchful attention, seizing on every weak point in the opposite case; his quickness and readiness; his sound and excellent judgment; his keen insight into character and motives, his almost intuitive knowledge of men; his ingenious and powerful cross-examinations; his adroitness in turning aside troublesome testimony, and availing himself of every favorable point; his quick sense of the ridiculous; his pathetic appeals to the feelings; his sustained eloquence, and remarkably energetic declamation,—all mark him for a 'leader.'

"From the beginning to the end of the trial of a case, nothing with him is neglected which can by possibility honorably conduce to success. His manner is always respectful and deferential to the court, captivating to the jury, and calculated to conciliate the good will even of those who would be otherwise indifferent spectators. In short, he plays the part of a successful actor; successful, because he always identifies himself with his part, and in him it is not acting.

"Perhaps, as would be expected by those who know his generosity of heart, and his scorn of everything like oppression or extortion, he is most powerful in his indignant denunciations of fraud or injustice, and his addresses to the feelings in behalf of the poor and lowly, and the sufferers under wrong. I remember to have heard of his extraordinary power on one occasion, when a person who had offered to procure arrears of a pension for revolutionary services had appropriated to himself a most unreasonable share of the money. General Pierce spoke of the frequency of these instances, and, before the numerous audience, offered his aid, freely and gratuitously, to redress the wrongs of any widow or representative of a revolutionary officer or soldier who had been made the subject of such extortion.

"The reply of the poor man, in the anecdote related by Lord Campbell of Harry Erskine, would be applicable, as exhibiting a feeling kindred to that with which General Pierce is regarded: 'There's no a puir man in a' Scotland need to want a friend or fear an enemy, sae lang as Harry Erskine lives!'"

We next give his aspect as seen from the bench, in the following carefully prepared and discriminating article, from the chief justice of New Hampshire:—

"In attempting to estimate the character and qualifications of Mr. Pierce as a lawyer and an advocate, we undertake a delicate, but, at the same time, an agreeable task. The profession of the law, practised by men of liberal and enlightened minds, and unstained by the sordidness which more or less affects all human pursuits, invariably confers honor upon and is honored by its followers. An integrity above suspicion, an eloquence alike vigorous and persuasive, and an intuitive sagacity have earned for Mr. Pierce the reputation that always follows them.

"The last case of paramount importance in which he was engaged as counsel was that of Morrison v. Philbrick, tried in the month of February, 1852, at the Court of Common Pleas for the county of Belknap. There was on both sides an array of eminent professional talent, Messrs. Pierce, Bell, and Bellows appearing for the defendant, and Messrs. Atherton and Whipple for the plaintiff. The case was one of almost unequalled interest to the public generally, and to the inhabitants of the country lying around the lower part of Lake Winnipiscogee. A company, commonly called the Lake Company, had become the owners of many of the outlets of the streams supplying the lake, and by means of their works at such places, and at Union Bridge, a few miles below, were enabled to keep back the waters of the lake, and to use them as occasion should require to supply the mills at Lowell. The plaintiff alleged that the dam at Union Bridge had caused the water to rise higher than was done by the dam that existed in the year 1828, and that he was essentially injured thereby. The case had been on trial nearly seven weeks. Evidence equivalent to the testimony of one hundred and eighty witnesses had been laid before the jury. Upon this immense mass of facts, involving a great number of issues, Mr. Pierce was to meet his most formidable opponent in the state, Mr. Atherton. In that gentleman are united many of the rarest qualifications of an advocate. Of inimitable self-possession; with a coolness and clearness of intellect which no sudden emergencies can disturb; with that confidence in his resources which nothing but native strength, aided by the most thorough training, can bestow; with a felicity and fertility of illustration, the result alike of an exquisite natural taste and a cultivation of those studies which refine while they strengthen the mind for forensic contests,—Mr. Atherton's argument was listened to with an earnestness and interest which showed the conviction of his audience that no ordinary man was addressing them.

"No one who witnessed that memorable trial will soon forget the argument of Mr. Pierce on that occasion. He was the counsel for the defendant, and was therefore to precede Mr. Atherton. He was to analyze and unfold to the jury this vast body of evidence under the watchful eyes of an opponent at once enterprising and cautious, and before whom it was necessary to be both bold and skilful. He was to place himself in the position of the jury, to see the evidence as they would be likely to regard it, to understand the character of their minds and what views would be the most likely to impress them. He was not only to be familiar with his own case, but to anticipate that of his opponent, and answer as he best might the argument of the counsel. And most admirably did he discharge the duties he had assumed on behalf of his client. Eminently graceful and attractive in his manner at all times, his demeanor was then precisely what it should have been, showing a manly confidence in himself and his case, and a courteous deference to the tribunal he was addressing. His erect and manly figure, his easy and unembarrassed air, bespoke the favorable attention of his audience. His earnest devotion to his cause, his deep emotion, evidently suppressed, but for that very reason all the more interesting, diffused themselves like electricity through his hearers. And when, as often happened, in the course of his argument, his clear and musical accents fell upon the ear in eloquent and pointed sentences, gratifying the taste while they satisfied the reason, no man could avoid turning to his neighbor, and expressing by his looks that pleasure which the very depth of his interest forbade him to express in words. And when the long trial was over, every one remembered with satisfaction that these two distinguished gentlemen had met each other during a most exciting and exhausting trial of seven weeks, and that no unkind words, or captious passages, had occurred between them to diminish their mutual respect, or that in which they were held by their fellow-citizens.

"In the above remarks, we have indicated a few of Mr. Pierce's characteristics as an advocate; but he possesses other endowments, to which we have not alluded. In the first place, as he is a perfectly fearless man, so he is a perfectly fearless advocate; and true courage is as necessary to the civilian as to the soldier, and smiles and frowns Mr. Pierce disregards alike in the undaunted discharge of his duty. He never fears to uphold his client, however unpopular his cause may seem to be for the moment. It is this courage which kindles his eloquence, inspires his conduct, and gives direction and firmness to his skill. This it is which impels him onward, at all risks, to lay bare every 'mystery of iniquity' which he believes is threatening his case. He does not ask himself whether his opponent be not a man of wealth and influence, of whom it might be for his interest to speak with care and circumspection;

but he devotes himself with a ready zeal to his cause, careless of aught but how he may best discharge his duty. His argumentative powers are of the highest order. He never takes before the court a position which he believes untenable. He has a quick and sure perception of his points, and the power of enforcing them by apt and pertinent illustrations. He sees the relative importance and weight of different views, and can assign to each its proper place, and brings forward the main body of his reasoning in prominent relief, without distracting the attention by unimportant particulars. And above all, he has the good sense, so rarely shown by many, to stop when he has said all that is necessary for the elucidation of his subject. With a proper confidence in his own perceptions, he states his views so pertinently and in such precise and logical terms, that they cannot but be felt and appreciated. He never mystifies; he never attempts to pervert words from their proper and legitimate meaning to answer a temporary purpose.

"His demeanor at the bar nay be pronounced faultless. His courtesy in the court house, like his courtesy elsewhere, is that which springs from self-respect and from a kindly heart, disposing its owner to say and do kindly things. But he would be a courageous man who, presuming upon the affability of Mr. Pierce's manner, would venture a second time to attack him; for he would long remember the rebuke that followed his first attack. There is a ready repartee and a quick and cutting sarcasm in his manner when he chooses to display it, which it requires a man of considerable nerve to withstand. He is peculiarly happy in the examination of witnesses—that art in which so few excel. He never browbeats, he never attempts to terrify. He is never rude or discourteous. But the equivocating witness soon discovers that his falsehood is hunted out of its recesses with an unsparing determination. If he is dogged and surly, he is met by a spirit as resolute as his own. If he is smooth and plausible, the veil is lifted from him by a firm but graceful hand. If he is pompous and vain, no ridicule was ever more perfect than that to which he listens with astonished and mortified ears.

"The eloquence of Mr. Pierce is of a character not to be easily forgotten. He understands men, their passions and their feelings. He knows the way to their hearts, and can make them vibrate to his touch. His language always attracts the hearer. A graceful and manly carriage, bespeaking him at once the gentleman and the true man; a manner warmed by the ardent glow of an earnest belief; an enunciation ringing, distinct, and impressive beyond that of most men; a command of brilliant and expressive language; and an accurate taste, together with a sagacious and instinctive insight into the points of his case, are the secrets of his success. It is thus that audiences are moved and truth ascertained; and he will ever be the most successful advocate who can approach the nearest to this lofty and difficult position.

"Mr. Pierce's views as a constitutional lawyer are such as have been advocated by the ablest minds of America. They are those which, taking their rise in the heroic age of the country, were transmitted to him by a noble father, worthy of the times in which he lived, worthy of that Revolution which he assisted in bringing about. He believes that the Constitution was made, not to be subverted, but to be sacredly preserved; that a republic is perfectly consistent with the conservation of law, of rational submission to right authority, and of true self-government. Equally removed from that malignant hostility to order which characterizes the demagogues who are eager to rise upon the ruins even of freedom, and from that barren and bigoted narrowness which would oppose all rational freedom of opinion, he is, in its loftiest and most ennobling sense, a friend of that Union, without which the honored name of American citizen would become a by-word among the nations. And if, as we fervently pray and confidently expect he will, Mr. Pierce shall display before the great tribunals of the nation the courage, the consistency, the sagacity, and the sense of honor, which have already secured for him so many thousands of devoted friends, and which have signalized both his private and professional life, his administration will long be held in grateful remembrance as one of which the sense of right and the sagacity to perceive it, a clear insight into the true destinies of the country and a determination to uphold them at whatever sacrifice, were the predominant characteristics."

It may appear singular that Franklin Pierce has not taken up his residence in some metropolis, where his great forensic abilities would so readily find a more conspicuous theatre, and a far richer remuneration than heretofore. He himself, it is understood, has sometimes contemplated a removal, and, two or three years since, had almost determined on settling in Baltimore. But his native state, where he is known so well, and regarded with so much familiar affection, which he has served so faithfully, and which rewards him so generously with its confidence, New Hampshire, with its granite hills, must always be his home. He will dwell there, except when public duty for a season shall summon him away; he will die there, and give his dust to its soil.

It was at his option, in 1846, to accept the highest legal position in the country, setting aside the bench, and the one which undoubtedly would most have gratified his professional aspirations. President Polk, with whom he had been associated on the most friendly terms in Congress, now offered him the post of attorney general of the United States. "In tendering to you this position in my cabinet," writes the President, "I have been governed by the high estimate which I place upon your character and eminent qualifications to fill it." The letter, in which this proposal is declined, shows so much of the writer's real self that we quote a portion of it.

"Although the early years of my manhood were devoted to public life, it was never really suited to my taste. I longed, as I am sure you must often have done, for the quiet and independence that belong only to the private citizen; and now, at forty, I feel that desire stronger than ever.

"Coming so unexpectedly as this offer does, it would be difficult, if not impossible, to arrange the business of an extensive practice, between this and the first of November, in a manner at all satisfactory to myself, or to those who have committed their interests to my care, and who rely on my services. Besides, you know that Mrs. Pierce's health, while at Washington, was very delicate. It is, I fear, even more so now; and the responsibilities which the proposed change would necessarily impose upon her ought, probably, in themselves, to constitute an insurmountable objection to leaving our quiet home for a public station at Washington.

"When I resigned my seat in the Senate in 1842, I did it with the fixed purpose never again to be voluntarily separated from my family for any considerable length of time, except at the call of my country in time of war; and yet this consequence, for the reason before stated, and on account of climate, would be very likely to result from my acceptance.

"These are some of the considerations which have influenced my decision. You will, I am sure, appreciate my motives. You will not believe that I have weighed my personal convenience and case against the public interest, especially as the office is one which, if not sought, would be readily accepted by gentlemen who could bring to your aid attainments and qualifications vastly superior to mine."

Previous to the offer of the attorney-generalship, the appointment of United States Senator had been tendered to Pierce by Governor Steele, and declined. It is unquestionable that, at this period, he hoped and expected to spend a life of professional toil in a private station, undistinguished except by the exercise of his great talents in peaceful pursuits. But such was not his destiny. The contingency to which he referred in the above letter, as the sole exception to his purpose of never being separated from his family, was now about to occur. Nor did he fail to comport himself as not only that intimation, but the whole tenor of his character, gave reason to anticipate.

During the years embraced in this chapter,—between 1842 and 1847,—he had constantly taken an efficient interest in the politics of the state, but had uniformly declined the honors which New Hampshire was at all times ready to confer upon him. A democratic convention nominated him for governor, but could not obtain his acquiescence. One of the occasions on which he most strenuously exerted himself was in holding the democratic party loyal to its principles, in opposition to the course of John P. Hale. This gentleman, then a representative in Congress, had broken with his party on no less important a point than the annexation of Texas. He has never since acted with the Democracy, and has long been a leader of the free soil party.

In 1844 died Frank Robert, son of Franklin Pierce, aged four years, a little boy of rare beauty and promise, and whose death was the greatest affliction that his father has experienced. His only surviving child is a son, now eleven years old.

CHAPTER IV.

THE MEXICAN WAR.

When Franklin Pierce declined the honorable offer of the attorney-generalship of the United States, he intimated that there might be one contingency in which he would feel it his duty to give up the cherished purpose of spending the remainder of his life in a private station. That exceptional case was brought about, in 1847, by the Mexican War. He showed his readiness to redeem the pledge by enrolling himself as the earliest volunteer of a company raised in Concord, and went through the regular drill, with his fellow-soldiers, as a private in the ranks. On the passage of the bill for the increase of the army, he received the appointment of colonel of the Ninth Regiment, which was the quota of New England towards the ten that were to be raised. And shortly afterwards,—in March, 1847,—he was commissioned as brigadier-general in the army; his brigade consisting of regiments from the extreme north, the extreme west, and the extreme south of the Union.

There is nothing in any other country similar to what we see in our own, when the blast of the trumpet at once converts men of peaceful pursuits into warriors. Every war in which America has been engaged has done this; the valor that wins our battles is not the trained hardihood of veterans, but a native and spontaneous fire; and there is surely a chivalrous beauty in the devotion of the citizen soldier to his country's cause, which the man who makes arms his profession, and is but doing his regular business on the field of battle, cannot pretend to rival. Taking the Mexican War as a specimen, this peculiar composition of an American army, as well in respect to its officers as its private soldiers, seems to create a spirit of romantic adventure which more than supplies the place of disciplined courage.

The author saw General Pierce in Boston, on the eve of his departure for Vera Cruz. He had been intensely occupied, since his appointment, in effecting the arrangements necessary on leaving his affairs, as well as by the preparations, military and personal, demanded by the expedition. The transports were waiting at Newport to receive the troops. He was now in the midst of bustle, with some of the officers of his command about him, mingled with the friends whom he was to leave behind. The severest point of the crisis was over, for he had already bidden his family farewell. His spirits appeared to have risen with the occasion. He was evidently in his element; nor, to say the truth, dangerous as was the path before him, could it be regretted that his life was now to have the opportunity of that species of success which—in his youth, at least—he had considered the best worth struggling for. He looked so fit to be a soldier, that it was impossible to doubt—not merely his good conduct, which was as certain before the event as afterwards, but—his good fortune in the field, and his fortunate return.

He sailed from Newport on the 27th of May, in the bark Kepler, having on board three companies of the Ninth Regiment of Infantry, together with Colonel Ransom, its commander, and the officers belonging to the detachment. The passage was long and tedious, with protracted calms, and so smooth a sea that a sail-boat might have performed the voyage in safety. The Kepler arrived at Vera Cruz in precisely a month after her departure from the United States, without speaking a single vessel from the south during her passage, and, of course, receiving no intelligence as to the position and state of the army which these reenforcements were to join.

From a journal kept by General Pierce, and intended only for the perusal of his family and friends, we present some extracts. They are mere hasty jottings-down in camp, and at the intervals of weary marches, but will doubtless bring the reader closer to the man than any narrative which we could substitute. [In this reprint it has been thought expedient to omit the passages from General Pierce's journal.]

* * * * * *

General Pierce's journal here terminates. In its clear and simple narrative the reader cannot fail to see—although it was written with no purpose of displaying them—the native qualities of a born soldier, together with the sagacity of an experienced one. He had proved himself, moreover, physically apt for war, by his easy endurance of the fatigues of the march; every step of which (as was the case with few other officers) was performed either on horseback or on foot. Nature, indeed, has endowed him with a rare elasticity both of mind and body; he springs up from pressure like a well-tempered sword. After the severest toil, a single night's rest does as much for him, in the way of refreshment, as a week could do for most other men.

His conduct on this adventurous march received the high encomiums of military men, and was honored with the commendation of the great soldier who is now his rival in the presidential contest. He reached the main army at Puebla on the 7th of August, with twenty-four hundred men, in fine order, and without the loss of a single wagon.

CHAPTER V.

HIS SERVICES IN THE VALLEY OF MEXICO.

General Scott, who was at Puebla with the main army awaiting this reenforcement, began his march towards the city of Mexico on the day after General Pierce's arrival. The battle of Contreras was fought on the 19th of August.

The enemy's force consisted of about seven thousand men, posted in a strongly-intrenched camp, under General Valencia, one of the bravest and ablest of the Mexican commanders. The object of the commanding general appears to have been to cut off the communications of these detached troops with Santa Anna's main army, and thus to have them entirely at his mercy. For this purpose a portion of the American forces were ordered to move against Valencia's left flank, and, by occupying strong positions in the villages and on the roads towards the city, to prevent reenforcements from reaching him. In the mean time, to draw the enemy's attention from this movement, a vigorous onset was made upon his front; and as the operations upon his flank were not immediately and fully carried out according to the plan, this front demonstration assumed the character of a fierce and desperate attack, upon which the fortunes of the day much depended. General Pierce's brigade formed a part of the force engaged in this latter movement, in which four thousand newly-recruited men, unable to bring their artillery to bear, contended against seven thousand disciplined soldiers, protected by intrenchments, and showering round shot and shells against the assailing troops.

The ground in front was of the rudest and roughest character. The troops made their way with difficulty over a broken tract called the Pedregal, bristling with sharp points of rocks, and which is represented as having been the crater of a now exhausted and extinct volcano. The enemy had thrown out skirmishers, who were posted in great force among the crevices and inequalities of this broken ground, and vigorously resisted the American advance; while the artillery of the intrenched camp played upon our troops, and shattered the very rocks over which they were to pass.

General Pierce's immediate command had never before been under such a fire of artillery. The enemy's range was a little too high, or the havoc in our ranks must have been dreadful. In the midst of this fire, General Pierce, being the only officer mounted in the brigade, leaped his horse upon an abrupt eminence, and addressed the colonels and captains of the regiments, as they passed, in a few stirring words,—reminding them of the honor of their country, of the victory their steady valor would contribute to achieve. Pressing forward to the head of the column, he had nearly reached the practicable ground that lay beyond, when his horse slipped among the rocks, thrust his foot into a crevice, and fell, breaking his own leg, and crushing his rider heavily beneath him.

Pierce's mounted orderly soon came to his assistance. The general was stunned, and almost insensible. When partially recovered, he found himself suffering from severe bruises, and especially from a sprain of the left knee, which was undermost when the horse came down. The orderly assisted him to reach the shelter of a projecting rock; and as they made their way thither, a shell fell close beside them and exploded, covering them with earth. "That was a lucky miss," said Pierce calmly. Leaving him in such shelter as the rock afforded, the orderly went in search of aid, and was fortunate to meet with Dr. Ritchie, of Virginia, who was attached to Pierce's brigade, and was following in close proximity to the advancing column. The doctor administered to him as well as the circumstances would admit. Immediately on recovering his full consciousness, General Pierce had become anxious to rejoin his troops; and now, in opposition to Dr. Ritchie's advice and remonstrances, he determined to proceed to the front.

With pain and difficulty, and leaning on his orderly's arm, he reached the battery commanded by Captain McGruder, where he found the horse of Lieutenant Johnson, who had just before received a mortal wound. In compliance with his wishes, he was assisted into the saddle; and, in answer to a remark that he would be unable to keep his seat, "Then," said the general, "you must tie me on." Whether his precaution was actually taken is a point upon which authorities differ; but at all events, with injuries so severe as would have sent almost any other man to the hospital, he rode forward into the battle.

The contest was kept up until nightfall, without forcing Valencia's intrenchment. General Pierce remained in the saddle until eleven o'clock at night. Finding himself, at nine o'clock, the senior officer in the field, he, in that capacity, withdrew the troops from their advanced position, and concentrated them at the point where they were to pass the night. At eleven, beneath a torrent of rain, destitute of a tent or other protection, and without food or refreshment, he lay down on an ammunition wagon, but was prevented by the pain of his injuries, especially that of his wounded knee, from finding any repose. At one o'clock came orders from General Scott to put the brigade into a new position, in front of the enemy's works, preparatory to taking part in the contemplated operations of the next morning. During the night, the troops appointed for that service, under Riley, Shields, Smith, and Cadwallader, had occupied the villages and roads between Valencia's position and the city; so that, with daylight, the commanding general's scheme of the battle was ready to be carried out, as it had originally existed in his mind.

At daylight, accordingly, Valencia's intrenched camp was assaulted. General Pierce was soon in the saddle at the head of his brigade, which retained its position in front, thus serving to attract the enemy's attention, and divert him from the true point of attack. The camp was stormed in the rear by the American troops, led on by Riley, Cadwallader, and Dimmick; and in the short space of seventeen minutes it had fallen into the hands of the assailants, together with a multitude of prisoners. The remnant of the routed enemy fled towards Churubusco. As Pierce led his brigade in pursuit, crossing the battle-field, and passing through the works that had just been stormed, he found the road and adjacent fields everywhere strewn with the dead and dying. The pursuit was continued until one o'clock, when the foremost of the

Americans arrived in front of the strong Mexican positions at Churubusco and San Antonio, where Santa Alma's army had been compelled to make a stand, and where the great conflict of the day commenced.

General Santa Anna entertained the design of withdrawing his forces towards the city. In order to intercept this movement, Pierce's brigade, with other troops, was ordered to pursue a route by which the enemy could be attacked in the rear. Colonel Noah E. Smith (a patriotic American, long resident in Mexico, whose local and topographical knowledge proved eminently serviceable) had offered to point out the road, and was sent to summon General Pierce to the presence of the commander-in-chief. When he met Pierce, near Coyacan, at the head of his brigade, the heavy fire of the batteries had commenced. "He was exceedingly thin," writes Colonel Smith, "worn down by the fatigue and pain of the day and night before, and then evidently suffering severely. Still there was a glow in his eye, as the cannon boomed, that showed within him a spirit ready for the conflict." He rode up to General Scott, who was at this time sitting on horseback beneath a tree, near the church of Coyacan, issuing orders to different individuals of his staff. Our account of this interview is chiefly taken from the narrative of Colonel Smith, corroborated by other testimony.

The commander-in-chief had already heard of the accident that befell Pierce the day before; and as the latter approached, General Scott could not but notice the marks of pain and physical exhaustion against which only the sturdiest constancy of will could have enabled him to bear up. "Pierce, my dear fellow," said he,—and that epithet of familiar kindness and friendship, upon the battle-field, was the highest of military commendation from such a man,—"you are badly injured; you are not fit to be in your saddle." "Yes, general, I am," replied Pierce, "in a case like this." "You cannot touch your foot to the stirrup," said Scott. "One of them I can," answered Pierce. The general looked again at Pierce's almost disabled figure, and seemed on the point of taking his irrevocable resolution. "You are rash, General Pierce," said he; "we shall lose you, and we cannot spare you. It is my duty to order you back to St. Augustine." "For God's sake, general," exclaimed Pierce, "don't say that! This is the last great battle, and I must lead my brigade!" The commander-in-chief made no further remonstrance, but gave the order for Pierce to advance with his brigade.

The way lay through thick standing corn, and over marshy ground intersected with ditches, which were filled, or partially so, with water. Over some of the narrower of these Pierce leaped his horse. When the brigade had advanced about a mile, however, it found itself impeded by a ditch ten or twelve feet wide, and six or eight feet deep. It being impossible to leap it, General Pierce was lifted from his saddle, and in some incomprehensible way, hurt as he was, contrived to wade or scramble across this obstacle, leaving his horse on the hither side. The troops were now under fire. In the excitement of the battle he forgot his injury, and hurried forward, leading the brigade, a distance of two or three hundred yards. But the exhaustion of his frame, and particularly the anguish of his knee,—made more intolerable by such free use of it,— was greater than any strength of nerve, or any degree of mental energy, could struggle against. He fell, faint and almost insensible, within full range of the enemy's fire. It was proposed to bear him off the field; but, as some of his soldiers approached to lift him, he became aware of their purpose, and was partially revived by his determination to resist it. "No," said he, with all the strength he had left, "don't carry me off! Let me lie here!" And there he lay, under the tremendous fire of Churubusco, until the enemy, in total rout, was driven from the field.

Immediately after the victory, when the city of Mexico lay at the mercy of the American commander, and might have been entered that very night, Santa Anna sent a flag of truce, proposing an armistice, with a view to negotiation for peace. It cannot be considered in any other light than as a very high and signal compliment to his gallantry in the field that General Pierce was appointed, by the commander-in-chief, one of the commissioners on our part, together with General Quitman and General Persifer F. Smith, to arrange the terms of this armistice. Pierce was unable to walk, or to mount his horse without assistance, when intelligence of his appointment reached him. He had not taken off his spurs nor slept an hour, for two nights; but he immediately obeyed the summons, was assisted into the saddle, and rode to Tacubaya, where, at the house of the British consul-general, the American and Mexican commissioners were assembled. The conference began late in the afternoon, and continued till four o'clock the next morning, when the articles were signed. Pierce then proceeded to the quarters of General Worth, in the village of Tacubaya, where he obtained an hour or two of repose.

The expectation of General Scott, that further bloodshed might be avoided by means of the armistice, proved deceptive. Military operations, after a temporary interruption, were actively renewed; and on the 8th of September was fought the bloody battle of Molino del Rey, one of the fiercest and most destructive of the war.

In this conflict General Worth, with three thousand troops, attacked and routed fourteen thousand Mexicans, driving them under the protection of the Castle of Chepultepec. Perceiving the obstinacy with which the field was contested, the commander-in-chief dispatched an order to General Pierce to advance to the support of General Worth's division. He moved forward with rapidity; and although the battle was won just as he reached the field, he interposed his brigade between Worth and the retreating enemy, and thus drew upon himself the fire of Chepultepec. A shell came streaming from the castle, and, bursting within a few feet of him, startled his horse, which was near plunging over an adjacent precipice. Continuing a long time under fire, Pierce's brigade was engaged in removing the wounded and the captured ammunition. While thus occupied, he led a portion of his command to repel the attacks of the enemy's skirmishers.

There remained but one other battle,—that of Chepultepec,—which was fought on the 13th of September. On the preceding day (although the injuries and the over-exertion resulting from previous marches and battles had greatly enfeebled him), General Pierce had acted with his brigade. In obedience to orders, it had occupied the field of Molino del Rey. Contrary to expectation, it was found that the enemy's force had been withdrawn from this position. Pierce remained in the field until noon, when, it being certain that the anticipated attack would not take place before the following day, he returned to the quarters of General Worth, which were near at hand. There he became extremely ill, and was unable to leave his bed for the thirty-six hours next ensuing. In the mean time, the Castle of Chepultepec was stormed by the troops under Generals Pillow and Quitman. Pierce's brigade behaved itself gallantly, and suffered severely; and that accomplished officer, Colonel Ransom, leading the Ninth Regiment to the attack, was shot through the head, and fell, with many other brave men, in that last battle of the war.

The American troops, under Quitman and Worth, had established themselves within the limits of the city, having possession of the gates of Belen and of San Cosma, but, up till nightfall, had met with a vigorous resistance from the Mexicans, led on by Santa Anna in person. They had still, apparently, a desperate task before them. It was anticipated that, with the next morning's light, our troops would be ordered to storm the citadel, and the city of Mexico itself. When this was told to Pierce, upon his sick-bed, he rose, and attempted to dress himself; but Captain Hardcastle, who had brought the intelligence from Worth, prevailed upon him to remain in bed, and not to exhaust his scanty strength until the imminence of the occasion should require his presence. Pierce acquiesced for the time, but again arose, in the course of the night, and made his way to the trenches, where he reported himself to General Quitman, with whose division was a part of his brigade. Quitman's share in the anticipated assault, it was supposed, owing to the position which his troops occupied, would be more perilous than that of Worth.

But the last great battle had been fought. In the morning, it was discovered that the citadel had been abandoned, and that Santa Anna had withdrawn his army from the city.

There never was a more gallant body of officers than those who came from civil life into the army on occasion of the Mexican War. All of them, from the rank of general downward, appear to have been animated by the spirit of young knights, in times of chivalry, when fighting for their spurs. Hitherto known only as peaceful citizens, they felt it incumbent on them, by daring and desperate valor, to prove their fitness to be intrusted with the guardianship of their country's honor. The old and trained soldier, already distinguished on former fields, was free to be discreet as well as brave; but these untried warriors were in a different position, and therefore rushed on perils with a recklessness that found its penalty on every battle-field—not one

53

of which was won without a grievous sacrifice of the best blood of America. In this band of gallant men, it is not too much to say, General Pierce was as distinguished for what we must term his temerity in personal exposure, as for the higher traits of leadership, wherever there was an opportunity for their display.

He had manifested, moreover, other and better qualities than these, and such as it affords his biographer far greater pleasure to record. His tenderness of heart, his sympathy, his brotherly or paternal care for his men, had been displayed in a hundred instances, and had gained him the enthusiastic affection of all who served under his command. During the passage from America, under the tropics, he would go down into the stifling air of the hold, with a lemon, a cup of tea, and, better and more efficacious than all, a kind word for the sick. While encamped before Vera Cruz, he gave up his own tent to a sick comrade, and went himself to lodge in the pestilential city. On the march, and even on the battle-field, he found occasion to exercise those feelings of humanity which show most beautifully there. And, in the hospitals of Mexico, he went among the diseased and wounded soldiers, cheering them with his voice and the magic of his kindness, inquiring into their wants, and relieving them to the utmost of his pecuniary means. There was not a man of his brigade but loved him, and would have followed him to death, or have sacrificed his own life in his general's defence.

The officers of the old army, whose profession was war, and who well knew what a soldier was and ought to be, fully recognized his merit. An instance of their honorable testimony in his behalf may fitly be recorded here. It was after General Pierce had returned to the United States. At a dinner in the halls of Montezuma, at which forty or fifty of the brave men above alluded to were present, a young officer of the New England Regiment was called on for a toast. He made an address, in which he spoke with irrepressible enthusiasm of General Pierce, and begged to propose his health. One of the officers of the old line rose, and observed that none of the recently appointed generals commanded more unanimous and universal respect; that General Pierce had appreciated the scientific knowledge of the regular military men, and had acquired their respect by the independence, firmness, and promptitude with which he exercised his own judgment, and acted on the intelligence derived from them. In concluding this tribute of high, but well-considered praise, the speaker very cordially acquiesced in the health of General Pierce, and proposed that it should be drunk standing, with three times three.

General Pierce remained in Mexico until December, when, as the warfare was over, and peace on the point of being concluded, he set out on his return. In nine months, crowded full of incident, he had seen far more of actual service than many professional soldiers during their whole lives. As soon as the treaty of peace was signed, he gave up his commission, and returned to the practice of the law, again proposing to spend the remainder of his days in the bosom of his family. All the dreams of his youth were now fulfilled; the military ardor, that had struck an hereditary root in his breast, had enjoyed its scope, and was satisfied; and he flattered himself that no circumstances could hereafter occur to draw him from the retirement of domestic peace. New Hampshire received him with even more enthusiastic affection than ever. At his departure, he had received a splendid sword at the hands of many of his friends, in token of their confidence; he had shown himself well worthy to wear and able to use a soldier's weapon; and his native state now gave him another, the testimonial of approved valor and warlike conduct.

CHAPTER VI.

THE COMPROMISE AND OTHER MATTERS.

The intervening years, since General Pierce's return from Mexico, and until the present time, have been spent in the laborious exercise of the legal profession,—an employment scarcely varied or interrupted, except by those episodes of political activity which a man of public influence finds it impossible to avoid, and in which, if his opinions are matter of conscience with him, he feels it his duty to interest himself.

In the presidential canvass of 1848 he used his best efforts (and with success, so far as New Hampshire was concerned) in behalf of the candidate of his party. A truer and better speech has never been uttered on a similar occasion than one which he made (during a hurried half hour, snatched from the court rooms) in October of the above year, before the democratic state convention, then in session at Concord. It is an invariable characteristic of General Pierce's popular addresses, that they evince a genuine respect for the people; he makes his appeal to their intelligence, their patriotism, and their integrity, and, never doubtful of their upright purpose, proves his faith in the great mind and heart of the country both by what he says and by what he refrains from saying. He never yet was guilty of an effort to cajole his fellow-citizens, to operate upon their credulity, or to trick them even into what was right; and therefore all the victories which he has ever won in popular assemblies have been triumphs doubly honored, being as creditable to his audiences as to himself.

When the series of measures known under the collective term of The Compromise were passed by Congress in 1850, and put to so searching a test here at the North the reverence of the people for the Constitution and their attachment to the Union, General Pierce was true to the principles which he had long ago avowed. At an early period of his congressional service he had made known, with the perfect frankness of his character, those opinions upon the slavery question which he has never since seen occasion to change in the slightest degree. There is an unbroken consistency in his action with regard to this matter. It is entirely of a piece, from his first entrance upon public life until the moment when he came forward, while many were faltering, to throw the great weight of his character and influence into the scale in favor of those measures through which it was intended to redeem the pledges of the Constitution, and to preserve and renew the old love and harmony among the sisterhood of States. His approval embraced the whole series of these acts, as well those which bore hard upon northern views and sentiments as those in which the South deemed itself to have made more than reciprocal concessions.

No friend nor enemy that know Franklin Pierce would have expected him to act otherwise. With his view of the whole subject, whether looking at it through the medium of his conscience, his feelings, or his intellect, it was impossible for him not to take his stand as the unshaken advocate of Union, and of the mutual steps of compromise which that great object unquestionably demanded. The fiercest, the least scrupulous, and the most consistent of those who battle against slavery recognize the same fact that he does. They see that merely human wisdom and human efforts cannot subvert it, except by tearing to pieces the Constitution, breaking the pledges which it sanctions, and severing into distracted fragments that common country which Providence brought into one nation, through a continued miracle of almost two hundred years, from the first settlement of the American wilderness until the Revolution. In the days when, a young member of Congress, he first raised his voice against agitation, Pierce saw these perils and their consequences. He considered, too, that the evil would be certain, while the good was, at best, a contingency, and (to the clear, practical foresight with which he looked into the future) scarcely so much as that, attended as the movement was and must be during its progress, with the aggravated injury of those whose condition it aimed to ameliorate, and terminating, in its possible triumph,— if such possibility there were,—with the ruin of two races which now dwelt together in greater peace and affection, it is not too much to say, than had ever elsewhere existed between the taskmaster and the serf.

Of course, there is another view of all these matters. The theorist may take that view in his closet; the philanthropist by profession may strive to act upon it uncompromisingly, amid the tumult and warfare of his life. But the statesman of practical sagacity—who loves his country as it is, and evolves good from things as they exist, and who demands to feel his firm grasp upon a better reality before he quits the one already gained— will be likely here, with all the greatest statesmen of America, to stand in the attitude of a conservative. Such, at all events, will be the attitude of Franklin Pierce. We have sketched some of the influences amid which he grew up, inheriting his father's love of country, mindful of the old patriot's valor in so many conflicts of the Revolution, and having close before his eyes the example of brothers and relatives, more than one of whom have bled for America, both at the extremest north and farthest south; himself, too, in early manhood, serving the Union in its legislative halls, and, at a maturer age, leading his fellow-citizens, his brethren, from the widest-sundered states, to redden the same battle-fields with their kindred blood, to unite their breath into one shout of victory, and perhaps to sleep, side by side, with the same sod over them. Such a man, with such hereditary recollections, and such a personal experience, must not narrow himself to adopt the cause of one section of his native country against another. He will stand up, as he has always stood, among the patriots of the whole land. And if the work of antislavery agitation, which it is undeniable leaves most men who earnestly engage in it with only half a country in their affections,—if this work must be done, let others do it.

Those northern men, therefore, who deem the great causes of human welfare as represented and involved in this present hostility against southern institutions, and who conceive that the world stands still except so far as that goes forward,—these, it may be allowed, can scarcely give their sympathy or their confidence to the subject of this memoir. But there is still another view, and probably as wise a one. It looks upon slavery as one of those evils which divine Providence does not leave to be remedied by human contrivances, but which, in its own good time, by some means impossible to be anticipated, but of the simplest and easiest operation, when all its uses shall have been fulfilled, it causes to vanish like a dream. There is no instance, in all history, of the human will and intellect having perfected any great moral reform by methods which it adapted to that end; but the progress of the world, at every step, leaves some evil or wrong on the path behind it, which the wisest of mankind, of their own set purpose, could never have found the way to rectify. Whatever contributes to the great cause of good, contributes to all its subdivisions and varieties; and, on this score, the lover of his race, the enthusiast, the philanthropist of whatever theory, might lend his aid to put a man, like the one before us, into the leadership of the world's affairs.

How firm and conscientious was General Pierce's support of The Compromise may be estimated from his conduct in reference to the Reverend John Atwood. In the foregoing pages it has come oftener in our way to illustrate the bland and prepossessing features of General Pierce's character, than the sterner ones which must necessarily form the bones, so to speak, the massive skeleton, of any man who retains an upright attitude amidst the sinister influences of public life. The transaction now alluded to affords a favorable opportunity for indicating some of these latter traits.

58

In October, 1850, a democratic convention, held at Concord, nominated Mr. Atwood as the party's regular candidate for governor. The Compromise, then recent, was inevitably a prominent element in the discussions of the convention; and a series of resolutions were adopted, bearing reference to this great subject, fully and unreservedly indorsing the measures comprehended under it, and declaring the principles on which the Democracy of the state was about to engage in the gubernatorial contest. Mr. Atwood accepted the nomination, acceding to the platform thus tendered him, taking exceptions to none of the individual resolutions, and, of course, pledging himself to the whole by the very act of assuming the candidacy, which was predicated upon them.

The reverend candidate, we should conceive, is a well-meaning, and probably an amiable man. In ordinary circumstances, he would, doubtless, have gone through the canvass triumphantly, and have administered the high office to which he aspired with no discredit to the party that had placed him at its head. But the disturbed state of the public mind on the Compromise question rendered the season a very critical one; and Mr. Atwood, unfortunately, had that fatal weakness of character, which, however respectably it may pass in quiet times, is always bound to make itself pitiably manifest under the pressure of a crisis. A letter was addressed to him by a committee, representing the party opposed to The Compromise, and with whom, it may be supposed, were included those who held the more thorough-going degrees of antislavery sentiment. The purpose of the letter was to draw out an expression of Mr. Atwood's opinion on the abolition movement generally, and with an especial reference to the Fugitive Slave Law, and whether, as chief magistrate of the state, he would favor any attempt for its repeal. In an answer of considerable length the candidate expressed sentiments that brought him unquestionably within the free soil pale, and favored his correspondents, moreover, with a pretty decided judgment as to the unconstitutional, unjust, and oppressive character of the Fugitive Slave Law.

During a space of about two months, this very important document was kept from the public eye. Rumors of its existence, however, became gradually noised abroad, and necessarily attracted the attention of Mr. Atwood's democratic friends. Inquiries being made, he acknowledged the existence of the letter, but averred that it had never been delivered, that it was merely a rough draught, and that he had hitherto kept it within his own control, with a view to more careful consideration. In accordance with the advice of friends, he expressed a determination, and apparently in good faith, to suppress the letter, and thus to sever all connection with the antislavery party. This, however, was now beyond his power. A copy of the letter had been taken; it was published, with high commendations, in the antislavery newspapers; and Mr. Atwood was exhibited in the awkward predicament of directly avowing sentiments on the one hand which he had implicitly disavowed on the other, of accepting a nomination based on principles diametrically opposite.

The candidate appears to have apprehended this disclosure, and he hurried to Concord, and sought counsel of General Pierce, with whom he was on terms of personal kindness, and between whom and himself, heretofore, there had never been a shade of political difference. An interview with the general and one or two other gentlemen ensued. Mr. Atwood was cautioned against saying or writing a word that might be repugnant to his feelings or his principles; but, voluntarily, and at his own suggestion, he now wrote for publication a second letter, in which he retracted every objectionable feature of his former one, and took decided ground in favor of The Compromise, including all its individual measures. Had he adhered to this latter position, he might have come out of the affair, if not with the credit of consistency, yet, at least, as a successful candidate in the impending election. But his evil fate, or, rather, the natural infirmity of his character, was not so to be thrown off. The very next day, unhappily, he fell into the hands of some of his antislavery friends, to whom he avowed a constant adherence to the principles of his first letter, describing the second as having been drawn from him by importunity, in an excited state of his mind, and without a full realization of its purport.

It would be needlessly cruel to Mr. Atwood to trace with minuteness the further details of this affair. It is impossible to withhold from him a certain sympathy, or to avoid feeling that a very worthy man, as the world goes, had entangled himself in an inextricable knot of duplicity and tergiversation, by an ill-advised effort to be two opposite things at once. For the sake of true manhood, we gladly turn to consider the course adopted by General Pierce.

The election for governor was now at a distance of only a few weeks; and it could not be otherwise than a most hazardous movement for the democratic party, at so late a period, to discard a candidate with whom the people had become familiar. It involved nothing less than the imminent peril of that political supremacy which the party had so long enjoyed. With Mr. Atwood as candidate, success might be considered as certain. To a short-sighted and a weak man, it would have appeared the obvious policy to patch up the difficulty, and, at all events, to conquer, under whatever leadership, and with whatever allies. But it was one of those junctures which test the difference between the man of principle and the mere politician—the man of moral courage and him who yields to temporary expediency. General Pierce could not consent that his party should gain a nominal triumph, at the expense of what he looked upon as its real integrity and life. With this view of the matter, he had no hesitation in his course; nor could the motives which otherwise would have been strongest with him—pity for the situation of an unfortunate individual, a personal friend, a Democrat, as Mr. Atwood describes himself, of nearly fifty years' standing—incline him to mercy where it would have been fatal to his sense of right. He took decided ground against Mr. Atwood. The convention met again, and satisfactory to all parties; and one of his political opponents (Professor Sanborn, of Dartmouth College) has ably sketched him, both in that aspect and as a debater.

"In drawing the portraits of the distinguished members of the constitutional convention," writes the professor, "to pass Frank Pierce unnoticed would be as absurd as to enact one of Shakespeare's dramas without its principal hero. I give my impressions of the man as I saw him in the convention; for I would not undertake to vouch for the truth or falsehood of those veracious organs of public sentiment, at the capital, which have loaded him in turn with indiscriminate praise and abuse. As a presiding officer, it would be difficult to find his equal. In proposing questions to the house, he never hesitates or blunders. In deciding points of order, he is both prompt and impartial. His treatment of every member of the convention was characterized by uniform courtesy and kindness. The deportment of the presiding officer of a deliberative body usually gives tone to the debates. If he is harsh, morose, or abrupt in his manner, the speakers are apt to catch his spirit by the force of involuntary sympathy. The same is true, to some extent, of the principal debaters in such a body. When a man of strong prejudices and harsh temper rises to address a public assembly, his indwelling antipathies speak from every feature of his face and from every motion of his person. The audience at once brace themselves against his assaults, and condemn his opinions before they are heard. The well-known character of an orator persuades or dissuades quite as forcibly as the language he utters. Some men never rise to address a deliberative assembly without conciliating good will in advance. The smile that plays upon the speaker's face awakens emotions of complacency in those who hear, even before he speaks. So does that weight of character, which is the matured fruit of long public services and acknowledged worth, soothe, in advance, the irritated and angry crowd.

"Mr. Pierce possesses unquestionable ability as a public speaker. Few men, in our country, better understand the means of swaying a popular assembly, or employ them with greater success. His forte lies in moving the passions of those whom he addresses. He knows how to call into vigorous action both the sympathies and antipathies of those who listen to him. I do not mean to imply by these remarks that his oratory is deficient in argument or sound reasoning. On the contrary, he seizes with great power upon the strong points of his subject, and presents them clearly, forcibly, and eloquently. As a prompt and ready debater, always prepared for assault or defence, he has few equals. In these encounters, he appears to great advantage, from his happy faculty of turning little incidents, unexpectedly occurring, to his own account. A word carelessly dropped, or an unguarded allusion to individuals or parties by an opponent, is frequently converted into a powerful weapon of assault, by this skilful advocate. He has been so much in office that he may be said to have been educated in public life. He is most thoroughly versed in all the tactics of debate. He is not only remarkably fluent in his elocution, but remarkably correct. He seldom miscalls or repeats a word. His style is not overloaded with ornament, and yet he draws liberally upon the treasury of rhetoric. His figures are often beautiful and striking, never incongruous. He is always listened to with respectful attention, if he does not always command conviction. From his whole course in the convention, a disinterested spectator could not fail to form a very favorable opinion, not only of his talent and eloquence, but of his generosity and magnanimity."

Among other antiquated relics of the past, and mouldy types of prejudices that ought now to be forgotten, and of which it was the object of the present convention to purge the Constitution of New Hampshire, there is a provision that certain state offices should be held only by Protestants. Since General Pierce's nomination for the presidency, the existence of this religious test has been brought as a charge against him, as if, in spite of his continued efforts to remove it, he were personally responsible for its remaining on the statute book.

General Pierce has naturally a strong endowment of religious feeling. At no period of his life, as is well known to his friends, have the sacred relations of the human soul been a matter of indifference with him; and, of more recent years, whatever circumstances of good or evil fortune may have befallen him, they have alike served to deepen this powerful sentiment. Whether in sorrow or success, he has learned, in his own behalf, the great lesson, that religious faith is the most valuable and most sacred of human possessions; but, with this sense, there has come no narrowness or illiberality, but a wide-embracing sympathy for the modes of Christian worship, and a reverence for individual belief, as a matter between the Deity and man's soul, and with which no other has a right to interfere. With the feeling here described, and with his acute intellectual perception of the abortive character of all intolerant measures, as defeating their own ends, it strikes one as nothing less than ludicrous that he should be charged with desiring to retain this obsolete enactment, standing, as it does, as a merely gratuitous and otherwise inoperative stigma upon the fair reputation of his native state. Even supposing no higher motives to have influenced him, it would have sufficed to secure his best efforts for the repeal of the religious test that so many of the Catholics have always been found in the advance-guard of freedom, marching onward with the progressive party; and that, whether in peace or war, they have performed for their adopted country the hard toil and the gallant services which she has a right to expect from her most faithful citizens.

The truth is that, ever since his entrance upon public life, on all occasions,—and often making the occasion where he found none,—General Pierce has done his utmost to obliterate this obnoxious feature from the

Constitution. He has repeatedly advocated the calling of a convention mainly for this purpose. In that of 1850, he both spoke and voted in favor of the abolition of the test, and, with the aid of Judge Woodbury and other democratic members, attained his purpose, so far as the convention possessed any power or responsibility in the matter. That the measure was ultimately defeated is due to other causes, either temporary or of long continuance; and to some of them it is attributable that the enlightened public sentiment of New Hampshire was not, long since, made to operate upon this enactment, so anomalous in the fundamental law of a free state.

In order to the validity of the amendments passed by the convention, it was necessary that the people should subsequently act upon them, and pass a vote of two thirds in favor of their adoption. The amendments proposed by the convention of 1850 were numerous. The Constitution had been modified in many and very important particulars, in respect to which the popular mind had not previously been made familiar, and on which it had not anticipated the necessity of passing judgment. In March, 1851, when the vote of the people was taken upon these measures, the Atwood controversy was at its height, and threw all matters of less immediate interest into the background. During the interval since the adjournment of the convention, the whig newspapers had been indefatigable in their attempts to put its proceedings in an odious light before the people. There had been no period, for many years, in which sinister influences rendered it so difficult to draw out an efficient expression of the will of the Democracy as on this occasion. It was the result of all these obstacles that the doings of the constitutional convention were rejected in the mass.

In the ensuing April, the convention reassembled, in order to receive the unfavorable verdict of the people upon its proposed amendments. At the suggestion of General Pierce, the amendment abolishing the religious test was again brought forward, and, in spite of the opposition of the leading whig members, was a second time submitted to the people. Nor did the struggle in behalf of this enlightened movement terminate here.

At the democratic caucus, in Concord, preliminary to the town meeting, he urged upon his political friends the repeal of the test, as a party measure;

64

and again, at the town meeting itself, while the balloting was going forward, he advocated it on the higher ground of religious freedom, and of reverence for what is inviolable in the human soul. Had the amendment passed, the credit would have belonged to no man more than to General Pierce; and that it failed, and that the free Constitution of New Hampshire is still disgraced by a provision which even monarchical England has cast off, is a responsibility which must rest elsewhere than on his head.

In September, 1851, died that eminent statesman and jurist, Levi Woodbury, then occupying the elevated post of judge of the Supreme Court of the United States. The connection between him and General Pierce, beginning in the early youth of the latter, had been sustained through all the subsequent years. They sat together, with but one intervening chair between, in the national Senate; they were always advocates of the same great measures, and held, through life, a harmony of opinion and action, which was never more conspicuous than in the few months that preceded Judge Woodbury's death. At a meeting of the bar, after his decease, General Pierce uttered some remarks, full of sensibility, in which he referred to the circumstances that had made this friendship an inheritance on his part. Had Judge Woodbury survived, it is not improbable that his more advanced age, his great public services, and equally distinguished zeal in behalf of the Union might have placed him in the position now occupied by the subject of this memoir. Fortunate the state which, after losing such a son, can still point to another, not less worthy to take upon him the charge of the nation's welfare.

We have now finished our record of Franklin Pierce's life, and have only to describe the posture of affairs which, without his own purpose and against his wish, has placed him before the people of the United States as a candidate for the presidency.

CHAPTER VII.

HIS NOMINATION FOR THE PRESIDENCY.

On the 12th of June, 1852, the democratic national convention assembled at Baltimore, in order to select a candidate for the presidency of the United States. Many names, eminently distinguished in peace and war, had been brought before the public, during several months previous; and among them, though by no means occupying a very prominent place, was the name of Franklin Pierce. In January of this year, the Democracy of New Hampshire had signified its preference of General Pierce as a presidential candidate in the approaching canvass—a demonstration which drew from him the following response, addressed to his friend, Mr. Atherton:—

"I am far from being insensible to the generous confidence so often manifested towards me by the people of this state; and although the object indicated in the resolution, having particular reference to myself, be not one of desire on my part, the expression is not on that account less gratifying.

"Doubtless the spontaneous and just appreciation of an intelligent people is the best earthly reward for earnest and cheerful services rendered to one's state and country; and while it is a matter of unfeigned regret that my life has been so barren of usefulness, I shall ever hold this and similar tributes among my most cherished recollections.

"To these, my sincere and grateful acknowledgments, I desire to add that the same motives which induced me, several years ago, to retire from public life, and which since that time controlled my judgment in this respect, now impel me to say that the use of my name in any event, before the democratic national convention at Baltimore, to which you are a delegate, would be utterly repugnant to my taste and wishes."

The sentiments expressed in the above letter were genuine, and from his heart. He had looked long and closely at the effects of high public station on the character and happiness, and on what is the innermost and dearest part of a man's possessions—his independence; and he had satisfied himself that office, however elevated, should be avoided for one's own sake, or accepted only as a good citizen would make any other sacrifice, at the call and at the need of his country.

As the time for the assembling of the national convention drew near, there were other sufficient indications of his sincerity in declining a stake in the great game. A circular letter was addressed, by Major Scott, of Virginia, to the distinguished Democrats whose claims had heretofore been publicly discussed, requesting a statement of their opinions on several points, and inquiring what would be the course of each of these gentlemen, in certain contingencies, in case of his attaining the presidency. These queries, it may be presumed, were of such a nature that General Pierce might have answered them, had he seen fit to do so, to the satisfaction of Major Scott himself, or to that of the southern democratic party, whom it seemed his purpose to represent. With not more than one exception, the other statesmen and soldiers, to whom the circular had been sent, made a response. General Pierce preserved an unbroken silence. It was equivalent to the withdrawal of all claims which he might be supposed to possess, in reference to the contemplated office; and he thereby repeated, to the delegates of the national party, the same avowal of distaste for public life which he had already made known to the Democracy of his native state. He had thus done everything in his power, actively or passively,—everything that he could have done, without showing such an estimate of his position before the country as was inconsistent with the modesty of his character,—to avoid the perilous and burdensome honor of the candidacy.

The convention met, at the date above mentioned, and continued its sessions during four days. Thirty-five ballotings were held, with a continually decreasing prospect that the friends of any one of the gentlemen hitherto prominent before the people would succeed in obtaining the two-thirds vote that was requisite for a nomination. Thus far, not a vote had been thrown for General Pierce; but, at the thirty-sixth ballot, the delegation of old Virginia brought forward his name. In the course of several more trials, his strength increased, very gradually at first, but afterwards with a growing impetus, until, at the forty-ninth ballot, the votes were for Franklin Pierce two hundred and eighty-two, and eleven for all other candidates. Thus Franklin Pierce became the nominee of the convention; and as quickly as the lightning flash could blazon it abroad his name was on every tongue, from end to end of this vast country. Within an hour he grew to be illustrious.

It would be a pretension, which we do not mean to put forward, to assert that, whether considering the length and amount of his public services, or his prominence before the country, General Pierce stood on equal ground with several of the distinguished men whose claims, to use the customary phrase, had been rejected in favor of his own. But no man, be his public services or sacrifices what they might, ever did or ever could possess, in the slightest degree, what we may term a legitimate claim to be elevated to the rulership of a free people. The nation would degrade itself, and violate every principle upon which its institutions are founded, by offering its majestic obedience to one of its citizens as a reward for whatever splendor of achievement. The conqueror may assert a claim, such as it is, to the sovereignty of the people whom he subjugates; but, with us Americans, when a statesman comes to the chief direction of affairs, it is at the summons of the nation, addressed to the servant whom it deems best fitted to spend his wisdom, his strength, and his life in its behalf. On this principle, which is obviously the correct one, a candidate's previous services are entitled to consideration only as they indicate the qualities which may enable him to render higher services in the position which his countrymen choose that he shall occupy. What he has done is of no importance, except as proving what he can do. And it is on this score, because they see in his public course the irrefragable evidences of patriotism, integrity, and courage, and because they recognize in him the noble gift of natural authority, and have a prescience of the stately endowment of administrative genius, that his fellow-citizens are about to summon Franklin Pierce to the presidency. To those who know him well, the event comes, not like accident, but as a consummation which might have been anticipated, from its innate fitness, and as the final step of a career which, all along, has tended thitherward.

It is not as a reward that he will take upon him the mighty burden of this office, of which the toil and awful responsibility whiten the statesman's head, and in which, as in more than one instance we have seen, the warrior encounters a deadlier risk than in the battle-field. When General Pierce received the news of his nomination, it affected him with no thrill of joy, but a sadness, which, for many days, was perceptible in his deportment. It awoke in his heart the sense of religious dependence—a sentiment that has been growing continually stronger, through all the trials and experiences of his life; and there was nothing feigned in that passage of his beautiful letter, accepting the nomination, in which he expresses his reliance upon heavenly support.

The committee, appointed by the Baltimore convention, conveyed to him the intelligence of his nomination in the following terms:—

"A national convention of the democratic republican party, which met at Baltimore on the first Tuesday in June, unanimously nominated you as a candidate for the high trust of the President of the United States. We have been delegated to acquaint you with the nomination, and earnestly to request that you will accept it. Persuaded as we are that this office should never be pursued by an unchastened ambition, it cannot be refused by a dutiful patriotism.

"The circumstances under which you will be presented for the canvass of your countrymen seem to be propitious to the interests which the Constitution intrusts to our Federal Union, and must be auspicious to your own name. You come before the people without the impulse of personal wishes, and free from selfish expectations. You are identified with none of the distractions which have recently disturbed our country, whilst you are known to be faithful to the Constitution—to all its guaranties and compromises. You will be free to exercise your tried abilities, within the path of duty, in protecting that repose we happily enjoy, and in giving efficacy and control to those cardinal principles that have already illustrated the party which has now selected you as its leader—principles that regard the security and prosperity of the whole country, and the paramount power of its laws, as indissolubly associated with the perpetuity of our civil and religious liberties.

"The convention did not pretermit the duty of reiterating those principles, and you will find them prominently set forth in the resolutions it adopted. To these we respectfully invite your attention.

"It is firmly believed that to your talents and patriotism the security of our holy Union, with its expanded and expanding interests, may be wisely trusted, and that, amid all the perils which may assail the Constitution, you will have the heart to love and the arm to defend it."

We quote likewise General Pierce's reply:—

"I have the honor to acknowledge your personal kindness in presenting me, this day, your letter, officially informing me of my nomination, by the democratic national convention, as a candidate for the presidency of the United States. The surprise with which I received the intelligence of my nomination was not unmingled with painful solicitude; and yet it is proper for me to say that the manner in which it was conferred was peculiarly gratifying.

"The delegation from New Hampshire, with all the glow of state pride, and with all the warmth of personal regard, would not have submitted my name to the convention, nor would they have cast a vote for me, under circumstances other than those which occurred.

"I shall always cherish with pride and gratitude the recollection of the fact that the voice which first pronounced, and pronounced alone, came from the Mother of States—a pride and gratitude rising above any consequences that can betide me personally. May I not regard it as a fact pointing to the overthrow of sectional jealousies, and looking to the permanent life and vigor of the Union, cemented by the blood of those who have passed to their reward?—a Union wonderful in its formation, boundless in its hopes, amazing in its destiny.

"I accept the nomination, relying upon an abiding devotion to the interests, honor, and glory of the whole country, but, above and beyond all, upon a Power superior to all human might—a Power which, from the first gun of the Revolution, in every crisis through which we have passed, in every hour of acknowledged peril, when the dark clouds had shut down over us, has interposed as if to baffle human wisdom, outmarch human forecast, and bring out of darkness the rainbow of promise. Weak myself, faith and hope repose there in security.

"I accept the nomination upon the platform adopted by the convention, not because this is expected of me as a candidate, but because the principles it embraces command the approbation of my judgment; and with them, I believe I can safely say, there has been no word or act of my life in conflict."

70

The news of his nomination went abroad over the Union, and, far and wide, there came a response, in which was distinguishable a truer appreciation of some of General Pierce's leading traits than could have been anticipated, considering the unobtrusive tenor of his legislative life, and the lapse of time since he had entirely withdrawn himself from the nation's eye. It was the marvellous and mystic influence of character, in regard to which the judgment of the people is so seldom found erroneous, and which conveys the perception of itself through some medium higher and deeper than the intellect. Everywhere the country knows that a man of steadfast will, true heart, and generous qualities has been brought forward, to receive the suffrages of his fellow-citizens.

He comes before the people of the United States at a remarkable era in the history of this country and of the world. The two great parties of the nation appear—at least to an observer somewhat removed from both—to have nearly merged into one another; for they preserve the attitude of political antagonism rather through the effect of their old organizations than because any great and radical principles are at present in dispute between them. The measures advocated by the one party, and resisted by the other, through a long series of years, have now ceased to be the pivots on which the election turns. The prominent statesmen, so long identified with those measures, will henceforth relinquish their controlling influence over public affairs. Both parties, it may likewise be said, are united in one common purpose,—that of preserving our sacred Union, as the immovable basis from which the destinies, not of America alone, but of mankind at large, may be carried upward and consummated. And thus men stand together, in unwonted quiet and harmony, awaiting the new movement in advance which all these tokens indicate.

It remains for the citizens of this great country to decide, within the next few weeks, whether they will retard the steps of human progress by placing at its head an illustrious soldier, indeed, a patriot, and one indelibly stamped into the history of the past, but who has already done his work, and has not in him the spirit of the present or of the coming time; or whether they will put their trust in a new man, whom a life of energy and various activity has tested, but not worn out, and advance with him into the auspicious epoch upon which we are about to enter.

NOTE.

We have done far less than justice to Franklin Pierce's college standing, in our statement in Chapter I. Some circumstances connected with this matter are too characteristic not to be reported.

During the first two years, Pierce was extremely inattentive to his college duties, bestowing only such modicum of time upon them as was requisite to supply the merest superficial acquaintance with the course of study for the recitation room. The consequence was that when the relative standing of the members of the class was first authoritatively ascertained, in the junior year, he found himself occupying precisely the lowest position in point of scholarship. In the first mortification of wounded pride, he resolved never to attend another recitation, and accordingly absented himself from college exercises of all kinds for several days, expecting and desiring that some form of punishment, such as suspension or expulsion, would be the result. The faculty of the college, however, with a wise lenity, took no notice of this behavior; and at last, having had time to grow cool, and moved by the grief of his friend Little and another classmate, Pierce determined to resume the routine of college duties. "But," said he to his friends, "if I do so, you shall see a change!"

Accordingly, from that time forward, he devoted himself to study. His mind, having run wild for so long a period, could be reclaimed only by the severest efforts of an iron resolution; and for three months afterwards, he rose at four in the morning, toiled all day over his books, and retired only at midnight, allowing himself but four hours for sleep. With habit and exercise, he acquired command over his intellectual powers, and was no longer under the necessity of application so intense. But from the moment when he made his resolve until the close of his college life, he never incurred a censure, never was absent (and then unavoidably) but from two college exercises, never went into the recitation room without a thorough acquaintance with the subject to be recited, and finally graduated as the third scholar of his class. Nothing save the low standard of his previous scholarship prevented his taking a yet higher rank.

The moral of this little story lies in the stern and continued exercise of self-controlling will, which redeemed him from indolence, completely changed the aspect of his character, and made this the turning point of his life.

CHIEFLY ABOUT WAR MATTERS.

By a Peaceable Man.

[This article appeared in the "Atlantic Monthly" for July, 1862, and is now first reprinted among Hawthorne's collected writings. The editor of the magazine objected to sundry paragraphs in the manuscript, and these were cancelled with the consent of the author, who himself supplied all the footnotes that accompanied the article when it was published. It has seemed best to retain them in the present reproduction. One of the suppressed passages, in which President Lincoln is described, has since been printed, and is therefore restored to its proper place in the following pages.—G. P. L.]

Here is no remoteness of life and thought, no hermetically sealed seclusion, except possibly, that of the grave, into which the disturbing influences of this war do not penetrate. Of course, the general heart-quake of the country long ago knocked at my cottage-door, and compelled me, reluctantly, to suspend the contemplation of certain fantasies, to which, according to my harmless custom, I was endeavoring to give a sufficiently life-like aspect to admit of their figuring in a romance. As I make no pretensions to state-craft or soldiership, and could promote the common weal neither by valor nor counsel, it seemed, at first, a pity that I should be debarred from such unsubstantial business as I had contrived for myself, since nothing more genuine was to be substituted for it. But I magnanimously considered that there is a kind of treason in insulating one's self from the universal fear and sorrow, and thinking one's idle thoughts in the dread time of civil war; and could a man be so cold and hardhearted, he would better deserve to be sent to Fort Warren than many who have found their way thither on the score of violent, but misdirected sympathies. I remembered the touching rebuke administered by King Charles to that rural squire the echo of whose hunting-horn came to the poor monarch's ear on the morning before a battle, where the sovereignty and constitution of England were to be set at a stake. So I gave myself up to reading newspapers and listening to the click of the telegraph, like other people; until, after a great many months of such pastime, it grew so abominably irksome that I determined to look a little more closely at matters with my own eyes.

Accordingly we set out—a friend and myself—towards Washington, while it was still the long, dreary January of our Northern year, though March in name; nor were we unwilling to clip a little margin off the five months' winter, during which there is nothing genial in New England save the fireside. It was a clear, frosty morning, when we started. The sun shone brightly on snow-covered hills in the neighborhood of Boston, and burnished the surface of frozen ponds; and the wintry weather kept along with us while we trundled through Worcester and Springfield, and all those old, familiar towns, and through the village-cities of Connecticut. In New York the streets were afloat with liquid mud and slosh. Over New Jersey there was still a thin covering of snow, with the face of Nature visible through the rents in her white shroud, though with little or no symptom of reviving life. But when we reached Philadelphia, the air was mild and balmy; there was but a patch or two of dingy winter here and there, and the bare, brown fields about the city were ready to be green. We had met the Spring half-way, in her slow progress from the South; and if we kept onward at the same pace, and could get through the Rebel lines, we should soon come to fresh grass, fruit-blossoms, green peas, strawberries, and all such delights of early summer.

On our way, we heard many rumors of the war, but saw few signs of it. The people were staid and decorous, according to their ordinary fashion; and business seemed about as brisk as usual,—though, I suppose, it was considerably diverted from its customary channels into warlike ones. In the cities, especially in New York, there was a rather prominent display of military goods at the shop windows,—such as swords with gilded scabbards and trappings, epaulets, carabines, revolvers, and sometimes a great iron cannon at the edge of the pavement, as if Mars had dropped one of his pocket-pistols there, while hurrying to the field. As railway-companions, we had now and then a volunteer in his French-gray great-coat, returning from furlough, or a new-made officer travelling to join his regiment, in his new-made uniform, which was perhaps all of the military character that he had about him,—but proud of his eagle-buttons and likely enough to do them honor before the gilt should be wholly dimmed. The country, in short, so far as bustle and movement went, was more quiet than in ordinary times, because so large a proportion of its restless elements had been drawn towards the seat of the conflict. But the air was full of a vague disturbance. To me, at least, it seemed so, emerging from such a solitude as has been hinted at, and the more impressible by rumors and indefinable presentiments, since I had not lived, like other men, in an atmosphere of continual talk about the war. A battle was momentarily expected on the Potomac; for, though our army was still on the hither side of the river, all of us were looking towards the mysterious and terrible Manassas, with the idea that somewhere in its neighborhood lay a ghastly battle-field, yet to be fought, but foredoomed of old to be bloodier than the one where we had reaped such shame. Of all haunted places, methinks such a destined field should be thickest thronged with ugly phantoms, ominous of mischief through ages beforehand.

Beyond Philadelphia there was a much greater abundance of military people. Between Baltimore and Washington a guard seemed to hold every station along the railroad; and frequently, on the hill-sides, we saw a collection of weather-beaten tents, the peaks of which, blackened with smoke, indicated that they had been made comfortable by stove-heat throughout the winter. At several commanding positions we saw fortifications, with the muzzles of cannon protruding from the ramparts, the slopes of which were made of the yellow earth of that region, and still unsodded; whereas, till these troublous times, there have been no forts but what were grass-grown with the lapse of at least a lifetime of peace. Our stopping-places were thronged with soldiers, some of whom came through the cars asking for newspapers that contained accounts of the battle between the Merrimack and Monitor, which had been fought the day before. A railway-train met us, conveying a regiment out of Washington to some unknown point; and reaching the capital, we filed out of the station between lines of soldiers, with shouldered muskets, putting us in mind of similar spectacles at the gates of European cities. It was not without sorrow that we saw the free circulation of the nation's life-blood (at the very heart, moreover) clogged with such strictures as these, which have caused chronic diseases in almost all countries save our own. Will the time ever come again, in America, when we may live half a score of years without once seeing the likeness of a soldier, except it be in the festal march of a company on its summer tour? Not in this generation, I fear, nor in the next, nor till the Millennium; and even that blessed epoch, as the prophecies seem to intimate, will advance to the sound of the trumpet.

One terrible idea occurs in reference to this matter. Even supposing the war should end to-morrow, and the army melt into the mass of the population within the year, what an incalculable preponderance will there be of military titles and pretensions for at least half a century to come! Every country-neighborhood will have its general or two, its three or four colonels, half a dozen majors, and captains without end,—besides non-commissioned officers and privates, more than the recruiting offices ever knew of,—all with their campaign-stories, which will become the staple of fireside talk forevermore. Military merit, or rather, since that is not so readily estimated, military notoriety, will be the measure of all claims to civil distinction.— One bullet-headed general will succeed another in the Presidential chair; and veterans will hold the offices at home and abroad, and sit in Congress and the state legislatures, and fill all the avenues of public life. And yet I do not speak of this deprecatingly, since, very likely, it may substitute something more real and genuine, instead of the many shams on which men have heretofore founded their claims to public regard; but it behooves civilians to consider their wretched prospects in the future, and assume the military button before it is too late.

We were not in time to see Washington as a camp. On the very day of our arrival sixty thousand men had crossed the Potomac on their march towards Manassas; and almost with their first step into the Virginia mud, the phantasmagory of a countless host and impregnable ramparts, before which they had so long remained quiescent, dissolved quite away. It was as if General McClellan had thrust his sword into a gigantic enemy, and, beholding him suddenly collapse, had discovered to himself and the world that he had merely punctured an enormously swollen bladder. There are instances of a similar character in old romances, where great armies are long kept at bay by the arts of necromancers, who build airy towers and battlements, and muster warriors of terrible aspect, and thus feign a defence of seeming impregnability, until some bolder champion of the besiegers dashes forward to try an encounter with the foremost foeman, and finds him melt away in the death grapple. With such heroic adventures let the march upon Manassas be hereafter reckoned. The whole business, though connected with the destinies of a nation, takes inevitably a tinge of the ludicrous. The vast preparation of men and warlike material,—the majestic patience and docility with which the people waited through those weary and dreary months,—the martial skill, courage, and caution, with which our movement was ultimately made,—and, at last, the tremendous shock with which we were brought suddenly up against nothing at all! The Southerners show little sense of humor nowadays, but I think they must have meant to provoke a laugh at our expense, when they planted those Quaker guns. At all events, no other Rebel artillery has played upon us with such overwhelming effect.

The troops being gone, we had the better leisure and opportunity to look into other matters. It is natural enough to suppose that the centre and heart of Washington is the Capitol; and certainly, in its outward aspect, the world has not many statelier or more beautiful edifices, nor any, I should suppose, more skilfully adapted to legislative purposes, and to all accompanying needs. But, etc., etc. [We omit several paragraphs here, in which the author speaks of some prominent Members of Congress with a freedom that seems to have been not unkindly meant, but might be liable to misconstruction. As he admits that he never listened to an important debate, we can hardly recognize his qualifications to estimate these gentlemen, in their legislative and oratorical capacities.

* * * * * *

We found one man, however, at the Capitol, who was satisfactorily adequate to the business which brought him thither. In quest of him, we went through halls, galleries, and corridors, and ascended a noble staircase, balustraded with a dark and beautifully variegated marble from Tennessee, the richness of which is quite a sufficient cause for objecting to the secession of that State. At last we came to a barrier of pine boards, built right across the stairs. Knocking at a rough, temporary door, we thrust a card beneath; and in a minute or two it was opened by a person in his shirt-sleeves, a middle-aged figure, neither tall nor short, of Teutonic build and aspect, with an ample beard of a ruddy tinge and chestnut hair. He looked at us, in the first place, with keen and somewhat guarded eyes, as if it were not his practice to vouchsafe any great warmth of greeting, except upon sure ground of observation. Soon, however, his look grew kindly and genial (not that it had ever been in the least degree repulsive, but only reserved), and Leutze allowed us to gaze at the cartoon of his great fresco, and talked about it unaffectedly, as only a man of true genius can speak of his own works. Meanwhile the noble design spoke for itself upon the wall. A sketch in color, which we saw afterwards, helped us to form some distant and flickering notion of what the picture will be, a few months hence, when these bare outlines, already so rich in thought and suggestiveness, shall glow with a fire of their own,—a fire which, I truly believe, will consume every other pictorial decoration of the Capitol, or, at least, will compel us to banish those stiff and respectable productions to some less conspicuous gallery. The work will be emphatically original and American, embracing characteristics that neither art nor literature have yet dealt with, and producing new forms of artistic beauty from the natural features of the Rocky-Mountain region, which Leutze seems to have studied broadly and minutely. The garb of the hunters and wanderers of those deserts, too, under his free and natural management, is shown as the most picturesque of costumes. But it would be doing this admirable painter no kind office to overlay his picture with any more of my colorless and uncertain words; so I shall merely add that it looked full of energy, hope, progress, irrepressible movement onward, all represented in a momentary pause of triumph; and it was most cheering to feel its good augury at this dismal time, when our country might seem to have arrived at such a deadly stand-still.

It was an absolute comfort, indeed, to find Leutze so quietly busy at this great national work, which is destined to glow for centuries on the walls of the Capitol, if that edifice shall stand, or must share its fate, if treason shall succeed in subverting it with the Union which it represents. It was delightful to see him so calmly elaborating his design, while other men doubted and feared, or hoped treacherously, and whispered to one another that the nation would exist only a little longer, or that, if a remnant still held together, its centre and seat of government would be far northward and westward of Washington.

But the artist keeps right on, firm of heart and hand, drawing his outlines with an unwavering pencil, beautifying and idealizing our rude, material life, and thus manifesting that we have an indefeasible claim to a more enduring national existence. In honest truth, what with the hope-inspiring influence of the design, and what with Leutze's undisturbed evolvement of it, I was exceedingly encouraged, and allowed these cheerful auguries to weigh against a sinister omen that was pointed out to me in another part of the Capitol. The freestone walls of the central edifice are pervaded with great cracks, and threaten to come thundering down, under the immense weight of the iron dome,—an appropriate catastrophe enough if it should occur on the day when we drop the Southern stars out of our flag.

Everybody seems to be at Washington, and yet there is a singular dearth of imperatively noticeable people there. I question whether there are half a dozen individuals, in all kinds of eminence, at whom a stranger, wearied with the contact of a hundred moderate celebrities, would turn round to snatch a second glance. Secretary Seward, to be sure,—a pale, large-nosed, elderly man, of moderate stature, with a decided originality of gait and aspect, and a cigar in his mouth,—etc., etc. [We are again compelled to interfere with our friend's license of personal description and criticism. Even Cabinet Ministers (to whom the next few pages of the article were devoted) had their private immunities, which ought to be conscientiously observed,—unless, indeed, the writer chanced to have some very piquant motives for violating them.]

* * * * * *

Of course, there was one other personage, in the class of statesmen, whom I should have been truly mortified to leave Washington without seeing; since (temporarily, at least, and by force of circumstances) he was the man of men. But a private grief had built up a barrier about him, impeding the customary free intercourse of Americans with their chief magistrate; so that I might have come away without a glimpse of his very remarkable physiognomy, save for a semi-official opportunity of which I was glad to take advantage. The fact is, we were invited to annex ourselves, as supernumeraries, to a deputation that was about to wait upon the President, from a Massachusetts whip-factory, with a present of a splendid whip.

Our immediate party consisted only of four or five (including Major Ben Perley Poore, with his note-book and pencil), but we were joined by several other persons, who seemed to have been lounging about the precincts of the White House, under the spacious porch, or within the hall, and who swarmed in with us to take the chances of a presentation. Nine o'clock had been appointed as the time for receiving the deputation, and we were punctual to the moment; but not so the President, who sent us word that he was eating his breakfast, and would come as soon as he could. His appetite, we were glad to think, must have been a pretty fair one; for we waited about half an hour in one of the antechambers, and then were ushered into a reception-room, in one corner of which sat the Secretaries of War and of the Treasury, expecting, like ourselves, the termination of the Presidential breakfast. During this interval there were several new additions to our group, one or two of whom were in a working-garb, so that we formed a very miscellaneous collection of people, mostly unknown to each other, and without any common sponsor, but all with an equal right to look our head-servant in the face.

By and by there was a little stir on the staircase and in the passage-way, and in lounged a tall, loose-jointed figure, of an exaggerated Yankee port and demeanor, whom (as being about the homeliest man I ever saw, yet by no means repulsive or disagreeable) it was impossible not to recognize as Uncle Abe.

Unquestionably, Western man though he be, and Kentuckian by birth, President Lincoln is the essential representative of all Yankees, and the veritable specimen, physically, of what the world seems determined to regard as our characteristic qualities. It is the strangest and yet the fittest thing in the jumble of human vicissitudes, that he, out of so many millions, unlooked for, unselected by any intelligible process that could be based upon his genuine qualities, unknown to those who chose him, and unsuspected of what endowments may adapt him for his tremendous responsibility, should have found the way open for him to fling his lank personality into the chair of state,—where, I presume, it was his first impulse to throw his legs on the council-table, and tell the Cabinet Ministers a story. There is no describing his lengthy awkwardness, nor the uncouthness of his movement; and yet it seemed as if I had been in the habit of seeing him daily, and had shaken hands with him a thousand times in some village street; so true was he to the aspect of the pattern American, though with a certain extravagance which, possibly, I exaggerated still further by the delighted eagerness with which I took it in. If put to guess his calling and livelihood, I should have taken him for a country schoolmaster as soon as anything else. He was dressed in a rusty black frock-coat and pantaloons, unbrushed, and worn so faithfully that the suit had adapted itself to the curves and angularities of his figure, and had grown to be an outer skin of the man. He had shabby slippers on his feet. His hair was black, still unmixed with gray, stiff, somewhat bushy, and had apparently been acquainted with neither brush nor comb that morning, after the disarrangement of the pillow; and as to a night-cap, Uncle Abe probably knows nothing of such effeminacies. His complexion is dark and sallow, betokening, I fear, an insalubrious atmosphere around the White House; he has thick black eyebrows and an impending brow; his nose is large, and the lines about his mouth are very strongly defined.

The whole physiognomy is as coarse a one as you would meet anywhere in the length and breadth of the States; but, withal, it is redeemed, illuminated, softened, and brightened by a kindly though serious look out of his eyes, and an expression of homely sagacity, that seems weighted with rich results of village experience. A great deal of native sense; no bookish cultivation, no refinement; honest at heart, and thoroughly so, and yet, in some sort, sly,— at least, endowed with a sort of tact and wisdom that are akin to craft, and would impel him, I think, to take an antagonist in flank, rather than to make a bull-run at him right in front. But, on the whole, I like this sallow, queer, sagacious visage, with the homely human sympathies that warmed it; and, for my small share in the matter, would as lief have Uncle Abe for a ruler as any man whom it would have been practicable to put in his place.

Immediately on his entrance the President accosted our member of Congress, who had us in charge, and, with a comical twist of his face, made some jocular remark about the length of his breakfast. He then greeted us all round, not waiting for an introduction, but shaking and squeezing everybody's hand with the utmost cordiality, whether the individual's name was announced to him or not. His manner towards us was wholly without pretence, but yet had a kind of natural dignity, quite sufficient to keep the forwardest of us from clapping him on the shoulder and asking him for a story. A mutual acquaintance being established, our leader took the whip out of its case, and began to read the address of presentation. The whip was an exceedingly long one, its handle wrought in ivory (by some artist in the Massachusetts State Prison, I believe), and ornamented with a medallion of the President, and other equally beautiful devices; and along its whole length there was a succession of golden bands and ferrules. The address was shorter than the whip, but equally well made, consisting chiefly of an explanatory description of these artistic designs, and closing with a hint that the gift was a suggestive and emblematic one, and that the President would recognize the use to which such an instrument should be put.

This suggestion gave Uncle Abe rather a delicate task in his reply, because, slight as the matter seemed, it apparently called for some declaration, or intimation, or faint foreshadowing of policy in reference to the conduct of the war, and the final treatment of the Rebels. But the President's Yankee aptness and not-to-be-caughtness stood him in good stead, and he jerked or wiggled himself out of the dilemma with an uncouth dexterity that was entirely in character; although, without his gesticulation of eye and month,— and especially the flourish of the whip, with which he imagined himself touching up a pair of fat horses,—I doubt whether his words would be worth recording, even if I could remember them. The gist of the reply was, that he accepted the whip as an emblem of peace; not punishment; and, this great affair over, we retired out of the presence in high good-humor, only regretting that we could not have seen the President sit down and fold up his legs (which is said to be a most extraordinary spectacle), or have heard him tell one of those delectable stories for which he is so celebrated. A good many of them are afloat upon the common talk of Washington, and are certainly the aptest, pithiest, and funniest little things imaginable; though, to be sure, they smack of the frontier freedom, and would not always bear repetition in a drawing-room, or on the immaculate page of the Atlantic.

[The above passage relating to President Lincoln was one of those omitted from the article as originally published, and the following note was appended to explain the omission, which had been indicated by a line of points:—

We are compelled to omit two or three pages, in which the author describes the interview, and gives his idea of the personal appearance and deportment of the President. The sketch appears to have been written in a benign spirit, and perhaps conveys a not inaccurate impression of its august subject; but it lacks reverence, and it pains us to see a gentleman of ripe age, and who has spent years under the corrective influence of foreign institutions, falling into the characteristic and most ominous fault of Young America.]

Good Heavens! what liberties have I been taking with one of the potentates of the earth, and the man on whose conduct more important consequences depend than on that of any other historical personage of the century! But with whom is an American citizen entitled to take a liberty, if not with his own chief magistrate? However, lest the above allusions to President Lincoln's little peculiarities (already well known to the country and to the world) should be misinterpreted, I deem it proper to say a word or two in regard to him, of unfeigned respect and measurable confidence. He is evidently a man of keen faculties, and, what is still more to the purpose, of powerful character. As to his integrity, the people have that intuition of it which is never deceived. Before he actually entered upon his great office, and for a considerable time afterwards, there is no reason to suppose that he adequately estimated the gigantic task about to be imposed on him, or, at least, had any distinct idea how it was to be managed; and I presume there may have been more than one veteran politician who proposed to himself to take the power out of President Lincoln's hands into his own, leaving our honest friend only the public responsibility for the good or ill success of the career. The extremely imperfect development of his statesmanly qualities, at that period, may have justified such designs. But the President is teachable by events, and has now spent a year in a very arduous course of education; he has a flexible mind, capable of much expansion, and convertible towards far loftier studies and activities than those of his early life; and if he came to

Washington a backwoods humorist, he has already transformed himself into as good a statesman (to speak moderately) as his prime-minister.

Among other excursions to camps and places of interest in the neighborhood of Washington, we went, one day, to Alexandria. It is a little port on the Potomac, with one or two shabby wharves and docks, resembling those of a fishing-village in New England, and the respectable old brick town rising gently behind. In peaceful times it no doubt bore an aspect of decorous quietude and dulness; but it was now thronged with the Northern soldiery, whose stir and bustle contrasted strikingly with the many closed warehouses, the absence of citizens from their customary haunts, and the lack of any symptom of healthy activity, while army-wagons trundled heavily over the pavements, and sentinels paced the sidewalks, and mounted dragoons dashed to and fro on military errands. I tried to imagine how very disagreeable the presence of a Southern army would be in a sober town of Massachusetts; and the thought considerably lessened my wonder at the cold and shy regards that are cast upon our troops, the gloom, the sullen demeanor, the declared or scarcely hidden sympathy with rebellion, which are so frequent here. It is a strange thing in human life, that the greatest errors both of men and women often spring from their sweetest and most generous qualities; and so, undoubtedly, thousands of warm-hearted, sympathetic, and impulsive persons have joined the Rebels, not from any real zeal for the cause, but because, between two conflicting loyalties, they chose that which necessarily lay nearest the heart. There never existed any other government against which treason was so easy, and could defend itself by such plausible arguments, as against that of the United States. The anomaly of two allegiances (of which that of the State comes nearest home to a man's feelings, and includes the altar and the hearth, while the General Government claims his devotion only to an airy mode of law, and has no symbol but a flag) is exceedingly mischievous in this point of view; for it has converted crowds of honest people into traitors, who seem to themselves not merely innocent but patriotic, and who die for a bad cause with as quiet a conscience as if it were the best. In the vast extent of our country,—too vast by far to be taken into one small human heart,— we inevitably limit to our own State, or, at farthest, to our own section, that sentiment of physical love for the soil which renders an Englishman, for example, so intensely sensitive to the dignity and well-being of his little island, that one hostile foot, treading anywhere upon it, would make a bruise on each individual breast. If a man loves his individual State, therefore, and is content to be ruined with her, let us shoot him if we can, but allow him an honorable burial in the soil he fights for.

[We do not thoroughly comprehend the author's drift in the foregoing paragraph, but are inclined to think its tone reprehensible, and its tendency impolitic in the present stage of our national difficulties.]

In Alexandria we visited the tavern in which Colonel Ellsworth was killed, and saw the spot where he fell, and saw the stairs below, whence Jackson fired the fatal shot, and where he himself was slain a moment afterwards; so that the assassin and his victim must have met on the threshold of the spirit-world, and perhaps came to a better understanding before they had taken many steps on the other side. Ellsworth was too generous to bear an immortal grudge for a deed like that, done in hot blood, and by no skulking enemy. The memorial-hunters have completely cut away the original wood-work around the spot, with their pocket-knives; and the staircase, balustrade, and floor, as well as the adjacent doors and door-frames, have recently been renewed; the walls, moreover, are covered with new paper-hangings, the former having been torn off in tatters; and thus it becomes something like a metaphysical question whether the place of the murder actually exists.

Driving out of Alexandria, we stopped on the edge of the city to inspect an old slave-pen, which is one of the lions of the place, but a very poor one; and a little farther on, we came to a brick church, where Washington used sometimes to attend service,—a pre-Revolutionary edifice, with ivy growing over its walls, though not very luxuriantly. Reaching the open country, we saw forts and camps on all sides; some of the tents being placed immediately on the ground, while others were raised over a basement of logs, laid lengthwise, like those of a log-hut, or driven vertically into the soil in a circle,—thus forming a solid wall, the chinks closed up with Virginia mud, and above it the pyramidal shelter of the tent. Here were in progress all the occupations, and all the idleness, of the soldier in the tented field: some were cooking the company-rations in pots hung over fires in the open air; some played at ball, or developed their muscular power by gymnastic exercise; some read newspapers; some smoked cigars or pipes; and many were cleaning their arms or accoutrements,—the more carefully, perhaps, because their division was to be reviewed by the Commander-in-Chief that afternoon; others sat on the ground, while their comrades cut their hair,—it being a soldierly fashion (and for excellent reasons) to crop it within an inch of the skull; others, finally, lay asleep in breast-high tents, with their legs protruding into the open air.

We paid a visit to Fort Ellsworth, and from its ramparts (which have been heaped up out of the muddy soil within the last few months, and will require still a year or two to make them verdant) we had a beautiful view of the Potomac, a truly majestic river, and the surrounding country. The fortifications, so numerous in all this region, and now so unsightly with their bare, precipitous sides, will remain as historic monuments, grass-grown and picturesque memorials of an epoch of terror and suffering: they will serve to make our country dearer and more interesting to us, and afford fit soil for poetry to root itself in: for this is a plant which thrives best in spots where blood has been spilt long ago, and grows in abundant clusters in old ditches, such as the moat around Fort Ellsworth will be a century hence. It may seem to be paying dear for what many will reckon but a worthless weed; but the more historical associations we can link with our localities, the richer will be the daily life that feeds upon the past, and the more valuable the things that have been long established: so that our children will be less prodigal than their fathers in sacrificing good institutions to passionate impulses and impracticable theories. This herb of grace, let us hope, will be found in the old footprints of the war.

Even in an aesthetic point of view, however, the war has done a great deal of enduring mischief, by causing the devastation of great tracts of woodland scenery, in which this part of Virginia would appear to be very rich. Around all the encampments, and everywhere along the road, we saw the bare sites of what had evidently been tracts of hard-wood forest, indicated by the unsightly stumps of well-grown trees, not smoothly felled by regular axe-men, but hacked, haggled, and unevenly amputated, as by a sword or other miserable tool, in an unskilful hand. Fifty years will not repair this desolation. An army destroys everything before and around it, even to the very grass; for the sites of the encampments are converted into barren esplanades, like those of the squares in French cities, where not a blade of grass is allowed to grow. As to the other symptoms of devastation and obstruction, such as deserted houses, unfenced fields, and a general aspect of nakedness and ruin, I know not how much may be due to a normal lack of neatness in the rural life of Virginia, which puts a squalid face even upon a prosperous state of things; but undoubtedly the war must have spoilt what was good, and made the bad a great deal worse. The carcasses of horses were scattered along the wayside.

One very pregnant token of a social system thoroughly disturbed was presented by a party of contrabands, escaping out of the mysterious depths of Secessia; and its strangeness consisted in the leisurely delay with which they trudged forward, as dreading no pursuer, and encountering nobody to turn them back. They were unlike the specimens of their race whom we are accustomed to see at the North, and, in my judgment, were far more agreeable. So rudely were they attired,—as if their garb had grown upon them spontaneously,—so picturesquely natural in manners, and wearing such a crust of primeval simplicity (which is quite polished away from the Northern black man), that they seemed a kind of creature by themselves, not altogether human, but perhaps quite as good, and akin to the fawns and rustic deities of olden times. I wonder whether I shall excite anybody's wrath by saying this. It is no great matter. At all events, I felt most kindly towards these poor fugitives, but knew not precisely what to wish in their behalf, nor in the least how to help them. For the sake of the manhood which is latent in them, I would not have turned them back; but I should have felt almost as reluctant, on their own account, to hasten them forward to the stranger's land; and I think my prevalent idea was, that, whoever may be benefited by the results of this war, it will not be the present generation of negroes, the childhood of whose race is now gone forever, and who must henceforth fight a hard battle with the world, on very unequal terms. On behalf of my own race, I am glad and can only hope that an inscrutable Providence means good to both parties.

There is an historical circumstance, known to few, that connects the children of the Puritans with these Africans of Virginia in a very singular way. They are our brethren, as being lineal descendants from the Mayflower, the fated womb of which, in her first voyage, sent forth a brood of Pilgrims on Plymouth Rock, and, in a subsequent one, spawned slaves upon the Southern soil,—a monstrous birth, but with which we have an instinctive sense of kindred, and so are stirred by an irresistible impulse to attempt their rescue, even at the cost of blood and ruin. The character of our sacred ship, I fear, may suffer a little by this revelation; but we must let her white progeny offset her dark one,—and two such portents never sprang from an identical source before.

While we drove onward, a young officer on horseback looked earnestly into the carriage, and recognized some faces that he had seen before; so he rode along by our side, and we pestered him with queries and observations, to which he responded more civilly than they deserved. He was on General McClellan's staff; and a gallant cavalier, high-booted, with a revolver in his belt, and mounted on a noble horse, which trotted hard and high without disturbing the rider in his accustomed seat. His face had a healthy hue of exposure and an expression of careless hardihood; and, as I looked at him, it seemed to me that the war had brought good fortune to the youth of this epoch, if to none beside; since they now make it their daily business to ride a horse and handle a sword, instead of lounging listlessly through the duties, occupations, pleasures—all tedious alike—to which the artificial state of society limits a peaceful generation. The atmosphere of the camp and the smoke of the battle-field are morally invigorating; the hardy virtues flourish in them, the nonsense dies like a wilted weed. The enervating effects of centuries of civilization vanish at once, and leave these young men to enjoy a life of hardship, and the exhilarating sense of danger,—to kill men blamelessly, or to be killed gloriously,—and to be happy in following out their native instincts of destruction, precisely in the spirit of Homer's heroes, only with some considerable change of mode. One touch of Nature makes not only the whole world, but all time, akin. Set men face to face, with weapons in their hands, and they are as ready to slaughter one another now, after playing at peace and good-will for so many years, as in the rudest ages, that never heard of peace-societies, and thought no wine so delicious as what they quaffed from an enemy's skull. Indeed, if the report of a Congressional committee may be trusted, that old-fashioned kind of goblet has again come into use at the expense of our Northern head-pieces,—a costly drinking-cup to him that furnishes it! Heaven forgive me for seeming to jest upon such a subject!—only, it is so odd, when we measure our advances from barbarism, and find ourselves just here! [We hardly expected this outbreak in favor of war from the Peaceable Man; but the justness of our cause makes us all soldiers at heart, however quiet in our outward life. We have heard of twenty Quakers in a single company of a Pennsylvania regiment.]

We now approached General McClellan's head-quarters, which, at that time, were established at Fairfield Seminary. The edifice was situated on a gentle elevation, amid very agreeable scenery, and, at a distance, looked like a gentleman's seat. Preparations were going forward for reviewing a division of ten or twelve thousand men, the various regiments composing which had begun to array themselves on an extensive plain, where, methought, there was a more convenient place for a battle than is usually found in this broken and difficult country. Two thousand cavalry made a portion of the troops to be reviewed. By and by we saw a pretty numerous troop of mounted officers, who were congregated on a distant part of the plain, and whom we finally ascertained to be the Commander-in-Chief's staff, with McClellan himself at their head. Our party managed to establish itself in a position conveniently close to the General, to whom, moreover, we had the honor of an introduction; and he bowed, on his horseback, with a good deal of dignity and martial courtesy, but no airs nor fuss nor pretension beyond what his character and rank inevitably gave him.

Now, at that juncture, and in fact, up to the present moment, there was, and is, a most fierce and bitter outcry, and detraction loud and low, against General McClellan, accusing him of sloth, imbecility, cowardice, treasonable purposes, and, in short, utterly denying his ability as a soldier, and questioning his integrity as a man. Nor was this to be wondered at; for when before, in all history, do we find a general in command of half a million of men, and in presence of an enemy inferior in numbers and no better disciplined than his own troops, leaving it still debatable, after the better part of a year, whether he is a soldier or no? The question would seem to answer itself in the very asking. Nevertheless, being most profoundly ignorant of the art of war, like the majority of the General's critics, and, on the other hand, having some considerable impressibility by men's characters, I was glad of the opportunity to look him in the face, and to feel whatever influence might reach me from his sphere. So I stared at him, as the phrase goes, with all the eyes I had; and the reader shall have the benefit of what I saw, —to which he is the more welcome, because, in writing this article, I feel disposed to be singularly frank, and can scarcely restrain myself from telling truths the utterance of which I should get slender thanks for.

The General was dressed in a simple, dark-blue uniform, without epaulets, booted to the knee, and with a cloth cap upon his head; and, at first sight, you might have taken him for a corporal of dragoons, of particularly neat and soldier-like aspect, and in the prime of his age and strength. He is only of middling stature, but his build is very compact and sturdy, with broad shoulders and a look of great physical vigor, which, in fact, he is said to possess,—he and Beauregard having been rivals in that particular, and both distinguished above other men. His complexion is dark and sanguine, with dark hair. He has a strong, bold, soldierly face, full of decision; a Roman nose, by no means a thin prominence, but very thick and firm; and if he follows it (which I should think likely), it may be pretty confidently trusted to guide him aright. His profile would make a more effective likeness than the full face, which, however, is much better in the real man than in any photograph that I have seen. His forehead is not remarkably large, but comes forward at the eyebrows; it is not the brow nor countenance of a prominently intellectual man (not a natural student, I mean, or abstract thinker), but of one whose office it is to handle things practically and to bring about tangible results. His face looked capable of being very stern, but wore, in its repose, when I saw it, an aspect pleasant and dignified; it is not, in its character, an American face, nor an English one. The man on whom he fixes his eye is conscious of him. In his natural disposition, he seems calm and self-possessed, sustaining his great responsibilities cheerfully, without shrinking, or weariness, or spasmodic effort, or damage to his health, but all with quiet, deep-drawn breaths; just as his broad shoulders would bear up a heavy burden without aching beneath it.

After we had had sufficient time to peruse the man (so far as it could be done with one pair of very attentive eyes), the General rode off, followed by his cavalcade, and was lost to sight among the troops. They received him with loud shouts, by the eager uproar of which—now near, now in the centre, now on the outskirts of the division, and now sweeping back towards us in a great volume of sound—we could trace his progress through the ranks. If he is a coward, or a traitor, or a humbug, or anything less than a brave, true, and able man, that mass of intelligent soldiers, whose lives and honor he had in charge, were utterly deceived, and so was this present writer; for they believed in him, and so did I; and had I stood in the ranks, should have shouted with the lustiest of them. Of course I may be mistaken; my opinion on such a point is worth nothing, although my impression may be worth a little more; neither do I consider the General's antecedents as bearing very decided testimony to his practical soldiership. A thorough knowledge of the science of war seems to be conceded to him; he is allowed to be a good military critic; but all this is possible without his possessing any positive qualities of a great general, just as a literary critic may show the profoundest acquaintance with the principles of epic poetry without being able to produce a single stanza of an epic poem. Nevertheless, I shall not give up my faith in General McClellan's soldiership until he is defeated, nor in his courage and integrity even then.

Another of our excursions was to Harper's Ferry,—the Directors of the Baltimore and Ohio Railroad having kindly invited us to accompany them on the first trip over the newly laid track, after its breaking up by the Rebels. It began to rain, in the early morning, pretty soon after we left Washington, and continued to pour a cataract throughout the day; so that the aspect of the country was dreary, where it would otherwise have been delightful, as we entered among the hill-scenery that is formed by the subsiding swells of the Alleghanies. The latter part of our journey lay along the shore of the Potomac, in its upper course, where the margin of that noble river is bordered by gray, over-hanging crags, beneath which—and sometimes right through them—the railroad takes its way. In one place the Rebels had attempted to arrest a train by precipitating an immense mass of rock down upon the track, by the side of which it still lay, deeply imbedded in the ground, and looking as if it might have lain there since the Deluge. The scenery grew even more picturesque as we proceeded, the bluffs becoming very bold in their descent upon the river, which, at Harper's Ferry, presents as striking a vista among the hills as a painter could desire to see. But a beautiful landscape is a luxury, and luxuries are thrown away amid discomfort; and when we alighted in the tenacious mud and almost fathomless puddle, on the hither side of the Ferry (the ultimate point to which the cars proceeded, since the railroad bridge had been destroyed by the Rebels), I cannot remember that any very rapturous emotions were awakened by the scenery.

We paddled and floundered over the ruins of the track, and, scrambling down an embankment, crossed the Potomac by a pontoon-bridge, a thousand feet in length, over the narrow line of which—level with the river, and rising and subsiding with it—General Banks had recently led his whole army, with its ponderous artillery and heavy laden wagons. Yet our own tread made it vibrate. The broken bridge of the railroad was a little below us, and at the base of one of its massive piers, in the rocky bed of the river, lay a locomotive, which the Rebels had precipitated there.

As we passed over, we looked towards the Virginia shore, and beheld the little town of Harper's Ferry, gathered about the base of a round hill and climbing up its steep acclivity; so that it somewhat resembled the Etruscan cities which I have seen among the Apennines, rushing, as it were, down an apparently breakneck height. About midway of the ascent stood a shabby brick church, towards which a difficult path went scrambling up the precipice, indicating, one would say; a very fervent aspiration on the part of the worshippers, unless there was some easier mode of access in another direction. Immediately on the shore of the Potomac, and extending back towards the town, lay the dismal ruins of the United States arsenal and armory, consisting of piles of broken bricks and a waste of shapeless demolition, amid which we saw gun-barrels in heaps of hundreds together. They were the relics of the conflagration, bent with the heat of the fire, and rusted with the wintry rain to which they had since been exposed. The brightest sunshine could not have made the scene cheerful, nor have taken away the gloom from the dilapidated town; for, besides the natural shabbiness, and decayed, unthrifty look of a Virginian village, it has an inexpressible forlornness resulting from the devastations of war and its occupation by both armies alternately. Yet there would be a less striking contrast between Southern and New England villages, if the former were as much in the habit of using white paint as we are. It is prodigiously efficacious in putting a bright face upon a bad matter.

There was one small shop which appeared to have nothing for sale. A single man and one or two boys were all the inhabitants in view, except the Yankee sentinels and soldiers, belonging to Massachusetts regiments, who were scattered about pretty numerously. A guard-house stood on the slope of the hill; and in the level street at its base were the offices of the Provost-Marshal and other military authorities, to whom we forthwith reported ourselves. The Provost-Marshal kindly sent a corporal to guide us to the little building which John Brown seized upon as his fortress, and which, after it was stormed by the United States marines, became his temporary prison. It is an old engine-house, rusty and shabby, like every other work of man's hands in this God-forsaken town, and stands fronting upon the river, only a short distance from the bank, nearly at the point where the pontoon-bridge touches the Virginia shore. In its front wall, on each side of the door, are two or three ragged loop-holes, which John Brown perforated for his defence, knocking out merely a brick or two, so as to give himself and his garrison a sight over their rifles. Through these orifices the sturdy old man dealt a good deal of deadly mischief among his assailants, until they broke down the door by thrusting against it with a ladder, and tumbled headlong in upon him. I shall not pretend to be an admirer of old John Brown, any farther than sympathy with Whittier's excellent ballad about him may go; nor did I expect ever to shrink so unutterably from any apophthegm of a sage, whose happy lips have uttered a hundred golden sentences, as from that saying (perhaps falsely attributed to so honored a source), that the death of this blood-stained fanatic has "made the Gallows as venerable as the Cross!" Nobody was ever more justly hanged. He won his martyrdom fairly, and took it firmly. He himself, I am persuaded (such was his natural integrity), would have acknowledged that Virginia had a right to take the life which he had staked and lost; although it would have been better for her, in the hour that is fast coming, if she could generously have forgotten the criminality of his attempt in its enormous folly. On the other hand, any common-sensible man, looking at the matter unsentimentally, must have felt a certain intellectual satisfaction in seeing him hanged, if it were only in requittal of his preposterous miscalculation of possibilities. [Can it be a son of old Massachusetts who utters this abominable sentiment? For shame.]

But, coolly as I seem to say these things, my Yankee heart stirred triumphantly when I saw the use to which John Brown's fortress and prison-house has now been put. What right have I to complain of any other man's foolish impulses, when I cannot possibly control my own? The engine-house is now a place of confinement for Rebel prisoners.

A Massachusetts soldier stood on guard, but readily permitted our whole party to enter. It was a wretched place. A room of perhaps twenty-five feet square occupied the whole interior of the building, having an iron stove in its centre, whence a rusty funnel ascended towards a hole in the roof, which served the purposes of ventilation, as well as for the exit of smoke. We found ourselves right in the midst of the Rebels, some of whom lay on heaps of straw, asleep, or, at all events, giving no sign of consciousness; others sat in the corners of the room, huddled close together, and staring with a lazy kind of interest at the visitors; two were astride of some planks, playing with the dirtiest pack of cards that I ever happened to see. There was only one figure in the least military among all these twenty prisoners of war,—a man with a dark, intelligent, moustached face, wearing a shabby cotton uniform, which he had contrived to arrange with a degree of soldierly smartness, though it had evidently borne the brunt of a very filthy campaign. He stood erect, and talked freely with those who addressed him, telling them his place of residence, the number of his regiment, the circumstances of his capture, and such other particulars as their Northern inquisitiveness prompted them to ask. I liked the manliness of his deportment; he was neither ashamed, nor afraid, nor in the slightest degree sullen, peppery, or contumacious, but bore himself as if whatever animosity he had felt towards his enemies was left upon the battle-field, and would not be resumed till he had again a weapon in his hand.

Neither could I detect a trace of hostile feeling in the countenance, words, or manner of any prisoner there. Almost to a man, they were simple, bumpkin-like fellows, dressed in homespun clothes, with faces singularly vacant of meaning, but sufficiently good-humored: a breed of men, in short, such as I did not suppose to exist in this country, although I have seen their like in some other parts of the world. They were peasants, and of a very low order; a class of people with whom our Northern rural population has not a single trait in common. They were exceedingly respectful,—more so than a rustic New-Englander ever dreams of being towards anybody, except perhaps his minister; and had they worn any hats they would probably have been self-constrained to take them off, under the unusual circumstance of being permitted to hold conversation with well-dressed persons. It is my belief that not a single bumpkin of them all (the moustached soldier always excepted) had the remotest comprehension of what they had been fighting for, or how they had deserved to be shut up in that dreary hole; nor, possibly, did they care to inquire into this latter mystery, but took it as a godsend to be suffered to lie here in a heap of unwashed human bodies, well warmed and well foddered to-day, and without the necessity of bothering themselves about the possible hunger and cold of to-morrow. Their dark prison-life may have seemed to them the sunshine of all their lifetime.

There was one poor wretch, a wild-beast of a man, at whom I gazed with greater interest than at his fellows; although I know not that each one of them, in their semi-barbarous moral state, might not have been capable of the same savage impulse that had made this particular individual a horror to all beholders. At the close of some battle or skirmish, a wounded Union soldier had crept on hands and knees to his feet, and besought his assistance,—not dreaming that any creature in human shape, in the Christian land where they had so recently been brethren, could refuse it. But this man (this fiend, if you prefer to call him so, though I would not advise it) flung a bitter curse at the poor Northerner, and absolutely trampled the soul out of his body, as he lay writhing beneath his feet. The fellow's face was horribly ugly; but I am not quite sure that I should have noticed it if I had not known his story. He spoke not a word, and met nobody's eye, but kept staring upward into the smoky vacancy towards the ceiling, where, it might be, he beheld a continual portraiture of his victim's horror-stricken agonies. I rather fancy, however, that his moral sense was yet too torpid to trouble him with such remorseful visions, and that, for his own part, he might have had very agreeable reminiscences of the soldier's death, if other eyes had not been bent reproachfully upon him and warned him that something was amiss. It was this reproach in other men's eyes that made him look aside. He was a wild-beast, as I began with saying,—an unsophisticated wild-beast,—while the rest of us are partially tamed, though still the scent of blood excites some of the savage instincts of our nature. What this wretch needed, in order to make him capable of the degree of mercy and benevolence that exists in us, was simply such a measure of moral and intellectual development as we have received; and, in my mind, the present war is so well justified by no other consideration as by the probability that it will free this class of Southern whites from a thraldom in which they scarcely begin to be responsible beings. So far as the education of the heart is concerned, the negroes have apparently the advantage of them; and as to other schooling, it is practically unattainable by black or white.

Looking round at these poor prisoners, therefore, it struck me as an immense absurdity that they should fancy us their enemies; since, whether we intend it so or no, they have a far greater stake on our success than we can possibly have. For ourselves, the balance of advantages between defeat and triumph may admit of question. For them, all truly valuable things are dependent on our complete success; for thence would come the regeneration of a people,—the removal of a foul scurf that has overgrown their life, and keeps then in a state of disease and decrepitude, one of the chief symptoms of which is, that, the more they suffer and are debased, the more they imagine themselves strong and beautiful. No human effort, on a grand scale, has ever yet resulted according to the purpose, of its projectors. The advantages are always incidental. Man's accidents are God's purposes. We miss the good we sought, and do the good we little cared for. [The author seems to imagine that he has compressed a great deal of meaning into these little, hard, dry pellets of aphoristic wisdom. We disagree with him. The counsels of wise and good men are often coincident with the purposes of Providence; and the present war promises to illustrate our remark.]

Our Government evidently knows when and where to lay its finger upon its most available citizens; for, quite unexpectedly, we were joined by some other gentlemen, scarcely less competent than ourselves, in a commission to proceed to Fortress Monroe and examine into things in general. Of course, official propriety compels us to be extremely guarded in our description of the interesting objects which this expedition opened to our view. There can be no harm, however, in stating that we were received by the commander of the fortress with a kind of acid good-nature, or mild cynicism, that indicated him to be a humorist, characterized by certain rather pungent peculiarities, yet of no unamiable cast. He is a small, thin, old gentleman, set off by a large pair of brilliant epaulets,—the only pair, so far as my observation went, that adorn the shoulders of any officer in the Union army. Either for our inspection, or because the matter had already been arranged, he drew out a regiment of Zouaves that formed the principal part of his garrison, and appeared at their head, sitting on horseback with rigid perpendicularity, and affording us a vivid idea of the disciplinarian of Baron Steuben's school.

There can be no question of the General's military qualities; he must have been especially useful in converting raw recruits into trained and efficient soldiers. But valor and martial skill are of so evanescent a character (hardly less fleeting than a woman's beauty), that Government has perhaps taken the safer course in assigning to this gallant officer, though distinguished in former wars, no more active duty than the guardianship of an apparently impregnable fortress. The ideas of military men solidify and fossilize so fast, while military science makes such rapid advances, that even here there might be a difficulty. An active, diversified, and therefore a youthful, ingenuity is required by the quick exigencies of this singular war. Fortress Monroe, for example, in spite of the massive solidity of its ramparts, its broad and deep moat, and all the contrivances of defence that were known at the not very remote epoch of its construction, is now pronounced absolutely incapable of resisting the novel modes of assault which may be brought to bear upon it. It can only be the flexible talent of a young man that will evolve a new efficiency out of its obsolete strength.

It is a pity that old men grow unfit for war, not only by their incapacity for new ideas, but by the peaceful and unadventurous tendencies that gradually possess themselves of the once turbulent disposition, which used to snuff the battle-smoke as its congenial atmosphere. It is a pity; because it would be such an economy of human existence, if time-stricken people (whose value I have the better right to estimate, as reckoning myself one of them) could snatch from their juniors the exclusive privilege of carrying on the war. In case of death upon the battle-field, how unequal would be the comparative sacrifice! On one part, a few unenjoyable years, the little remnant of a life grown torpid; on the other, the many fervent summers of manhood in its spring and prime, with all that they include of possible benefit to mankind. Then, too, a bullet offers such a brief and easy way, such a pretty little orifice, through which the weary spirit might seize the opportunity to be exhaled! If I had the ordering of these matters, fifty should be the tenderest age at which a recruit might be accepted for training; at fifty-five or sixty, I would consider him eligible for most kinds of military duty and exposure, excluding that of a forlorn hope, which no soldier should be permitted to volunteer upon, short of the ripe age of seventy. As a general rule, these venerable combatants should have the preference for all dangerous and honorable service in the order of their seniority, with a distinction in favor of those whose infirmities might render their lives less worth the keeping. Methinks there would be no more Bull Runs; a warrior with gout in his toe, or rheumatism in his joints, or with one foot in the grave, would make a sorry fugitive!

On this admirable system, the productive part of the population would be undisturbed even by the bloodiest war; and, best of all, those thousands upon thousands of our Northern girls, whose proper mates will perish in camp-hospitals or on Southern battle-fields, would avoid their doom of forlorn old-maidenhood. But, no doubt, the plan will be pooh-poohed down by the War Department; though it could scarcely be more disastrous than the one on which we began the war, when a young army was struck with paralysis through the age of its commander.

The waters around Fortress Monroe were thronged with a gallant array of ships of war and transports, wearing the Union flag,—"Old Glory," as I hear it called in these days. A little withdrawn from our national fleet lay two French frigates, and, in another direction, an English sloop, under that banner which always makes itself visible, like a red portent in the air, wherever there is strife. In pursuance of our official duty (which had no ascertainable limits), we went on board the flag-ship, and were shown over every part of her, and down into her depths, inspecting her gallant crew, her powerful armament, her mighty engines, and her furnaces, where the fires are always kept burning, as well at midnight as at noon, so that it would require only five minutes to put the vessel under full steam. This vigilance has been felt necessary ever since the Merrimack made that terrible dash from Norfolk. Splendid as she is, however, and provided with all but the very latest improvements in naval armament, the Minnesota belongs to a class of vessels that will be built no more, nor ever fight another battle,—being as much a thing of the past as any of the ships of Queen Elizabeth's time, which grappled with the galleons of the Spanish Armada.

On her quarter-deck, an elderly flag-officer was pacing to and fro, with a self-conscious dignity to which a touch of the gout or rheumatism perhaps contributed a little additional stiffness. He seemed to be a gallant gentleman, but of the old, slow, and pompous school of naval worthies, who have grown up amid rules, forms, and etiquette which were adopted full-blown from the British navy into ours, and are somewhat too cumbrous for the quick spirit of to-day. This order of nautical heroes will probably go down, along with the ships in which they fought valorously and strutted most intolerably. How can an admiral condescend to go to sea in an iron pot? What space and elbow-room can be found for quarter-deck dignity in the cramped lookout of the Monitor, or even in the twenty-feet diameter of her cheese-box? All the pomp and splendor of naval warfare are gone by. Henceforth there must come up a race of enginemen and smoke-blackened cannoneers, who will hammer away at their enemies under the direction of a single pair of eyes; and even heroism— so deadly a gripe is Science laying on our noble possibilities—will become a quality of very minor importance, when its possessor cannot break through the iron crust of his own armament and give the world a glimpse of it.

At no great distance from the Minnesota lay the strangest-looking craft I ever saw. It was a platform of iron, so nearly on a level with the water that the swash of the waves broke over it, under the impulse of a very moderate breeze; and on this platform was raised a circular structure, likewise of iron, and rather broad and capacious, but of no great height. It could not be called a vessel at all; it was a machine,—and I have seen one of somewhat similar appearance employed in cleaning out the docks; or, for lack of a better similitude, it looked like a gigantic rat-trap. It was ugly, questionable, suspicious, evidently mischievous, —nay, I will allow myself to call it devilish; for this was the new war-fiend, destined, along with others of the same breed, to annihilate whole navies and batter down old supremacies. The wooden walls of Old England cease to exist, and a whole history of naval renown reaches its period, now that the Monitor comes smoking into view; while the billows dash over what seems her deck, and storms bury even her turret in green water, as she burrows and snorts along, oftener under the surface than above. The singularity of the object has betrayed me into a more ambitious vein of description than I often indulge; and, after all, I might as well have contented myself with simply saying that she looked very queer.

Going on board, we were surprised at the extent and convenience of her interior accommodations. There is a spacious ward-room, nine or ten feet in height, besides a private cabin for the commander, and sleeping accommodations on an ample scale; the whole well lighted and ventilated, though beneath the surface of the water. Forward, or aft (for it is impossible to tell stem from stern), the crew are relatively quite as well provided for as the officers. It was like finding a palace, with all its conveniences, under the sea. The inaccessibility, the apparent impregnability, of this submerged iron fortress are most satisfactory; the officers and crew get down through a little hole in the deck, hermetically seal themselves, and go below; and until they see fit to reappear, there would seem to be no power given to man whereby they can be brought to light. A storm of cannon-shot damages them no more than a handful of dried peas. We saw the shot-marks made by the great artillery of the Merrimack on the outer casing of the iron tower; they were about the breadth and depth of shallow saucers, almost imperceptible dents, with no corresponding bulge on the interior surface. In fact, the thing looked altogether too safe; though it may not prove quite an agreeable predicament to be thus boxed up in impenetrable iron, with the possibility, one would imagine, of being sent to the bottom of the sea, and, even there, not drowned, but stifled. Nothing, however, can exceed the confidence of the officers in this new craft. It was pleasant to see their benign exultation in her powers of mischief, and the delight with which they exhibited the circumvolutory movement of the tower, the quick thrusting forth of the immense guns to deliver their ponderous missiles, and then the immediate recoil, and the security behind the closed port-holes. Yet even this will not long be the last and most terrible improvement in the science of war. Already we hear of vessels the armament of which is to act entirely beneath the surface of the water; so that, with no other external symptoms than a great bubbling and foaming, and gush of smoke, and belch of smothered thunder out of the yeasty waves, there shall be a deadly fight going on below,—and, by and by, a sucking whirlpool, as one of the ships goes down.

The Monitor was certainly an object of great interest; but on our way to Newport News, whither we next went, we saw a spectacle that affected us with far profounder emotion. It was the sight of the few sticks that are left of the frigate Congress, stranded near the shore,—and still more, the masts of the Cumberland rising midway out of the water, with a tattered rag of a pennant fluttering from one of them. The invisible hull of the latter ship seems to be careened over, so that the three masts stand slantwise; the rigging looks quite unimpaired, except that a few ropes dangle loosely from the yards. The flag (which never was struck, thank Heaven!) is entirely hidden under the waters of the bay, but is still doubtless waving in its old place, although it floats to and fro with the swell and reflex of the tide, instead of rustling on the breeze. A remnant of the dead crew still man the sunken ship, and sometimes a drowned body floats up to the surface.

That was a noble fight. When was ever a better word spoken than that of Commodore Smith, the father of the commander of the Congress, when he heard that his son's ship was surrendered? "Then Joe's dead!" said he; and so it proved. Nor can any warrior be more certain of enduring renown than the gallant Morris, who fought so well the final battle of the old system of naval

102

warfare, and won glory for his country and himself out of inevitable disaster and defeat. That last gun from the Cumberland, when her deck was half submerged, sounded the requiem of many sinking ships. Then went down all the navies of Europe and our own, Old Ironsides and all, and Trafalgar and a thousand other fights became only a memory, never to be acted over again; and thus our brave countrymen come last in the long procession of heroic sailors that includes Blake and Nelson, and so many mariners of England, and other mariners as brave as they, whose renown is our native inheritance. There will be other battles, but no more such tests of seamanship and manhood as the battles of the past; and, moreover, the Millennium is certainly approaching, because human strife is to be transferred from the heart and personality of man into cunning contrivances of machinery, which by and by will fight out our wars with only the clank and smash of iron, strewing the field with broken engines, but damaging nobody's little finger except by accident. Such is obviously the tendency of modern improvement. But, in the mean while, so long as manhood retains any part of its pristine value, no country can afford to let gallantry like that of Morris and his crew, any more than that of the brave Worden, pass unhonored and unrewarded. If the Government do nothing, let the people take the matter into their own hands, and cities give him swords, gold boxes, festivals of triumph, and, if he needs it, heaps of gold. Let poets brood upon the theme, and make themselves sensible how much of the past and future is contained within its compass, till its spirit shall flash forth in the lightning of a song!

From these various excursions, and a good many others (including one to Manassas), we gained a pretty lively idea of what was going on; but, after all, if compelled to pass a rainy day in the hall and parlors of Willard's Hotel, it proved about as profitably spent as if we had floundered through miles of Virginia mud, in quest of interesting matter. This hotel, in fact, may be much more justly called the centre of Washington and the Union than either the Capitol, the White House, or the State Department. Everybody may be seen there. It is the meeting-place of the true representatives of the country,—not such as are chosen blindly and amiss by electors who take a folded ballot from the hand of a local politician, and thrust it into the ballot-box unread, but men who gravitate or are attracted hither by real business, or a native impulse to breathe the intensest atmosphere of the nation's life, or a genuine anxiety to see how this life-and-death struggle is going to deal with us. Nor these only, but all manner of loafers. Never, in any other spot, was there such a miscellany of people. You exchange nods with governors of sovereign States; you elbow illustrious men, and tread on the toes of generals; you hear statesmen and orators speaking in their familiar tones. You are mixed up with office-seekers, wire-pullers, inventors, artists, poets, prosers (including editors, army-correspondents, attaches of foreign journals, and long-winded talkers), clerks, diplomatists, mail-contractors, railway-directors, until your own identity is lost among them. Occasionally you talk with a man whom you have never before heard of, and are struck with the brightness of a thought, and fancy that there is more wisdom hidden among the obscure than is anywhere revealed among the famous. You adopt the universal habit of the place, and call for mint-julep, a whiskey-skin, a gin-cocktail, a brandy smash, or a glass of pure Old Rye; for the conviviality of Washington sets in at an early hour, and, so far as I had opportunity of observing, never terminates at any hour, and all these drinks are continually in request by almost all these people. A constant atmosphere of cigar-smoke, too, envelops the motley crowd, and forms a sympathetic medium, in which men meet more closely and talk more frankly than in any other kind of air. If legislators would smoke in session, they might speak truer words, and fewer of them, and bring about more valuable results.

It is curious to observe what antiquated figures and costumes sometimes make their appearance at Willard's. You meet elderly men with frilled shirt-fronts, for example, the fashion of which adornment passed away from among the people of this world half a century ago. It is as if one of Stuart's portraits were walking abroad. I see no way of accounting for this, except that the trouble of the times, the impiety of traitors, and the peril of our sacred Union and Constitution have disturbed, in their honored graves, some of the venerable fathers of the country, and summoned them forth to protest against the meditated and half-accomplished sacrilege. If it be so, their wonted fires are not altogether extinguished in their ashes,—in their throats, I might rather say,—for I beheld one of these excellent old men quaffing such a horn of Bourbon whiskey as a toper of the present century would be loath to venture upon. But, really, one would be glad to know where these strange figures come from. It shows, at any rate, how many remote, decaying villages and country-neighborhoods of the North, and forest-nooks of the West, and old mansion-houses in cities, are shaken by the tremor of our native soil, so that men long hidden in retirement put on the garments of their youth and hurry out to inquire what is the matter. The old men whom we see here have generally more marked faces than the young ones, and naturally enough; since it must be an extraordinary vigor and renewability of life that can overcome the rusty sloth of age, and keep the senior flexible enough to take an interest in new things; whereas hundreds of commonplace young men come hither to stare with eyes of vacant wonder, and with vague hopes of finding out what they are fit for. And this war (we may say so much in its favor) has been the means of discovering that important secret to not a few.

We saw at Willard's many who had thus found out for themselves, that, when Nature gives a young man no other utilizable faculty, she must be understood as intending him for a soldier. The bulk of the army had moved out of Washington before we reached the city; yet it seemed to me that at least two thirds of the guests and idlers at the hotel were one or another token of the military profession. Many of them, no doubt, were self-commissioned officers, and had put on the buttons and the shoulder-straps, and booted themselves to the knees, merely because captain, in these days, is so good a travelling-name. The majority, however, had been duly appointed by the President, but might be none the better warriors for that. It was pleasant, occasionally, to distinguish a grizzly veteran among this crowd of carpet-knights,—the trained soldier of a lifetime, long ago from West Point, who had spent his prime upon the frontier, and very likely could show an Indian bullet-mark on his breast,—if such decorations, won in an obscure warfare, were worth the showing now.

The question often occurred to me,—and, to say the truth, it added an indefinable piquancy to the scene,—what proportion of all these people, whether soldiers or civilians, were true at heart to the Union, and what part were tainted, more or less, with treasonable sympathies and wishes, even if such had never blossomed into purpose. Traitors there were among them,—

no doubt of that,—civil servants of the public, very reputable persons, who yet deserved to dangle from a cord; or men who buttoned military coats over their breasts, hiding perilous secrets there, which might bring the gallant officer to stand pale-faced before a file of musketeers, with his open grave behind him. But, without insisting upon such picturesque criminality and punishment as this, an observer, who kept both his eyes and heart open, would find it by no means difficult to discern that many residents and visitors of Washington so far sided with the South as to desire nothing more nor better than to see everything reestablished a little worse than its former basis. If the cabinet of Richmond were transferred to the Federal city, and the North awfully snubbed, at least, and driven back within its old political limits, they would deem it a happy day. It is no wonder, and, if we look at the matter generously, no unpardonable crime. Very excellent people hereabouts remember the many dynasties in which the Southern character has been predominant, and contrast the genial courtesy, the warm and graceful freedom of that region, with what they call (though I utterly disagree with them) the frigidity of our Northern manners, and the Western plainness of the President. They have a conscientious, though mistaken belief, that the South was driven out of the Union by intolerable wrong on our part, and that we are responsible for having compelled true patriots to love only half their country instead of the whole, and brave soldiers to draw their swords against the Constitution which they would once have died for,—to draw them, too, with a bitterness of animosity which is the only symptom of brotherhood (since brothers hate each other best) that any longer exists. They whisper these things with tears in their eyes, and shake their heads, and stoop their poor old shoulders, at the tidings of another and another Northern victory, which, in their opinion, puts farther off the remote, the already impossible, chance of a reunion.

I am sorry for them, though it is by no means a sorrow without hope. Since the matter has gone so far, there seems to be no way but to go on winning victories, and establishing peace and a truer union in another generation, at the expense, probably, of greater trouble, in the present one, than any other people ever voluntarily suffered. We woo the South "as the Lion wooes his bride;" it is a rough courtship, but perhaps love and a quiet household may come of it at last. Or, if we stop short of that blessed consummation, heaven was heaven still, as Milton sings, after Lucifer and a third part of the angels had seceded from its golden palaces,—and perhaps all the more heavenly, because so many gloomy brows, and soured, vindictive hearts, had gone to plot ineffectual schemes of mischief elsewhere.

[We regret the innuendo in the concluding sentence. The war can never be allowed to terminate, except in the complete triumph of Northern principles. We hold the event in our own hands, and may choose whether to terminate it by the methods already so successfully used, or by other means equally within our control, and calculated to be still more speedily efficacious. In truth, the work is already done.

We should be sorry to cast a doubt on the Peaceable Man's loyalty, but he will allow us to say that we consider him premature in his kindly feelings towards traitors and sympathizers with treason. As the author himself says of John Brown (and, so applied, we thought it an atrociously cold-blooded dictum), "any common-sensible man would feel an intellectual satisfaction in seeing them hanged, were it only for their preposterous miscalculation of possibilities." There are some degrees of absurdity that put Reason herself into a rage, and affect us like an intolerable crime,—which this Rebellion is, into the bargain.]

ALICE DOANE'S APPEAL.

On a pleasant afternoon of June, it was my good fortune to be the companion of two young ladies in a walk. The direction of our course being left to me, I led them neither to Legge's Hill, nor to the Cold Spring, nor to the rude shores and old batteries of the Neck, nor yet to Paradise; though if the latter place were rightly named, my fair friends would have been at home there. We reached the outskirts of the town, and turning aside from a street of tanners and curriers, began to ascend a hill, which at a distance, by its dark slope and the even line of its summit, resembled a green rampart along the road. It was less steep than its aspect threatened. The eminence formed part of an extensive tract of pasture land, and was traversed by cow paths in various directions; but, strange to tell, though the whole slope and summit were of a peculiar deep green, scarce a blade of grass was visible from the base upward. This deceitful verdure was occasioned by a plentiful crop of "wood-wax," which wears the same dark and glossy green throughout the summer, except at one short period, when it puts forth a profusion of yellow blossoms. At that season, to a distant spectator, the hill appears absolutely overlaid with gold, or covered with a glory of sunshine, even beneath a clouded sky. But the curious wanderer on the hill will perceive that all the grass, and everything that should nourish man or beast, has been destroyed by this vile and ineradicable weed: its tufted roots make the soil their own, and permit nothing else to vegetate among them; so that a physical curse may be said to have blasted the spot, where guilt and frenzy consummated the most execrable scene that our history blushes to record. For this was the field where superstition won her darkest triumph; the high place where our fathers set up their shame, to the mournful gaze of generations far remote. The dust of martyrs was beneath our feet. We stood on Gallows Hill.

For my own part, I have often courted the historic influence of the spot. But it is singular how few come on pilgrimage to this famous hill; how many spend their lives almost at its base, and never once obey the summons of the shadowy past, as it beckons them to the summit. Till a year or two since, this portion of our history had been very imperfectly written, and, as we are not a people of legend or tradition, it was not every citizen of our ancient town that could tell, within half a century, so much as the date of the witchcraft delusion. Recently, indeed, an historian has treated the subject in a manner that will keep his name alive, in the only desirable connection with the errors of our ancestry, by converting the hill of their disgrace into an honorable monument of his own antiquarian lore, and of that better wisdom, which draws the moral while it tells the tale. But we are a people of the present, and have no heartfelt interest in the olden time. Every fifth of November, in commemoration of they know not what, or rather without an idea beyond the momentary blaze, the young men scare the town with bonfires on this haunted height, but never dream of paying funeral honors to those who died so wrongfully, and, without a coffin or a prayer, were buried here.

Though with feminine susceptibility, my companions caught all the melancholy associations of the scene, yet these could but imperfectly overcome the gayety of girlish spirits. Their emotions came and went with quick vicissitude, and sometimes combined to form a peculiar and delicious excitement, the mirth brightening the gloom into a sunny shower of feeling, and a rainbow in the mind. My own more sombre mood was tinged by theirs. With now a merry word and next a sad one, we trod among the tangled weeds, and almost hoped that our feet would sink into the hollow of a witch's grave. Such vestiges were to be found within the memory of man, but have vanished now, and with them, I believe, all traces of the precise spot of the executions. On the long and broad ridge of the eminence, there is no very decided elevation of any one point, nor other prominent marks, except the decayed stumps of two trees, standing near each other, and here and there the rocky substance of the hill, peeping just above the wood-wax.

There are few such prospects of town and village, woodland and cultivated field, steeples and country seats, as we beheld from this unhappy spot. No blight had fallen on old Essex; all was prosperity and riches, healthfully distributed. Before us lay our native town, extending from the foot of the hill to the harbor, level as a chess board, embraced by two arms of the sea, and filling the whole peninsula with a close assemblage of wooden roofs, overtopped by many a spire, and intermixed with frequent heaps of verdure, where trees threw up their shade from unseen trunks. Beyond was the bay and its islands, almost the only objects, in a country unmarked by strong natural features, on which time and human toil had produced no change. Retaining these portions of the scene, and also the peaceful glory and tender gloom of the declining sun, we threw, in imagination, a veil of deep forest over the land, and pictured a few scattered villages, and this old town itself a village, as when the prince of hell bore sway there. The idea thus gained of its former aspect, its quaint edifices standing far apart, with peaked roofs and projecting stories, and its single meeting-house pointing up a tall spire in the midst; the vision, in short, of the town in 1692, served to introduce a wondrous tale of those old times.

I had brought the manuscript in my pocket. It was one of a series written years ago, when my pen, now sluggish and perhaps feeble, because I have not munch to hope or fear, was driven by stronger external motives and a more passionate impulse within, than I am fated to feel again. Three or four of these tales had appeared in the "Token," after a long time and various adventures, but had encumbered me with no troublesome notoriety, even in my birthplace. One great heap had met a brighter destiny: they had fed the flames; thoughts meant to delight the world and endure for ages had perished in a moment, and stirred not a single heart but mine. The story now to be introduced, and another, chanced to be in kinder custody at the time, and thus, by no conspicuous merits of their own, escaped destruction.

The ladies, in consideration that I had never before intruded my performances on them, by any but the legitimate medium, through the press, consented to hear me read. I made them sit down on a moss-grown rock, close by the spot where we chose to believe that the death tree had stood. After a little hesitation on my part, caused by a dread of renewing my acquaintance with fantasies that had lost their charm in the ceaseless flux of mind, I began the tale, which opened darkly with the discovery of a murder.

A hundred years, and nearly half that time, have elapsed since the body of a murdered man was found, at about the distance of three miles, on the old road to Boston. He lay in a solitary spot, on the bank of a small lake, which

110

the severe frost of December had covered with a sheet of ice. Beneath this, it seemed to have been the intention of the murderer to conceal his victim in a chill and watery grave, the ice being deeply hacked, perhaps with the weapon that had slain him, though its solidity was too stubborn for the patience of a man with blood upon his hand. The corpse therefore reclined on the earth, but was separated from the road by a thick growth of dwarf pines. There had been a slight fall of snow during the night, and as if nature were shocked at the deed, and strove to hide it with her frozen tears, a little drifted heap had partly buried the body, and lay deepest over the pale dead face. An early traveller, whose dog had led him to the spot, ventured to uncover the features, but was affrighted by their expression. A look of evil and scornful triumph had hardened on them, and made death so life-like and so terrible, that the beholder at once took flight, as swiftly as if the stiffened corpse would rise up and follow.

I read on, and identified the body as that of a young man, a stranger in the country, but resident during several preceding months in the town which lay at our feet. The story described, at some length, the excitement caused by the murder, the unavailing quest after the perpetrator, the funeral ceremonies, and other commonplace matters, in the course of which, I brought forward the personages who were to move among the succeeding events. They were but three. A young man and his sister; the former characterized by a diseased imagination and morbid feelings; the latter, beautiful and virtuous, and instilling something of her own excellence into the wild heart of her brother, but not enough to cure the deep taint of his nature. The third person was a wizard; a small, gray, withered man, with fiendish ingenuity in devising evil, and superhuman power to execute it, but senseless as an idiot and feebler than a child to all better purposes. The central scene of the story was an interview between this wretch and Leonard Doane, in the wizard's hut, situated beneath a range of rocks at some distance from the town. They sat beside a smouldering fire, while a tempest of wintry rain was beating on the roof.

The young man spoke of the closeness of the tie which united him and Alice, the consecrated fervor of their affection from childhood upwards, their sense of lonely sufficiency to each other, because they only of their race had escaped death, in a night attack by the Indians. He related his discovery or suspicion of a secret sympathy between his sister and Walter Brome, and told how a distempered jealousy had maddened him. In the following passage, I threw a glimmering light on the mystery of the tale.

"Searching," continued Leonard, "into the breast of Walter Brome, I at length found a cause why Alice must inevitably love him. For he was my very counterpart! I compared his mind by each individual portion, and as a whole, with mine. There was a resemblance from which I shrunk with sickness, and loathing, and horror, as if my own features had come and stared upon me in a solitary place, or had met me in struggling through a crowd. Nay! the very same thoughts would often express themselves in the same words from our lips, proving a hateful sympathy in our secret souls. His education, indeed, in the cities of the old world, and mine in the rude wilderness, had wrought a superficial difference. The evil of his character, also, had been strengthened and rendered prominent by a reckless and ungoverned life, while mine had been softened and purified by the gentle and holy nature of Alice. But my soul had been conscious of the germ of all the fierce and deep passions, and of all the many varieties of wickedness, which accident had brought to their full maturity in him. Nor will I deny that, in the accursed one, I could see the withered blossom of every virtue, which, by a happier culture, had been made to bring forth fruit in me. Now, here was a man whom Alice might love with all the strength of sisterly affection, added to that impure passion which alone engrosses all the heart. The stranger would have more than the love which had been gathered to me from the many graves of our household—and I be desolate!"

Leonard Doane went on to describe the insane hatred that had kindled his heart into a volume of hellish flame. It appeared, indeed, that his jealousy had grounds, so far as that Walter Brome had actually sought the love of Alice, who also had betrayed an undefinable, but powerful interest in the unknown youth. The latter, in spite of his passion for Alice, seemed to return the loathful antipathy of her brother; the similarity of their dispositions made them like joint possessors of an individual nature, which could not become wholly the property of one, unless by the extinction of the other. At last, with the sane devil in each bosom, they chanced to meet, they two, on a lonely road. While Leonard spoke, the wizard had sat listening to what he already knew, yet with tokens of pleasurable interest, manifested by flashes of expression across his vacant features, by grisly smiles, and by a word here and there, mysteriously filling up some void in the narrative. But when the young man told how Walter Brome had taunted him with indubitable proofs of the shame of Alice, and, before the triumphant sneer could vanish from his face, had died by her brother's hand, the wizard laughed aloud. Leonard started, but just then a gust of wind came down the chimney, forming itself into a close resemblance of the slow, unvaried laughter, by which he had been interrupted. "I was deceived," thought he; and thus pursued his fearful story.

"I trod out his accursed soul, and knew that he was dead; for my spirit bounded as if a chain had fallen from it and left me free. But the burst of exulting certainty soon fled, and was succeeded by a torpor over my brain and a dimness before my eyes, with the sensation of one who struggles through a dream. So I bent down over the body of Walter Brome, gazing into his face, and striving to make my soul glad with the thought, that he, in very truth, lay dead before me. I know not what space of time I had thus stood, nor how the vision came. But it seemed to me that the irrevocable years since childhood had rolled back, and a scene, that had long been confused and broken in my memory, arrayed itself with all its first distinctness. Methought I stood a weeping infant by my father's hearth; by the cold and blood-stained hearth where he lay dead. I heard the childish wail of Alice, and my own cry arose with hers, as we beheld the features of our parent, fierce with the strife and distorted with the pain, in which his spirit had passed away. As I gazed, a cold wind whistled by, and waved my father's hair. Immediately I stood again in the lonesome road, no more a sinless child, but a man of blood, whose tears were falling fast over the face of his dead enemy. But the delusion was not wholly gone; that face still wore a likeness of my father; and because my soul shrank from the fixed glare of the eyes, I bore the body to the lake, and would have buried it there. But before his icy sepulchre was hewn, I heard the voices of two travellers and fled."

Such was the dreadful confession of Leonard Doane. And now tortured by the idea of his sister's guilt, yet sometimes yielding to a conviction of her purity; stung with remorse for the death of Walter Brome, and shuddering with a deeper sense of some unutterable crime, perpetrated, as he imagined, in madness or a dream; moved also by dark impulses, as if a fiend were whispering him to meditate violence against the life of Alice; he had sought this interview with the wizard, who, on certain conditions, had no power to withhold his aid in unravelling the mystery. The tale drew near its close.

The moon was bright on high; the blue firmament appeared to glow with an inherent brightness; the greater stars were burning in their spheres; the northern lights threw their mysterious glare far over the horizon; the few small clouds aloft were burdened with radiance; but the sky, with all its variety of light, was scarcely so brilliant as the earth. The rain of the preceding night had frozen as it fell, and, by that simple magic, had wrought wonders. The trees were hung with diamonds and many-colored gems; the houses were overlaid with silver, and the streets paved with slippery brightness; a frigid glory was flung over all familiar things, from the cottage chimney to the steeple of the meeting-house, that gleamed upward to the sky. This living world, where we sit by our firesides, or go forth to meet beings like ourselves, seemed rather the creation of wizard power, with so much of resemblance to known objects that a man might shudder at the ghostly shape of his old beloved dwelling, and the shadow of a ghostly tree before his door. One looked to behold inhabitants suited to such a town, glittering in icy garments, with motionless features, cold, sparkling eyes, and just sensation enough in their frozen hearts to shiver at each other's presence.

By this fantastic piece of description, and more in the same style, I intended to throw a ghostly glimmer round the reader, so that his imagination might view the town through a medium that should take off its every-day aspect, and make it a proper theatre for so wild a scene as the final one. Amid this unearthly show, the wretched brother and sister were represented as setting forth, at midnight, through the gleaming streets, and directing their steps to a graveyard, where all the dead had been laid from the first corpse in that ancient town, to the murdered man who was buried three days before.

As they went, they seemed to see the wizard gliding by their sides, or walking dimly on the path before them. But here I paused, and gazed into the faces of my two fair auditors, to judge whether, even on the hill where so many had been brought to death by wilder tales than this, I might venture to proceed. Their bright eyes were fixed on me; their lips apart. I took courage, and led the fated pair to a new made grave, where for a few moments, in the bright and silent midnight, they stood alone. But suddenly there was a multitude of people among the graves.

Each family tomb had given up its inhabitants, who, one by one, through distant years, had been borne to its dark chamber, but now came forth and stood in a pale group together. There was the gray ancestor, the aged mother, and all their descendants, some withered and full of years, like themselves, and others in their prime; there, too, were the children who went prattling to the tomb, and there the maiden who yielded her early beauty to death's embrace, before passion had polluted it. Husbands and wives arose, who had lain many years side by side, and young mothers who had forgotten to kiss their first babes, though pillowed so long on their bosoms. Many had been buried in the habiliments of life, and still wore their ancient garb; some were old defenders of the infant colony, and gleamed forth in their steel-caps and bright breastplates, as if starting up at an Indian war-cry; other venerable shapes had been pastors of the church, famous among the New England clergy, and now leaned with hands clasped over their gravestones, ready to call the congregation to prayer. There stood the early settlers, those old illustrious ones, the heroes of tradition and fireside legends, the men of history whose features had been so long beneath the sod that few alive could have remembered them. There, too, were faces of former townspeople, dimly recollected from childhood, and others, whom Leonard and Alice had wept in later years, but who now were most terrible of all, by their ghastly smile of recognition. All, in short, were there; the dead of other generations, whose moss-grown names could scarce be read upon their tombstones, and their successors, whose graves were not yet green; all whom black funerals had followed slowly thither now reappeared where the mourners left them. Yet none but souls accursed were there, and fiends counterfeiting the likeness of departed saints.

The countenances of those venerable men, whose very features had been hallowed by lives of piety, were contorted now by intolerable pain or hellish passion, and now by an unearthly and derisive merriment. Had the pastors prayed, all saintlike as they seemed, it had been blasphemy. The chaste matrons, too, and the maidens with untasted lips, who had slept in their virgin graves apart from all other dust, now wore a look from which the two trembling mortals shrank, as if the unimaginable sin of twenty worlds were collected there. The faces of fond lovers, even of such as had pined into the tomb, because there their treasure was, were bent on one another with glances of hatred and smiles of bitter scorn, passions that are to devils what love is to the blest. At times, the features of those who had passed from a holy life to heaven would vary to and fro, between their assumed aspect and the fiendish lineaments whence they had been transformed. The whole miserable multitude, both sinful souls and false spectres of good men, groaned horribly and gnashed their teeth, as they looked upward to the calm loveliness of the midnight sky, and beheld those homes of bliss where they must never dwell. Such was the apparition, though too shadowy for language to portray; for here would be the moonbeams on the ice, glittering through a warrior's breastplate, and there the letters of a tombstone, on the form that stood before it; and whenever a breeze went by, it swept the old men's hoary heads, the women's fearful beauty, and all the unreal throng, into one indistinguishable cloud together.

I dare not give the remainder of the scene, except in a very brief epitome. This company of devils and condemned souls had come on a holiday, to revel in the discovery of a complicated crime; as foul a one as ever was imagined in their dreadful abode. In the course of the tale, the reader had been permitted to discover that all the incidents were results of the machinations of the wizard, who had cunningly devised that Walter Brome should tempt his unknown sister to guilt and shame, and himself perish by the hand of his twin-brother. I described the glee of the fiends at this hideous conception, and their eagerness to know if it were consummated. The story concluded with the Appeal of Alice to the spectre of Walter Brome; his reply, absolving her from every stain; and the trembling awe with which ghost and devil fled as from the sinless presence of an angel.

116

The sun had gone down. While I held my page of wonders in the fading light, and read how Alice and her brother were left alone among the graves, my voice mingled with the sigh of a summer wind, which passed over the hill-top, with the broad and hollow sound as of the flight of unseen spirits. Not a word was spoken till I added that the wizard's grave was close beside us, and that the wood-wax had sprouted originally from his unhallowed bones. The ladies started; perhaps their cheeks might have grown pale had not the crimson west been blushing on them; but after a moment they began to laugh, while the breeze took a livelier motion, as if responsive to their mirth. I kept an awful solemnity of visage, being, indeed, a little piqued that a narrative which had good authority in our ancient superstitions, and would have brought even a church deacon to Gallows Hill, in old witch times, should now be considered too grotesque and extravagant for timid maids to tremble at. Though it was past supper time, I detained them a while longer on the hill, and made a trial whether truth were more powerful than fiction.

We looked again towards the town, no longer arrayed in that icy splendor of earth, tree, and edifice, beneath the glow of a wintry midnight, which shining afar through the gloom of a century had made it appear the very home of visions in visionary streets. An indistinctness had begun to creep over the mass of buildings and blend them with the intermingled tree-tops, except where the roof of a statelier mansion, and the steeples and brick towers of churches, caught the brightness of some cloud that yet floated in the sunshine. Twilight over the landscape was congenial to the obscurity of time. With such eloquence as my share of feeling and fancy could supply, I called back hoar antiquity, and bade my companions imagine an ancient multitude of people, congregated on the hillside, spreading far below, clustering on the steep old roofs, and climbing the adjacent heights, wherever a glimpse of this spot might be obtained. I strove to realize and faintly communicate the deep, unutterable loathing and horror, the indignation, the affrighted wonder, that wrinkled on every brow, and filled the universal heart. See! the whole crowd turns pale and shrinks within itself, as the virtuous emerge from yonder street. Keeping pace with that devoted company, I described them one by one; here tottered a woman in her dotage, knowing neither the crime imputed her, nor its punishment; there another, distracted by the universal madness, till feverish dreams were remembered as realities, and she almost believed her guilt. One, a proud man once, was so broken down by the intolerable hatred heaped upon him, that he seemed to hasten his steps, eager to hide himself in the grave hastily dug at the foot of the gallows. As they went slowly on, a mother looked behind, and beheld her peaceful dwelling; she cast her eyes elsewhere, and groaned inwardly yet with bitterest anguish, for there was her little son among the accusers. I watched the face of an ordained pastor, who walked onward to the same death; his lips moved in prayer; no narrow petition for himself alone, but embracing all his fellow-sufferers and the frenzied multitude; he looked to Heaven and trod lightly up the hill.

Behind their victims came the afflicted, a guilty and miserable band; villains who had thus avenged themselves on their enemies, and viler wretches, whose cowardice had destroyed their friends; lunatics, whose ravings had chimed in with the madness of the land; and children, who had played a game that the imps of darkness might have envied them, since it disgraced an age, and dipped a people's hands in blood. In the rear of the procession rode a figure on horseback, so darkly conspicuous, so sternly triumphant, that my hearers mistook him for the visible presence of the fiend himself; but it was only his good friend, Cotton Mather, proud of his well-won dignity, as the representative of all the hateful features of his time: the one bloodthirsty man, in whom were concentrated those vices of spirit and errors of opinion that sufficed to madden the whole surrounding multitude. And thus I marshalled them onward, the innocent who were to die, and the guilty who were to grow old in long remorse—tracing their every step, by rock, and shrub, and broken track, till their shadowy visages had circled round the hilltop, where we stood. I plunged into my imagination for a blacker horror, and a deeper woe, and pictured the scaffold——

But here my companions seized an arm on each side; their nerves were trembling; and, sweeter victory still, I had reached the seldom trodden places of their hearts, and found the well-spring of their tears. And now the past had done all it could. We slowly descended, watching the lights as they twinkled gradually through the town, and listening to the distant mirth of boys at play, and to the voice of a young girl warbling somewhere in the dusk, a pleasant sound to wanderers from old witch times. Yet, ere we left the hill, we could not but regret that there is nothing on its barren summit, no relic of old, nor lettered stone of later days, to assist the imagination in appealing to the heart. We build the memorial column on the height which our fathers made sacred with their blood, poured out in a holy cause. And here, in dark, funereal stone, should rise another monument, sadly commemorative of the errors of an earlier race, and not to be cast down while the human heart has one infirmity that may result in crime.

THE ANCESTRAL FOOTSTEP

Outlines of an English Romance.

INTRODUCTORY NOTE.

"Septimius Felton" was the outgrowth of a project, formed by Hawthorne during his residence in England, of writing a romance, the scene of which should be laid in that country; but this project was afterwards abandoned, giving place to a new conception in which the visionary search for means to secure an earthly immortality was to form the principal interest. The new conception took shape in the uncompleted "Dolliver Romance." The two themes, of course, were distinct, but, by a curious process of thought, one grew directly out of the other: the whole history constitutes, in fact, a chapter in what may be called the genealogy of a romance. There remained, after "Septimius Felton" had been published, certain manuscripts connected with the scheme of an English story. One of these manuscripts was written in the form of a journalized narrative; the author merely noting the date of what he wrote, as he went along. The other was a more extended sketch of much greater bulk, and without date, but probably produced several years later. It was not originally intended by those who at the time had charge of Hawthorne's papers that either of these incomplete writings should be laid before the public; because they manifestly had not been left by him in a form which he would have considered as warranting such a course. But since the second and larger manuscript has been published under the title of "Dr. Grimshawe's Secret," it has been thought best to issue the present sketch, so that the two documents may be examined together. Their appearance places in the hands of readers the entire process of development leading to the "Septimius" and "The Dolliver Romance." They speak for themselves much more efficiently than any commentator can expect to do; and little, therefore, remains to be said beyond a few words of explanation in regard to the following pages.

The Note-Books show that the plan of an English romance, turning upon the fact that an emigrant to America had carried away a family secret which should give his descendant the power to ruin the family in the mother country, had occurred to Hawthorne as early as April, 1855. In August of the same year he visited Smithell's Hall, in Bolton le Moors, concerning which he had already heard its legend of "The Bloody Footstep," and from that time on, the idea of this footprint on the threshold-stone of the ancestral mansion seems to have associated itself inextricably with the dreamy substance of his yet unshaped romance. Indeed, it leaves its mark broadly upon Sibyl Dacy's wild legend in "Septimius Felton," and reappears in the last paragraph of that story. But, so far as we can know at this day, nothing definite was done until after his departure for Italy. It was then, while staying in Rome, that he began to put upon paper that plot which had first occupied his thoughts three years before, in the scant leisure allowed him by his duties at the Liverpool consulate. Of leisure there was not a great deal at Rome, either; for, as the "French and Italian Note-Books" show, sight-seeing and social intercourse took up a good deal of his time, and the daily record in his journal likewise had to be kept up. But he set to work resolutely to embody, so far as he might, his stray imaginings upon the haunting English theme, and to give them connected form. April 1, 1858, he began; and then nearly two weeks passed before he found an opportunity to resume; April 13th being the date of the next passage. By May he gets fully into swing, so that day after day, with but slight breaks, he carries on the story, always increasing in interest for as who read as for him who improvised. Thus it continues until May 19th, by which time he has made a tolerably complete outline, filled in with a good deal of detail here and there. Although the sketch is cast in the form of a regular narrative, one or two gaps occur, indicating that the author had thought out certain points which he then took for granted without making note of them. Brief scenes, passages of conversation and of narration, follow one another after the manner of a finished story, alternating with synopses of the plot, and queries concerning particulars that needed further study; confidences of the romancer to himself which form certainly a valuable contribution to literary history. The manuscript closes with a rapid sketch of the conclusion, and the way in which it is to be executed. Succinctly, what we have is a romance in embryo; one, moreover, that never attained to a viable stature and constitution. During his lifetime it naturally would not have been put forward as demanding public attention; and, in consideration of that fact, it has since been withheld from the press by the decision of his daughter, in whom the title to it vests. Students of literary art, however, and many more general readers will, I think, be likely to discover in it a charm all the greater for its being in parts only indicated; since, as it stands, it presents the precise condition of a work of fiction in its first stage. The unfinished "Grimshawe" was another development of the same theme, and the "Septimius" a later sketch, with a new element introduced. But the present experimental fragment, to which it has been decided to give the title of "The Ancestral Footstep," possesses a freshness and spontaneity recalling the peculiar fascination of those chalk or pencil outlines with which great masters in the graphic art have been wont to arrest their fleeting glimpses of a composition still unwrought.

It would not be safe to conclude, from the large amount of preliminary writing done with a view to that romance, that Hawthorne always adopted this laborious mode of making several drafts of a book. On the contrary, it is understood that his habit was to mature a design so thoroughly in his mind before attempting to give it actual existence on paper that but little rewriting was needed. The circumstance that he was obliged to write so much that did not satisfy him in this case may account partly for his relinquishing the theme, as one which for him had lost its seductiveness through too much recasting.

It need be added only that the original manuscript, from which the following pages are printed through the medium of an exact copy, is singularly clear and fluent. Not a single correction occurs throughout; but here and there a word is omitted obviously by mere accident, and these omissions have been supplied. The correction in each case is marked by brackets in this printed reproduction. The sketch begins abruptly; but there is no reason to suppose that anything preceded it except the unrecorded musings in the author's mind, and one or two memoranda in the "English Note-Books." We must therefore imagine the central figure, Middleton, who is the American descendant of an old English family, as having been properly introduced, and then pass at once to the opening sentences. The rest will explain itself. G. P. L.

I.

April 1, 1858. Thursday.—He had now been travelling long in those rich portions of England where he would most have wished to find the object of his pursuit; and many had been the scenes which he would willingly have identified with that mentioned in the ancient, time-yellowed record which he bore about with him. It is to be observed that, undertaken at first half as the amusement, the unreal object of a grown man's play-day, it had become more and more real to him with every step of the way that he followed it up; along those green English lanes it seemed as if everything would bring him close to the mansion that he sought; every morning he went on with renewed hopes, nor did the evening, though it brought with it no success, bring with it the gloom and heaviness of a real disappointment. In all his life, including its earliest and happiest days, he had never known such a spring and zest as now filled his veins, and gave lightsomeness to his limbs; this spirit gave to the beautiful country which he trod a still richer beauty than it had ever borne, and he sought his ancient home as if he had found his way into Paradise and were there endeavoring to trace out the sight [site] of Eve's bridal bower, the birthplace of the human race and its glorious possibilities of happiness and high performance.

In these sweet and delightful moods of mind, varying from one dream to another, he loved indeed the solitude of his way; but likewise he loved the facility which his pursuit afforded him, of coming in contact with many varieties of men, and he took advantage of this facility to an extent which it was not usually his impulse to do. But now he came forth from all reserves, and offered himself to whomever the chances of the way offered to him, with a ready sensibility that made its way through every barrier that even English exclusiveness, in whatever rank of life, could set up. The plastic character of Middleton was perhaps a variety of American nature only presenting itself under an individual form; he could throw off the man of our day, and put on a ruder nature, but then it was with a certain fineness, that made this only [a] distinction between it and the central truth. He found less variety of form in the English character than he had been accustomed to see at home; but perhaps this was in consequence of the external nature of his acquaintance with it; for the view of one well accustomed to a people, and of a stranger to them, differs in this—that the latter sees the homogeneity, the one universal character, the ground work of the whole, while the former sees a thousand little differences, which distinguish the individual men apart to such a degree that they seem hardly to have any resemblance among themselves.

But just at the period of his journey when we take him up, Middleton had been for two or three days the companion of an old man who interested him more than most of his wayside companions; the more especially as he seemed to be wandering without an object, or with such a dreamy object as that which led Middleton's own steps onward. He was a plain old man enough, but with a pale, strong-featured face and white hair, a certain picturesqueness and venerableness, which Middleton fancied might have befitted a richer garb than he now wore. In much of their conversation, too, he was sensible that, though the stranger betrayed no acquaintance with literature, nor seemed to have conversed with cultivated minds, yet the results of such acquaintance and converse were here. Middleton was inclined to think him, however, an old man, one of those itinerants, such as Wordsworth represented in the "Excursion," who smooth themselves by the attrition of the world and gain a knowledge equivalent to or better than that of books from the actual intellect of man awake and active around them.

Often, during the short period since their companionship originated, Middleton had felt impelled to disclose to the old man the object of his journey, and the wild tale by which, after two hundred years, he had been blown as it were across the ocean, and drawn onward to commence this search. The old man's ordinary conversation was of a nature to draw forth such a confidence as this; frequently turning on the traditions of the wayside; the reminiscences that lingered on the battle-fields of the Roses, or of the Parliament, like flowers nurtured by the blood of the slain, and prolonging their race through the centuries for the wayfarer to pluck them; or the family histories of the castles, manor-houses, and seats which, of various epochs, had their park-gates along the roadside and would be seen with dark gray towers or ancient gables, or more modern forms of architecture, rising up among clouds of ancient oaks. Middleton watched earnestly to see if, in any of these tales, there were circumstances resembling those striking and singular ones which he had borne so long in his memory, and on which he was now acting in so strange a manner; but [though] there was a good deal of variety of incident in them, there never was any combination of incidents having the peculiarity of this.

"I suppose," said he to the old man, "the settlers in my country may have carried away with them traditions long since forgotten in this country, but which might have an interest and connection, and might even piece out the broken relics of family history, which have remained perhaps a mystery for hundreds of years. I can conceive, even, that this might be of importance in settling the heirships of estates; but which now, only the two insulated parts of the story being known, remain a riddle, although the solution of it is actually in the world, if only these two parts could be united across the sea, like the wires of an electric telegraph."

"It is an impressive idea," said the old man. "Do you know any such tradition as you have hinted at?"

April 13th.—Middleton could not but wonder at the singular chance that had established him in such a place, and in such society, so strangely adapted to the purposes with which he had been wandering through England. He had come hither, hoping as it were to find the past still alive and in action; and here it was so in this one only spot, and these few persons into the midst of whom he had suddenly been cast. With these reflections he looked forth from his window into the old-fashioned garden, and at the stone sun-dial, which had numbered all the hours—all the daylight and serene ones, at least—since his mysterious ancestor left the country. And [is] this, then, he thought to himself, the establishment of which some rumor had been preserved? Was it here that the secret had its hiding-place in the old coffer, in the cupboard, in the secret chamber, or whatever was indicated by the apparently idle words of the document which he had preserved? He still smiled at the idea, but it was with a pleasant, mysterious sense that his life had at last got out of the dusty real, and that strangeness had mixed itself up with his daily experience.

With such feelings he prepared himself to go down to dinner with his host. He found him alone at table, which was placed in a dark old room modernized with every English comfort and the pleasant spectacle of a table set with the whitest of napery and the brightest of glass and china. The friendly old gentleman, as he had found him from the first, became doubly and trebly so in that position which brings out whatever warmth of heart an Englishman has, and gives it to him if he has none. The impressionable and sympathetic character of Middleton answered to the kindness of his host; and by the time the meal was concluded, the two were conversing with almost as much zest and friendship as if they were similar in age, even fellow-countrymen, and had known one another all their lifetime. Middleton's secret, it may be supposed, came often to the tip of his tongue; but still he kept it within, from a natural repugnance to bring out the one romance of his life. The talk, however, necessarily ran much upon topics among which this one would have come in without any extra attempt to introduce it.

"This decay of old families," said the Master, "is much greater than would appear on the surface of things. We have such a reluctance to part with them, that we are content to see them continued by any fiction, through any indirections, rather than to dispense with old names. In your country, I suppose, there is no such reluctance; you are willing that one generation should blot out all that preceded it, and be itself the newest and only age of the world."

"Not quite so," answered Middleton; "at any rate, if there be such a feeling in the people at large, I doubt whether, even in England, those who fancy themselves possessed of claims to birth, cherish them more as a treasure than we do. It is, of course, a thousand times more difficult for us to keep alive a name amid a thousand difficulties sedulously thrown around it by our institutions, than for you to do, where your institutions are anxiously calculated to promote the contrary purpose. It has occasionally struck me, however, that the ancient lineage might often be found in America, for a family which has been compelled to prolong itself here through the female line, and through alien stocks."

"Indeed, my young friend," said the Master, "if that be the case, I should like to [speak?] further with you upon it; for, I can assure you, there are sometimes vicissitudes in old families that make me grieve to think that a man cannot be made for the occasion."

All this while, the young lady at table had remained almost silent; and Middleton had only occasionally been reminded of her by the necessity of performing some of those offices which put people at table under a Christian necessity of recognizing one another. He was, to say the truth, somewhat interested in her, yet not strongly attracted by the neutral tint of her dress, and the neutral character of her manners. She did not seem to be handsome, although, with her face full before him, he had not quite made up his mind on this point.

April 14th.—So here was Middleton, now at length seeing indistinctly a thread, to which the thread that he had so long held in his hand—the hereditary thread that ancestor after ancestor had handed down—might seem ready to join on. He felt as if they were the two points of an electric chain, which being joined, an instantaneous effect must follow. Earnestly, as he would have looked forward to this moment (had he in sober reason ever put any real weight on the fantasy in pursuit of which he had wandered so far) he now, that it actually appeared to be realizing itself, paused with a vague sensation of alarm. The mystery was evidently one of sorrow, if not of crime, and he felt as if that sorrow and crime might not have been annihilated even by being buried out of human sight and remembrance so long. He remembered to have heard or read, how that once an old pit had been dug open, in which were found the remains of persons that, as the shuddering by-standers traditionally remembered, had died of an ancient pestilence; and out of that old grave had come a new plague, that slew the far-off progeny of those who had first died by it. Might not some fatal treasure like this, in a moral view, be brought to light by the secret into which he had so strangely been drawn? Such were the fantasies with which he awaited the return of Alice, whose light footsteps sounded afar along the passages of the old mansion; and then all was silent.

At length he heard the sound, a great way off, as he concluded, of her returning footstep, approaching from chamber to chamber, and along the staircases, closing the doors behind her. At first, he paid no great attention to the character of these sounds, but as they drew nearer, he became aware that the footstep was unlike those of Alice; indeed, as unlike as could be, very regular, slow, yet not firm, so that it seemed to be that of an aged person, sauntering listlessly through the rooms. We have often alluded to Middleton's sensitiveness, and the quick vibrations of his sympathies; and there was something in this slow approach that produced a strange feeling within him; so that he stood breathlessly, looking towards the door by which these slow footsteps were to enter. At last, there appeared in the doorway a venerable figure, clad in a rich, faded dressing-gown, and standing on the threshold looked fixedly at Middleton, at the same time holding up a light in his left hand. In his right was some object that Middleton did not distinctly see. But he knew the figure, and recognized the face. It was the old man, his long since companion on the journey hitherward.

"So," said the old man, smiling gravely, "you have thought fit, at last, to accept the hospitality which I offered you so long ago. It might have been better for both of us—for all parties—if you had accepted it then!"

"You here!" exclaimed Middleton. "And what can be your connection with all the error and trouble, and involuntary wrong, through which I have wandered since our last meeting? And is it possible that you even then held the clue which I was seeking?"

"No,—no," replied Rothermel. "I was not conscious, at least, of so doing. And yet had we two sat down there by the wayside, or on that English stile, which attracted your attention so much; had we sat down there and thrown forth each his own dream, each his own knowledge, it would have saved much that we must now forever regret. Are you even now ready to confide wholly in me?"

"Alas," said Middleton, with a darkening brow, "there are many reasons, at this moment, which did not exist then, to incline me to hold my peace. And why has not Alice returned?—and what is your connection with her?"

"Let her answer for herself," said Rothermel; and he called her, shouting through the silent house as if she were at the furthest chamber, and he were in instant need: "Alice!—Alice!—Alice!—here is one who would know what is the link between a maiden and her father!"

Amid the strange uproar which he made Alice came flying back, not in alarm but only in haste, and put her hand within his own. "Hush, father," said she. "It is not time."

Here is an abstract of the plot of this story. The Middleton who emigrated to America, more than two hundred years ago, had been a dark and moody man; he came with a beautiful though not young woman for his wife, and left a family behind him. In this family a certain heirloom had been preserved, and with it a tradition that grew wilder and stranger with the passing generations. The tradition had lost, if it ever had, some of its connecting links; but it referred to a murder, to the expulsion of a brother from the hereditary house, in some strange way, and to a Bloody Footstep which he had left impressed into the threshold, as he turned about to make a last remonstrance. It was rumored, however, or vaguely understood, that the expelled brother was not altogether an innocent man; but that there had been wrong done as well as crime committed, insomuch that his reasons were strong that led him, subsequently, to imbibe the most gloomy religious views, and to bury himself in the Western wilderness. These reasons he had never fully imparted to his family; but had necessarily made allusions to them, which had been treasured up and doubtless enlarged upon. At last, one descendant of the family determines to go to England, with the purpose of searching out whatever ground there may be for these traditions, carrying with him certain ancient documents, and other relics; and goes about the country, half in earnest, and half in sport of fancy, in quest of the old family mansion. He makes singular discoveries, all of which bring the book to an end unexpected by everybody, and not satisfactory to the natural yearnings of novel readers. In the traditions that he brought over, there was a key to some family secrets that were still unsolved, and that controlled the descent of estates and titles. His influence upon these matters involves [him] in divers strange and perilous adventures; and at last it turns out that he himself is the rightful heir to the titles and estate, that had passed into another name within the last half-century. But he respects both, feeling that it is better to make a virgin soil than to try to make the old name grow in a soil that had been darkened with so much blood and misfortune as this.

April 27th, Tuesday.—It was with a delightful feeling of release from ordinary rules, that Middleton found himself brought into this connection with Alice; and he only hoped that this play-day of his life might last long enough to rest him from all that he had suffered. In the enjoyment of his position he almost forgot the pursuit that occupied him, nor might he have remembered for a long space if, one evening, Alice herself had not alluded to it. "You are wasting precious days," she suddenly said. "Why do you not renew your quest?"

"To what do you allude?" said Middleton in surprise. "What object do you suppose me to have?"

Alice smiled; nay, laughed outright. "You suppose yourself to be a perfect mystery, no doubt," she replied. "But do not I know you—have not I known you long—as the holder of the talisman, the owner of the mysterious cabinet that contains the blood-stained secret?"

"Nay, Alice, this is certainly a strange coincidence, that you should know even thus much of a foolish secret that makes me employ this little holiday time, which I have stolen out of a weary life, in a wild-goose chase. But, believe me, you allude to matters that are more a mystery to me than my affairs appear to be to you. Will you explain what you would suggest by this badinage?"

Alice shook her head. "You have no claim to know what I know, even if it would be any addition to your own knowledge. I shall not, and must not enlighten you. You must burrow for the secret with your own tools, in your own manner, and in a place of your own choosing. I am bound not to assist you."

"Alice, this is wilful, wayward, unjust," cried Middleton, with a flushed cheek. "I have not told you—yet you know well—the deep and real importance which this subject has for me. We have been together as friends, yet, the instant when there comes up an occasion when the slightest friendly feeling would induce you to do me a good office, you assume this altered tone."

"My tone is not in the least altered in respect to you," said Alice. "All along, as you know, I have reserved myself on this very point; it being, I candidly tell you, impossible for me to act in your interest in the matter alluded to. If you choose to consider this unfriendly, as being less than the terms on which you conceive us to have stood give you a right to demand of me—you must resent it as you please. I shall not the less retain for you the regard due to one who has certainly befriended me in very untoward circumstances."

This conversation confirmed the previous idea of Middleton, that some mystery of a peculiarly dark and evil character was connected with the family secret with which he was himself entangled; but it perplexed him to imagine in what way this, after the lapse of so many years, should continue to be a matter of real importance at the present day. All the actors in the original guilt—if guilt it were—must have been long ago in their graves; some in the churchyard of the village, with those moss-grown letters embossing their names; some in the church itself, with mural tablets recording their names over the family-pew, and one, it might be, far over the sea, where his grave was first made under the forest leaves, though now a city had grown up around it. Yet here was he, the remote descendant of that family, setting his foot at last in the country, and as secretly as might be; and all at once his mere presence seemed to revive the buried secret, almost to awake the dead who partook of that secret and had acted it. There was a vibration from the other world, continued and prolonged into this, the instant that he stepped upon the mysterious and haunted ground.

He knew not in what way to proceed. He could not but feel that there was something not exactly within the limits of propriety in being here, disguised—at least, not known in his true character—prying into the secrets of a proud and secluded Englishman. But then, as he said to himself on his own side of the question, the secret belonged to himself by exactly as ancient a tenure and by precisely as strong a claim, as to the Englishman. His rights here were just as powerful and well-founded as those of his ancestor had been, nearly three centuries ago; and here the same feeling came over him that he was that very personage, returned after all these ages, to see if his foot would fit this bloody footstep left of old upon the threshold. The result of all his cogitation was, as the reader will have foreseen, that he decided to continue his researches, and, his proceedings being pretty defensible, let the result take care of itself.

For this purpose he went next day to the hospital, and ringing at the Master's door, was ushered into the old-fashioned, comfortable library, where he had spent that well-remembered evening which threw the first ray of light on the pursuit that now seemed developing into such strange and unexpected consequences. Being admitted, he was desired by the domestic to wait, as his Reverence was at that moment engaged with a gentleman on business. Glancing through the ivy that mantled over the window, Middleton saw that this interview was taking place in the garden, where the Master and his visitor were walking to and fro in the avenue of box, discussing some matter, as it seemed to him, with considerable earnestness on both sides. He observed, too, that there was warmth, passion, a disturbed feeling on the stranger's part; while, on that of the Master, it was a calm, serious, earnest representation of whatever view he was endeavoring to impress on the other. At last, the interview appeared to come toward a climax, the Master addressing some words to his guest, still with undisturbed calmness, to which the latter replied by a violent and even fierce gesture, as it should seem of menace, not towards the Master, but some unknown party; and then hastily turning, he left the garden and was soon heard riding away. The Master looked after him awhile, and then, shaking his white head, returned into the house and soon entered the parlor.

He looked somewhat surprised, and, as it struck Middleton, a little startled, at finding him there; yet he welcomed him with all his former cordiality—indeed, with a friendship that thoroughly warmed Middleton's heart even to its coldest corner.

"This is strange!" said the old gentleman. "Do you remember our conversation on that evening when I first had the unlooked-for pleasure of receiving you as a guest into my house? At that time I spoke to you of a strange family story, of which there was no denouement, such as a novel-writer would desire, and which had remained in that unfinished posture for more than two hundred years! Well; perhaps it will gratify you to know that there seems a prospect of that wanting termination being supplied!"

"Indeed!" said Middleton.

"Yes," replied the Master. "A gentleman has just parted with me who was indeed the representative of the family concerned in the story. He is the descendant of a younger son of that family, to whom the estate devolved about a century ago, although at that time there was search for the heirs of the elder son, who had disappeared after the bloody incident which I related to you. Now, singular as it may appear, at this late day, a person claiming to be the descendant and heir of that eldest son has appeared, and if I may credit my friend's account, is disposed not only to claim the estate, but the dormant title which Eldredge himself has been so long preparing to claim for himself. Singularly enough, too, the heir is an American."

May 2d, Sunday.—"I believe," said Middleton, "that many English secrets might find their solution in America, if the two threads of a story could be brought together, disjoined as they have been by time and the ocean. But are you at liberty to tell me the nature of the incidents to which you allude?"

"I do not see any reason to the contrary," answered the Master; "for the story has already come in an imperfect way before the public, and the full and authentic particulars are likely soon to follow. It seems that the younger brother was ejected from the house on account of a love affair; the elder having married a young woman with whom the younger was in love, and, it is said, the wife disappeared on the bridal night, and was never heard of more. The elder brother remained single during the rest of his life; and dying childless, and there being still no news of the second brother, the inheritance and representation of the family devolved upon the third brother and his posterity. This branch of the family has ever since remained in possession; and latterly the representation has become of more importance, on account of a claim to an old title, which, by the failure of another branch of this ancient family, has devolved upon the branch here settled. Now, just at this juncture, comes another heir from America, pretending that he is the descendant of a marriage between the second son, supposed to have been murdered on the threshold of the manor-house, and the missing bride! Is it not a singular story?"

"It would seem to require very strong evidence to prove it," said Middleton. "And methinks a Republican should care little for the title, however he might value the estate."

"Both—both," said the Master, smiling, "would be equally attractive to your countryman. But there are further curious particulars in connection with this claim. You must know, they are a family of singular characteristics, humorists, sometimes developing their queer traits into something like insanity; though oftener, I must say, spending stupid hereditary lives here on their estates, rusting out and dying without leaving any biography whatever about them. And yet there has always been one very queer thing about this generally very commonplace family. It is that each father, on his death-bed, has had an interview with his son, at which he has imparted some secret that has evidently had an influence on the character and after life of the son, making him ever after a discontented man, aspiring for something he has never been able to find. Now the American, I am told, pretends that he has the clue which has always been needed to make the secret available; the key whereby the lock may be opened; the something that the lost son of the family carried away with him, and by which through these centuries he has impeded the progress of the race. And, wild as the story seems, he does certainly seem to bring something that looks very like the proof of what he says."

"And what are those proofs?" inquired Middleton, wonder-stricken at the strange reduplication of his own position and pursuits.

"In the first place," said the Master, "the English marriage-certificate by a clergyman of that day in London, after publication of the banns, with a reference to the register of the parish church where the marriage is recorded. Then, a certified genealogy of the family in New England, where such matters can be ascertained from town and church records, with at least as much certainty, it would appear, as in this country. He has likewise a manuscript in his ancestor's autograph, containing a brief account of the events which banished him from his own country; the circumstances which favored the idea that he had been slain, and which he himself was willing should be received as a belief; the fortune that led him to America, where he wished to found a new race wholly disconnected with the past; and this manuscript he sealed up, with directions that it should not be opened till two hundred years after his death, by which time, as it was probable to conjecture, it would matter little to any mortal whether the story was told or not. A whole generation has passed since the time when the paper was at last unsealed and read, so long it had no operation; yet now, at last, here comes the American, to disturb the succession of an ancient family!"

"There is something very strange in all this," said Middleton.

And indeed there was something stranger in his view of the matter than he had yet communicated to the Master. For, taking into consideration the relation in which he found himself with the present recognized representative of the family, the thought struck him that his coming hither had dug up, as it were, a buried secret that immediately assumed life and activity the moment that it was above ground again. For seven generations the family had vegetated in the quietude of English country gentility, doing nothing to make itself known, passing from the cradle to the tomb amid the same old woods that had waved over it before his ancestor had impressed the bloody footstep; and yet the instant that he came back, an influence seemed to be at work that was likely to renew the old history of the family. He questioned with himself whether it were not better to leave all as it was; to withdraw himself into the secrecy from which he had but half emerged, and leave the family to keep on, to the end of time perhaps, in its rusty innocence, rather than to interfere with his wild American character to disturb it. The smell of that dark crime— that brotherly hatred and attempted murder—seemed to breathe out of the ground as he dug it up. Was it not better that it should remain forever buried, for what to him was this old English title—what this estate, so far from his own native land, located amidst feelings and manners which would never be his own? It was late, to be sure—yet not too late for him to turn back: the vibration, the fear, which his footsteps had caused, would subside into peace! Meditating in this way, he took a hasty leave of the kind old Master, promising to see him again at an early opportunity. By chance, or however it was, his footsteps turned to the woods of ———— Chace, and there he wandered through its glades, deep in thought, yet always with a strange sense that he was treading on the soil where his ancestors had trodden, and where he himself had best right of all men to be. It was just in this state of feeling that he found his course arrested by a hand upon his shoulder.

"What business have you here?" was the question sounded in his ear; and, starting, he found himself in the grasp, as his blood tingled to know, of a gentleman in a shooting-dress, who looked at him with a wrathful brow. "Are you a poacher, or what?"

Be the case what it might, Middleton's blood boiled at the grasp of that hand, as it never before had done in the coarse of his impulsive life. He shook himself free, and stood fiercely before his antagonist, confronting him, with his uplifted stick, while the other, likewise, appeared to be shaken by a strange wrath.

"Fellow," muttered he—"Yankee blackguard!—imposter—take yourself off these grounds. Quick, or it will be the worse for you!"

Middleton restrained himself. "Mr. Eldredge," said he, "for I believe I speak to the man who calls himself owner of this land on which we stand, —Mr. Eldredge, you are acting under a strange misapprehension of my character. I have come hither with no sinister purpose, and am entitled, at the hands of a gentleman, to the consideration of an honorable antagonist, even if you deem me one at all. And perhaps, if you think upon the blue chamber and the ebony cabinet, and the secret connected. with it,"—

"Villain, no more!" said Eldredge; and utterly mad with rage, he presented his gun at Middleton; but even at the moment of doing so, he partly restrained himself, so far as, instead of shooting him, to raise the butt of his gun, and strike a blow at him. It came down heavily on Middleton's shoulder, though aimed at his head; and the blow was terribly avenged, even by itself, for the jar caused the hammer to come down; the gun went off, sending the bullet downwards through the heart of the unfortunate man, who fell dead upon the ground. Eldredge [Evidently a slip of the pen; Middleton being intended.] stood stupefied, looking at the catastrophe which had so suddenly occurred.

May 3d, Monday.—So here was the secret suddenly made safe in this so terrible way; its keepers reduced from two parties to one interest; the other who alone knew of this age-long mystery and trouble now carrying it into eternity, where a long line of those who partook of the knowledge, in each successive generation, might now be waiting to inquire of him how he had held his trust. He had kept it well, there was no doubt of it; for there he lay dead upon the ground, having betrayed it to no one, though by a method which none could have foreseen, the whole had come into the possession of him who had brought hither but half of it. Middleton looked down in horror upon the form that had just been so full of life and wrathful vigor—and now lay so quietly. Being wholly unconscious of any purpose to bring about the catastrophe, it had not at first struck him that his own position was in any manner affected by the violent death, under such circumstances, of the unfortunate man. But now it suddenly occurred to him, that there had been a train of incidents all calculated to make him the object of suspicion; and he felt that he could not, under the English administration of law, be suffered to go at large without rendering a strict account of himself and his relations with the deceased. He might, indeed, fly; he might still remain in the vicinity, and possibly escape notice. But was not the risk too great? Was it just even to be aware of this event, and not relate fully the manner of it, lest a suspicion of blood-guiltiness should rest upon some innocent head? But while he was thus cogitating, he heard footsteps approaching along the wood-path; and half-impulsively, half on purpose, he stept aside into the shrubbery, but still where he could see the dead body, and what passed near it.

The footsteps came on, and at the turning of the path, just where Middleton had met Eldredge, the new-comer appeared in sight. It was

Hoper, in his usual dress of velveteen, looking now seedy, poverty-stricken, and altogether in ill-case, trudging moodily along, with his hat pulled over his brows, so that he did not see the ghastly object before him till his foot absolutely trod upon the dead man's hand. Being thus made aware of the proximity of the corpse, he started back a little, yet evincing such small emotion as did credit to his English reserve; then uttering a low exclamation,—cautiously low, indeed,—he stood looking at the corpse a moment or two, apparently in deep meditation. He then drew near, bent down, and without evincing any horror at the touch of death in this horrid shape, he opened the dead man's vest, inspected the wound, satisfied himself that life was extinct, and then nodded his head and smiled gravely. He next proceeded to examine seriatim the dead man's pockets, turning each of them inside out and taking the contents, where they appeared adapted to his needs: for instance, a silken purse, through the interstices of which some gold was visible; a watch, which however had been injured by the explosion, and had stopt just at the moment—twenty-one minutes past five—when the catastrophe took place. Hoper ascertained, by putting the watch to his ear, that this was the case; then pocketing it, he continued his researches. He likewise secured a note-book, on examining which he found several bank-notes, and some other papers. And having done this, the thief stood considering what to do next; nothing better occurring to him, he thrust the pockets back, gave the corpse as nearly as he could the same appearance that it had worn before he found it, and hastened away, leaving the horror there on the wood-path.

He had been gone only a few minutes when another step, a light woman's step, [was heard] coming along the pathway, and Alice appeared, having on her usual white mantle, straying along with that fearlessness which characterized her so strangely, and made her seem like one of the denizens of nature. She was singing in a low tone some one of those airs which have become so popular in England, as negro melodies; when suddenly, looking before her, she saw the blood-stained body on the grass, the face looking ghastly upward. Alice pressed her hand upon her heart; it was not her habit to scream, not the habit of that strong, wild, self-dependent nature; and the exclamation which broke from her was not for help, but the voice of her heart crying out to herself. For an instant she hesitated, as [if] not knowing what to do; then approached, and with her white, maiden hand felt the brow of the dead man, tremblingly, but yet firm, and satisfied herself that life had wholly departed. She pressed her hand, that had just touched the dead man's, on her forehead, and gave a moment to thought.

What her decision might have been, we cannot say, for while she stood in this attitude, Middleton stept from his seclusion, and at the noise of his approach she turned suddenly round, looking more frightened and agitated than at the moment when she had first seen the dead body. She faced Middleton, however, and looked him quietly in the eye. "You see this!" said she, gazing fixedly at him. "It is not at this moment that you first discover it."

"No," said Middleton, frankly. "It is not. I was present at the catastrophe. In one sense, indeed, I was the cause of it; but, Alice, I need not tell you that I am no murderer."

"A murderer?—no," said Alice, still looking at him with the same fixed gaze. "But you and this man were at deadly variance. He would have rejoiced at any chance that would have laid you cold and bloody on the earth, as he is now; nay, he would most eagerly have seized on any fair-looking pretext that would have given him a chance to stretch you there. The world will scarcely believe, when it knows all about your relations with him, that his blood is not on your hand. Indeed," said she, with a strange smile, "I see some of it there now!"

And, in very truth, so there was; a broad blood-stain that had dried on Middleton's hand. He shuddered at it, but essayed vainly to rub it off.

"You see," said she. "It was foreordained that you should shed this man's blood; foreordained that, by digging into that old pit of pestilence, you should set the contagion loose again. You should have left it buried forever. But now what do you mean to do?"

"To proclaim this catastrophe," replied Middleton. "It is the only honest and manly way. What else can I do?"

"You can and ought to leave him on the wood-path, where he has fallen," said Alice, "and go yourself to take advantage of the state of things which Providence has brought about. Enter the old house, the hereditary house, where—now, at least—you alone have a right to tread. Now is the hour. All is within your grasp. Let the wrong of three hundred years be righted, and come back thus to your own, to these hereditary fields, this quiet, long-descended home; to title, to honor."

Yet as the wild maiden spoke thus, there was a sort of mockery in her eyes; on her brow; gleaming through all her face, as if she scorned what she thus pressed upon him, the spoils of the dead man who lay at their feet. Middleton, with his susceptibility, could not [but] be sensible of a wild and strange charm, as well as horror, in the situation; it seemed such a wonder that here, in formal, orderly, well-governed England, so wild a scene as this should have occurred; that they too [two?] should stand here, deciding on the descent of an estate, and the inheritance of a title, holding a court of their own.

"Come, then," said he, at length. "Let us leave this poor fallen antagonist in his blood, and go whither you will lead me. I will judge for myself. At all events, I will not leave my hereditary home without knowing what my power is."

"Come," responded Alice; and she turned back; but then returned and threw a handkerchief over the dead man's face, which while they spoke had assumed that quiet, ecstatic expression of joy which often is observed to overspread the faces of those who die of gunshot wounds, however fierce the passion in which their spirits took their flight. With this strange, grand, awful joy did the dead man gaze upward into the very eyes and hearts, as it were, of the two that now bent over him. They looked at one another.

"Whence comes this expression?" said Middleton, thoughtfully. "Alice, methinks he is reconciled to us now; and that we are members of one reconciled family, all of whom are in heaven but me."

140

Tuesday, May 4th.—"How strange is this whole situation between you and me," said Middleton, as they went up the winding pathway that led towards the house. "Shall I ever understand it? Do you mean ever to explain it to me? That I should find you here with that old man [The allusion here is apparently to the old man who proclaims himself Alice's father, in the portion dated April 14th. He figures hereafter as the old Hospitaller, Hammond. The reader must not take this present passage as referring to the death of Eldredge, which has just taken place in he preceding section. The author is now beginning to elaborate the relation of Middleton and Alice. As will be seen, farther on, the death of Eldredge is ignored and abandoned; Eldredge is revived, and the story proceeds in another way.—G. P. L.], so mysterious, apparently so poor, yet so powerful! What [is] his relation to you?"

"A close one," replied Alice sadly. "He was my father!"

"Your father!" repeated Middleton, starting back. "It does but heighten the wonder! Your father! And yet, by all the tokens that birth and breeding, and habits of thought and native character can show, you are my countrywoman. That wild, free spirit was never born in the breast of an Englishwoman; that slight frame, that slender beauty, that frail envelopment of a quick, piercing, yet stubborn and patient spirit,—are those the properties of an English maiden?"

"Perhaps not," replied Alice quietly. "I am your countrywoman. My father was an American, and one of whom you have heard—and no good, alas!—for many a year."

"And who then was he?" asked Middleton.

"I know not whether you will hate me for telling you," replied Alice, looking him sadly though firmly in the face. "There was a man—long years since, in your childhood—whose plotting brain proved the ruin of himself and many another; a man whose great designs made him a sort of potentate, whose schemes became of national importance, and produced results even upon the history of the country in which he acted. That man was my father; a man who sought to do great things, and, like many who have had similar aims, disregarded many small rights, strode over them, on his way to effect a gigantic purpose. Among other men, your father was trampled under foot, ruined, done to death, even, by the effects of his ambition."

"How is it possible!" exclaimed Middleton. "Was it Wentworth?"

"Even so," said Alice, still with the same sad calmness and not withdrawing her steady eyes from his face. "After his ruin; after the catastrophe that overwhelmed him and hundreds more, he took to flight; guilty, perhaps, but guilty as a fallen conqueror is; guilty to such an extent that he ceased to be a cheat, as a conqueror ceases to be a murderer. He came to England. My father had an original nobility of nature; and his life had not been such as to debase it, but rather such as to cherish and heighten that self-esteem which at least keeps the possessor of it from many meaner vices. He took nothing with him; nothing beyond the bare means of flight, with the world before him, although thousands of gold would not have been missed out of the scattered fragments of ruin that lay around him. He found his way hither, led, as you were, by a desire to reconnect himself with the place whence his family had originated; for he, too, was of a race which had something to do with the ancient story which has now been brought to a close. Arrived here, there were circumstances that chanced to make his talents and habits of business available to this Mr. Eldredge, a man ignorant and indolent, unknowing how to make the best of the property that was in his hands. By degrees, he took the estate into his management, acquiring necessarily a preponderating influence over such a man."

"And you," said Middleton. "Have you been all along in England? For you must have been little more than an infant at the time."

"A mere infant," said Alice, "and I remained in our own country under the care of a relative who left me much to my own keeping; much to the influences of that wild culture which the freedom of our country gives to its youth. It is only two years that I have been in England."

"This, then," said Middleton thoughtfully, "accounts for much that has seemed so strange in the events through which we have passed; for the knowledge of my identity and my half-defined purpose which has always glided before me, and thrown so many strange shapes of difficulty in my path. But whence,—whence came that malevolence which your father's conduct has so unmistakably shown? I had done him no injury, though I had suffered much."

"I have often thought," replied Alice, "that my father, though retaining a preternatural strength and acuteness of intellect, was really not altogether sane. And, besides, he had made it his business to keep this estate, and all the complicated advantages of the representation of this old family, secure to the person who was deemed to have inherited them. A succession of ages and generations might be supposed to have blotted out your claims from existence; for it is not just that there should be no term of time which can make security for lack of fact and a few formalities. At all events, he had satisfied himself that his duty was to act as he has done."

"Be it so! I do not seek to throw blame on him," said Middleton. "Besides, Alice, he was your father!"

"Yes," said she, sadly smiling; "let him [have] what protection that thought may give him, even though I lose what he may gain. And now here we are at the house. At last, come in! It is your own; there is none that can longer forbid you!"

They entered the door of the old mansion, now a farm-house, and there were its old hall, its old chambers, all before them. They ascended the staircase, and stood on the landing-place above; while Middleton had again that feeling that had so often made him dizzy,—that sense of being in one dream and recognizing the scenery and events of a former dream. So overpowering was this feeling, that he laid his hand on the slender arm of Alice, to steady himself; and she comprehended the emotion that agitated him, and looked into his eyes with a tender sympathy, which she had never before permitted to be visible,—perhaps never before felt. He steadied himself and followed her till they had entered an ancient chamber, but one that was finished with all the comfortable luxury customary to be seen in English homes.

"Whither have you led me now?" inquired Middleton.

"Look round," said Alice. "Is there nothing here that you ought to recognize?—nothing that you kept the memory of, long ago?"

He looked around the room again and again, and at last, in a somewhat shadowy corner, he espied an old cabinet made of ebony and inlaid with pearl; one of those tall, stately, and elaborate pieces of furniture that are rather articles of architecture than upholstery; and on which a higher skill, feeling, and genius than now is ever employed on such things, was expended. Alice drew near the stately cabinet and threw wide the doors, which, like the portals of a palace, stood between two pillars; it all seemed to be unlocked, showing within some beautiful old pictures in the panel of the doors, and a mirror, that opened a long succession of mimic halls, reflection upon reflection, extending to an interminable nowhere.

"And what is this?" said Middleton,—"a cabinet? Why do you draw my attention so strongly to it?"

"Look at it well," said she. "Do you recognize nothing there? Have you forgotten your description? The stately palace with its architecture, each pillar with its architecture, those pilasters, that frieze; you ought to know them all. Somewhat less than you imagined in size, perhaps; a fairy reality, inches for yards; that is the only difference. And you have the key?"

And there then was that palace, to which tradition, so false at once and true, had given such magnitude and magnificence in the traditions of the Middleton family, around their shifting fireside in America. Looming afar through the mists of time, the little fact had become a gigantic vision. Yes, here it was in miniature, all that he had dreamed of; a palace of four feet high!

"You have the key of this palace," said Alice; "it has waited—that is, its secret and precious chamber has, for you to open it, these three hundred years. Do you know how to find that secret chamber?"

Middleton, still in that dreamy mood, threw open an inner door of the cabinet, and applying the old-fashioned key at his watch-chain to a hole in the mimic pavement within, pressed one of the mosaics, and immediately the whole floor of the apartment sank, and revealed a receptacle withal. Alice had come forward eagerly, and they both looked into the hiding-place, expecting what should be there. It was empty! They looked into each other's faces with blank astonishment. Everything had been so strangely true, and so strangely false, up to this moment, that they could not comprehend this failure at the last moment. It was the strangest, saddest jest! It brought Middleton up with such a sudden revulsion that he grew dizzy, and the room swam round him and the cabinet dazzled before his eyes. It had been magnified to a palace; it had dwindled down to Liliputian size; and yet, up till now, it had seemed to contain in its diminutiveness all the riches which he had attributed to its magnitude. This last moment had utterly subverted it; the whole great structure seemed to vanish.

"See; here are the dust and ashes of it," observed Alice, taking something that was indeed only a pinch of dust out of the secret compartment. "There is nothing else."

II.

May 5th, Wednesday.—The father of these two sons, an aged man at the time, took much to heart their enmity; and after the catastrophe, he never held up his head again. He was not told that his son had perished, though such was the belief of the family; but imbibed the opinion that he had left his home and native land to become a wanderer on the face of the earth, and that some time or other he might return. In this idea he spent the remainder of his days; in this idea he died. It may be that the influence of this idea might be traced in the way in which he spent some of the latter years of his life, and a portion of the wealth which had become of little value in his eyes, since it had caused dissension and bloodshed between the sons of one household. It was a common mode of charity in those days—a common thing for rich men to do—to found an almshouse or a hospital, and endow it, for the support of a certain number of old and destitute men or women, generally such as had some claim of blood upon the founder, or at least were natives of the parish, the district, the county, where he dwelt. The Eldredge Hospital was founded for the benefit of twelve old men, who should have been wanderers upon the face of the earth; men, they should be, of some education, but defeated and hopeless, cast off by the world for misfortune, but not for crime. And this charity had subsisted, on terms varying little or nothing from the original ones, from that day to this; and, at this very time, twelve old men were not wanting, of various countries, of various fortunes, but all ending finally in ruin, who had centred here, to live on the poor pittance that had been assigned to them, three hundred years ago. What a series of chronicles it would have been if each of the beneficiaries of this charity, since its foundation, had left a record of the events which finally led him hither. Middleton often, as he talked with these old men, regretted that he himself had no turn for authorship, so rich a volume might he have compiled from the experience, sometimes sunny and triumphant, though always ending in shadow, which he gathered here. They were glad to talk to him, and would have been glad and grateful for any auditor, as they sat on one or another of the stone benches, in the sunshine of the garden; or at evening, around the great fireside, or within the chimney-corner, with their pipes and ale.

There was one old man who attracted much of his attention, by the venerableness of his aspect; by something dignified, almost haughty and commanding, in his air. Whatever might have been the intentions and expectations of the founder, it certainly had happened in these latter days that there was a difficulty in finding persons of education, of good manners, of evident respectability, to put into the places made vacant by deaths of members; whether that the paths of life are surer now than they used to be, and that men so arrange their lives as not to be left, in any event, quite without resources as they draw near its close; at any rate, there was a little tincture of the vagabond running through these twelve quasi gentlemen,—through several of them, at least. But this old man could not well be mistaken; in his manners, in his tones, in all his natural language and deportment, there was evidence that he had been more than respectable; and, viewing him, Middleton could not help wondering what statesman had suddenly vanished out of public life and taken refuge here, for his head was of the statesman-class, and his demeanor that of one who had exercised influence over large numbers of men. He sometimes endeavored to set on foot a familiar relation with this old man, but there was even a sternness in the manner in which he repelled these advances, that gave little encouragement for their renewal. Nor did it seem that his companions of the Hospital were more in his confidence than Middleton himself. They regarded him with a kind of awe, a shyness, and in most cases with a certain dislike, which denoted an imperfect understanding of him. To say the truth, there was not generally much love lost between any of the members of this family; they had met with too much disappointment in the world to take kindly, now, to one another or to anything or anybody. I rather suspect that they really had more pleasure in burying one another, when the time came, than in any other office of mutual kindness and brotherly love which it was their part to do; not out of hardness of heart, but merely from soured temper, and because, when people have met disappointment and have settled down into final unhappiness, with no more gush and spring of good spirits, there is nothing any more to create amiability out of.

So the old people were unamiable and cross to one another, and unamiable and cross to old Hammond, yet always with a certain respect; and the result seemed to be such as treated the old man well enough. And thus he moved about among them, a mystery; the histories of the others, in the general outline, were well enough known, and perhaps not very uncommon; this old man's history was known to none, except, of course, to the trustees of the charity, and to the Master of the Hospital, to whom it had necessarily been revealed, before the beneficiary could be admitted as an inmate. It was judged, by the deportment of the Master, that the old man had once held some eminent position in society; for, though bound to treat them all as gentlemen, he was thought to show an especial and solemn courtesy to Hammond.

Yet by the attraction which two strong and cultivated minds inevitably have for one another, there did spring up an acquaintanceship, an intercourse, between Middleton and this old man, which was followed up in many a conversation which they held together on all subjects that were supplied by the news of the day, or the history of the past. Middleton used to make the newspaper the opening for much discussion; and it seemed to him that the talk of his companion had much of the character of that of a retired statesman, on matters which, perhaps, he would look at all the more wisely, because it was impossible he could ever more have a personal agency in them. Their discussions sometimes turned upon the affairs of his own country, and its relations with the rest of the world, especially with England; and Middleton could not help being struck with the accuracy of the old man's knowledge respecting that country, which so few Englishmen know anything about; his shrewd appreciation of the American character,—shrewd and caustic, yet not without a good degree of justice; the sagacity of his remarks on the past, and prophecies of what was likely to happen,—prophecies which, in one instance, were singularly verified, in regard to a complexity which was then arresting the attention of both countries.

"You must have been in the United States," said he, one day.

"Certainly; my remarks imply personal knowledge," was the reply. "But it was before the days of steam."

"And not, I should imagine, for a brief visit," said Middleton. "I only wish the administration of this government had the benefit to-day of your knowledge of my countrymen. It might be better for both of these kindred nations."

"Not a whit," said the old man. "England will never understand America; for England never does understand a foreign country; and whatever you may say about kindred, America is as much a foreign country as France itself. These two hundred years of a different climate and circumstances— of life on a broad continent instead of in an island, to say nothing of the endless intermixture of nationalities in every part of the United States, except New England—have created a new and decidedly original type of national character. It is as well for both parties that they should not aim at any very intimate connection. It will never do."

"I should be very sorry to think so," said Middleton; "they are at all events two noble breeds of men, and ought to appreciate one another. And America has the breadth of idea to do this for England, whether reciprocated or not."

Thursday, May 6th.—Thus Middleton was established in a singular way among these old men, in one of the surroundings most unlike anything in his own country. So old it was that it seemed to him the freshest and newest thing that he had ever met with. The residence was made infinitely the more interesting to him by the sense that he was near the place—as all the indications warned him—which he sought, whither his dreams had tended from his childhood; that he could wander each day round the park within which were the old gables of what he believed was his hereditary home. He had never known anything like the dreamy enjoyment of these days; so quiet, such a contrast to the turbulent life from which he had escaped across the sea. And here he set himself, still with that sense of shadowiness in what he saw and in what he did, in making all the researches possible to him, about the neighborhood; visiting every little church that raised its square battlemented Norman tower of gray stone, for several miles round about; making himself acquainted with each little village and hamlet that surrounded these churches, clustering about the graves of those who had dwelt in the same cottages aforetime. He visited all the towns within a dozen miles; and probably there were few of the inhabitants who had so good an acquaintance with the neighborhood as this native American attained within a few weeks after his coming thither.

In course of these excursions he had several times met with a young woman,—a young lady, one might term her, but in fact he was in some doubt what rank she might hold, in England,—who happened to be wandering about the country with a singular freedom. She was always alone, always on foot; he would see her sketching some picturesque old church, some ivied ruin, some fine drooping elm. She was a slight figure, much more so than Englishwomen generally are; and, though healthy of aspect, had not the ruddy complexion, which he was irreverently inclined to call the coarse tint, that is believed the great charm of English beauty. There was a freedom in her step and whole little womanhood, an elasticity, an irregularity, so to speak, that made her memorable from first sight; and when he had encountered her three or four times, he felt in a certain way acquainted with her. She was very simply dressed, and quite as simple in her deportment; there had been one or two occasions, when they had both smiled at the same thing; soon afterwards a little conversation had taken place between them; and thus, without any introduction, and in a way that somewhat puzzled Middleton himself, they had become acquainted. It was so unusual that a young English girl should be wandering about the country entirely alone—so much less usual that she should speak to a stranger—that Middleton scarcely knew how to account for it, but meanwhile accepted the fact readily and willingly, for in truth he found this mysterious personage a very likely and entertaining companion. There was a strange quality of boldness in her remarks, almost of brusqueness, that he might have expected to find in a young countrywoman of his own, if bred up among the strong-minded, but was astonished to find in a young Englishwoman. Somehow or other she made him think more of home than any other person or thing he met with; and he could not but feel that she was in strange contrast with everything about her. She was no beauty; very piquant; very pleasing; in some points of view and at some moments pretty; always good-humored, but somewhat too self-possessed for Middleton's taste. It struck him that she had talked with him as if she had some knowledge of him and of the purposes with which he was there; not that this was expressed, but only implied by the fact that, on looking back to what had passed, he found many strange coincidences in what she had said with what he was thinking about.

He perplexed himself much with thinking whence this young woman had come, where she belonged, and what might be her history; when, the next day, he again saw her, not this time rambling on foot, but seated in an open barouche with a young lady. Middleton lifted his hat to her, and she nodded and smiled to him; and it appeared to Middleton that a conversation ensued about him with the young lady, her companion. Now, what still more interested him was the fact that, on the panel of the barouche were the arms of the family now in possession of the estate of Smithell's; so that the young lady, his new acquaintance, or the young lady, her seeming friend, one or the other, was the sister of the present owner of that estate. He was inclined to think that his acquaintance could not be the Miss Eldredge, of whose beauty he had heard many tales among the people of the neighborhood. The other young lady, a tall, reserved, fair-haired maiden, answered the description considerably better. He concluded, therefore, that his acquaintance must be a visitor, perhaps a dependent and companion; though the freedom of her thought, action, and way of life seemed hardly consistent with this idea.

However, this slight incident served to give him a sort of connection with the family, and he could but hope that some further chance would introduce him within what he fondly called his hereditary walls. He had come to think of this as a dreamland; and it seemed even more a dreamland now than before it rendered itself into actual substance, an old house of stone and timber standing within its park, shaded about with its ancestral trees.

But thus, at all events, he was getting himself a little wrought into the net-work of human life around him, secluded as his position had at first seemed to be, in the farm-house where he had taken up his lodgings. For, there was the Hospital and its old inhabitants, in whose monotonous existence he soon came to pass for something, with his liveliness of mind, his experience, his good sense, his patience as a listener, his comparative youth even—his power of adapting himself to these stiff and crusty characters, a power learned among other things in his political life, where he had acquired something of the faculty (good or bad as might be) of making himself all things to all men. But though he amused himself with them all, there was in truth but one man among them in whom he really felt much interest; and that one, we need hardly say, was Hammond. It was not often that he found the old gentleman in a conversible mood; always courteous, indeed, but generally cool and reserved; often engaged in his one room, to which Middleton had never yet been admitted, though he had more than once sent in his name, when Hammond was not apparent upon the bench which, by common consent of the Hospital, was appropriated to him.

One day, however, notwithstanding that the old gentleman was confined to his room by indisposition, he ventured to inquire at the door, and, considerably to his surprise, was admitted. He found Hammond in his easy-chair, at a table, with writing-materials before him: and as Middleton entered, the old gentleman looked at him with a stern, fixed regard, which, however, did not seem to imply any particular displeasure towards this visitor, but rather a severe way of regarding mankind in general. Middleton looked curiously around the small apartment, to see what modification the character of the man had had upon the customary furniture of the Hospital, and how much of individuality he had given to that general type. There was a shelf of books, and a row of them on the mantel-piece; works of political economy, they appeared to be, statistics and things of that sort; very dry reading, with which, however, Middleton's experience as a politician had made him acquainted. Besides there were a few works on local antiquities, a county-history borrowed from the Master's library, in which Hammond appeared to have been lately reading.

"They are delightful reading," observed Middleton, "these old county-histories, with their great folio volumes and their minute account of the affairs of families and the genealogies, and descents of estates, bestowing as much blessed space on a few hundred acres as other historians give to a principality. I fear that in my own country we shall never have anything of this kind. Our space is so vast that we shall never come to know and love it, inch by inch, as the English antiquarians do the tracts of country with which they deal; and besides, our land is always likely to lack the interest that belongs to English estates; for where land changes its ownership every few years, it does not become imbued with the personalities of the people who live on it. It is but so much grass; so much dirt, where a succession of people have dwelt too little to make it really their own. But I have found a pleasure that I had no conception of before, in reading some of the English local histories."

"It is not a usual course of reading for a transitory visitor," said Hammond. "What could induce you to undertake it?"

"Simply the wish, so common and natural with Americans," said Middleton— "the wish to find out something about my kindred—the local origin of my own family."

"You do not show your wisdom in this," said his visitor. "America had better recognize the fact that it has nothing to do with England, and look upon itself as other nations and people do, as existing on its own hook. I never heard of any people looking back to the country of their remote origin in the way the Anglo-Americans do. For instance, England is made up of many alien races, German, Danish, Norman, and what not: it has received large, accessions of population at a later date than the settlement of the United States. Yet these families melt into the great homogeneous mass of

Englishmen, and look back no more to any other country. There are in this vicinity many descendants of the French Huguenots; but they care no more for France than for Timbuctoo, reckoning themselves only Englishmen, as if they were descendants of the aboriginal Britons. Let it be so with you."

"So it might be," replied Middleton, "only that our relations with England remain far more numerous than our disconnections, through the bonds of history, of literature, of all that makes up the memories, and much that makes up the present interests of a people. And therefore I must still continue to pore over these old folios, and hunt around these precincts, spending thus the little idle time I am likely to have in a busy life. Possibly finding little to my purpose; but that is quite a secondary consideration."

"If you choose to tell me precisely what your aims are," said Hammond, "it is possible I might give you some little assistance."

May 7th, Friday.—Middleton was in fact more than half ashamed of the dreams which he had cherished before coming to England, and which since, at times, had been very potent with him, assuming as strong a tinge of reality as those [scenes?] into which he had strayed. He could not prevail with himself to disclose fully to this severe, and, as he thought, cynical old man how strong within him was the sentiment that impelled him to connect himself with the old life of England, to join on the broken thread of ancestry and descent, and feel every link well established. But it seemed to him that he ought not to lose this fair opportunity of gaining some light on the abstruse field of his researches; and he therefore explained to Hammond that he had reason, from old family traditions, to believe that he brought with him a fragment of a history that, if followed out, might lead to curious results. He told him, in a tone half serious, what he had heard respecting the quarrel of the two brothers, and the Bloody Footstep, the impress of which was said to remain, as a lasting memorial of the tragic termination of that enmity. At this point, Hammond interrupted him. He had indeed, at various points of the narrative, nodded and smiled mysteriously, as if looking into his mind and seeing something there analogous to what he was listening to. He now spoke.

"This is curious," said he. "Did you know that there is a manor-house in this neighborhood, the family of which prides itself on having such a blood-stained threshold as you have now described?"

"No, indeed!" exclaimed Middleton, greatly interested. "Where?"

"It is the old manor-house of Smithell's," replied Hammond, "one of those old wood and timber [plaster?] mansions, which are among the most ancient specimens of domestic architecture in England. The house has now passed into the female line, and by marriage has been for two or three generations in possession of another family. But the blood of the old inheritors is still in the family. The house itself, or portions of it, are thought to date back quite as far as the Conquest."

"Smithell's?" said Middleton. "Why, I have seen that old house from a distance, and have felt no little interest in its antique aspect. And it has a Bloody Footstep! Would it be possible for a stranger to get an opportunity to inspect it?"

"Unquestionably," said Hammond; "nothing easier. It is but a moderate distance from here, and if you can moderate your young footsteps, and your American quick walk, to an old man's pace, I would go there with you some day. In this languor and ennui of my life, I spend some time in local antiquarianism, and perhaps I might assist you in tracing out how far these traditions of yours may have any connection with reality. It would be curious, would it not, if you had come, after two hundred years, to piece out a story which may have been as much a mystery in England as there in America?"

An engagement was made for a walk to Smithell's the ensuing day; and meanwhile Middleton entered more fully into what he had received from family traditions and what he had thought out for himself on the matter in question.

"Are you aware," asked Hammond, "that there was formerly a title in this family, now in abeyance, and which the heirs have at various times claimed, and are at this moment claiming? Do you know, too,—but you can scarcely know it,—that it has been surmised by some that there is an insecurity in the title to the estate, and has always been; so that the possessors have lived in some apprehension, from time immemorial, that another heir would appear and take from them the fair inheritance? It is a singular coincidence."

"Very strange," exclaimed Middleton. "No; I was not aware of it; and, to say the truth, I should not altogether like to come forward in the light of a claimant. But this is a dream, surely!"

"I assure you, sir," continued the old man, "that you come here in a very critical moment; and singularly enough there is a perplexity, a difficulty, that has endured for as long a time as when your ancestors emigrated, that is still rampant within the bowels, as I may say, of the family. Of course, it is too like a romance that you should be able to establish any such claim as would have a valid influence on this matter; but still, being here on the spot, it may be worth while, if merely as a matter of amusement, to make some researches into this matter."

"Surely I will," said Middleton, with a smile, which concealed more earnestness than he liked to show; "as to the title, a Republican cannot be supposed to think twice about such a bagatelle. The estate!—that might be a more serious consideration."

They continued to talk on the subject; and Middleton learned that the present possessor of the estates was a gentleman nowise distinguished from hundreds of other English gentlemen; a country squire modified in accordance with the type of to-day, a frank, free, friendly sort of a person enough, who had travelled on the Continent, who employed himself much in field-sports, who was unmarried, and had a sister who was reckoned among the beauties of the county.

While the conversation was thus going on, to Middleton's astonishment there came a knock at the door of the room, and, without waiting for a response, it was opened, and there appeared at it the same young woman whom he had already met. She came in with perfect freedom and familiarity, and was received quietly by the old gentleman; who, however, by his manner towards Middleton, indicated that he was now to take his leave. He did so, after settling the hour at which the excursion of the next day was to take place. This arranged, he departed, with much to think of, and a light glimmering through the confused labyrinth of thoughts which had been unilluminated hitherto.

To say the truth, he questioned within himself whether it were not better to get as quickly as he could out of the vicinity; and, at any rate, not to put anything of earnest in what had hitherto been nothing more than a romance to him. There was something very dark and sinister in the events of family history, which now assumed a reality that they had never before worn; so much tragedy, so much hatred, had been thrown into that deep pit, and buried under the accumulated debris, the fallen leaves, the rust and dust of more than two centuries, that it seemed not worth while to dig it up; for perhaps the deadly influences, which it had taken so much time to hide, might still be lurking there, and become potent if he now uncovered them. There was something that startled him, in the strange, wild light, which gleamed from the old man's eyes, as he threw out the suggestions which had opened this prospect to him. What right had he—an American, Republican, disconnected with this country so long, alien from its habits of thought and life, reverencing none of the things which Englishmen reverenced—what right had he to come with these musty claims from the dim past, to disturb them in the life that belonged to them? There was a higher and a deeper law than any connected with ancestral claims which he could assert; and he had an idea that the law bade him keep to the country which his ancestor had chosen and to its institutions, and not meddle nor make with England. The roots of his family tree could not reach under the ocean; he was at most but a seedling from the parent tree. While thus meditating he found that his footsteps had brought him unawares within sight of the old manor-house of Smithell's; and that he was wandering in a path which, if he followed it further, would bring him to an entrance in one of the wings of the mansion. With a sort of shame upon him, he went forward, and, leaning against a tree, looked at what he considered the home of his ancestors.

May 9th, Sunday.—At the time appointed, the two companions set out on their little expedition, the old man in his Hospital uniform, the long black mantle, with the bear and ragged staff engraved in silver on the breast, and Middleton in the plain costume which he had adopted in these wanderings about the country. On their way, Hammond was not very communicative, occasionally dropping some shrewd remark with a good deal of acidity in it; now and then, too, favoring his companion with some reminiscence of local antiquity; but oftenest silent. Thus they went on, and entered the park of Pemberton Manor by a by-path, over a stile and one of those footways, which are always so well worth threading out in England, leading the pedestrian into picturesque and characteristic scenes, when the high-road would show him nothing except what was commonplace and uninteresting. Now the gables of the old manor-house appeared before them, rising amidst the hereditary woods, which doubtless dated from a time beyond the days which Middleton fondly recalled, when his ancestors had walked beneath their shade. On each side of them were thickets and copses of fern, amidst which they saw the hares peeping out to gaze upon them, occasionally running across the path, and comporting themselves like creatures that felt themselves under some sort of protection from the outrages of man, though they knew too much of his destructive character to trust him too far. Pheasants, too, rose close beside them, and winged but a little way before they alighted; they likewise knew, or seemed to know, that their hour was not yet come. On all sides in these woods, these wastes, these beasts and birds, there was a character that was neither wild nor tame. Man had laid his grasp on them all, and done enough to redeem them from barbarism, but had stopped short of domesticating them; although Nature, in the wildest thing there, acknowledged the powerful and pervading influence of cultivation.

Arriving at a side door of the mansion, Hammond rang the bell, and a servant soon appeared. He seemed to know the old man, and immediately acceded to his request to be permitted to show his companion the house; although it was not precisely a show-house, nor was this the hour when strangers were usually admitted. They entered; and the servant did not give himself the trouble to act as a cicerone to the two visitants, but carelessly said to the old gentleman that he knew the rooms, and that he would leave him to discourse to his friend about them. Accordingly, they went into the old hall, a dark oaken-panelled room, of no great height, with many doors opening into it. There was a fire burning on the hearth; indeed, it was the custom of the house to keep it up from morning to night; and in the damp, chill climate of England, there is seldom a day in some part of which a fire is not pleasant to feel. Hammond here pointed out a stuffed fox, to which some story of a famous chase was attached; a pair of antlers of enormous size; and some old family pictures, so blackened with time and neglect that Middleton could not well distinguish their features, though curious to do so, as hoping to see there the lineaments of some with whom he might claim kindred. It was a venerable apartment, and gave a good foretaste of what they might hope to find in the rest of the mansion.

But when they had inspected it pretty thoroughly, and were ready to proceed, an elderly gentleman entered the hall, and, seeing Hammond, addressed him in a kindly, familiar way; not indeed as an equal friend, but with a pleasant and not irksome conversation. "I am glad to see you here again," said he. "What? I have an hour of leisure; for, to say the truth, the day hangs rather heavy till the shooting season begins. Come; as you have a friend with you, I will be your cicerone myself about the house, and show you whatever mouldy objects of interest it contains."

He then graciously noticed the old man's companion, but without asking or seeming to expect an introduction; for, after a careless glance at him, he had evidently set him down as a person without social claims, a young man in the rank of life fitted to associate with an inmate of Pemberton's Hospital. And it must be noticed that his treatment of Middleton was not on that account the less kind, though far from being so elaborately courteous as if he had met him as an equal. "You have had something of a walk," said he, "and it is a rather hot day. The beer of Pemberton Manor has been reckoned good these hundred years; will you taste it?"

Hammond accepted the offer, and the beer was brought in a foaming tankard; but Middleton declined it, for in truth there was a singular emotion in his breast, as if the old enmity, the ancient injuries, were not yet atoned for, and as if he must not accept the hospitality of one who represented his hereditary foe. He felt, too, as if there were something unworthy, a certain want of fairness, in entering clandestinely the house, and talking with its occupant under a veil, as it were; and had he seen clearly how to do it, he would perhaps at that moment have fairly told Mr. Eldredge that he brought with him the character of kinsman, and must be received in that grade or none. But it was not easy to do this; and after all, there was no clear reason why he should do it; so he let the matter pass, merely declining to take the refreshment, and keeping himself quiet and retired.

Squire Eldredge seemed to be a good, ordinary sort of gentleman, reasonably well educated, and with few ideas beyond his estate and neighborhood, though he had once held a seat in Parliament for part of a term. Middleton could not but contrast him, with an inward smile, with the shrewd, alert politicians, their faculties all sharpened to the utmost, whom he had known and consorted with in the American Congress. Hammond had slightly informed him that his companion was an American; and Mr. Eldredge immediately gave proof of the extent of his knowledge of that country, by inquiring whether he came from the State of New England, and whether Mr. Webster was still President of the United States; questions to which Middleton returned answers that led to no further conversation.

These little preliminaries over, they continued their ramble through the house, going through tortuous passages, up and down little flights of steps, and entering chambers that had all the charm of discoveries of hidden regions; loitering about, in short, in a labyrinth calculated to put the head into a delightful confusion. Some of these rooms contained their time-honored furniture, all in the best possible repair, heavy, dark, polished; beds that had been marriage beds and dying beds over and over again; chairs with carved backs; and all manner of old world curiosities; family pictures, and samplers, and embroidery; fragments of tapestry; an inlaid floor; everything having a story to it, though, to say the truth, the possessor of these curiosities made but a bungling piece of work in telling the legends connected with them. In one or two instances Hammond corrected him.

By and by they came to what had once been the principal bed-room of the house; though its gloom, and some circumstances of family misfortune that had happened long ago, had caused it to fall into disrepute, in latter times; and it was now called the Haunted Chamber, or the Ghost's Chamber. The furniture of this room, however, was particularly rich in its antique magnificence; and one of the principal objects was a great black cabinet of ebony and ivory, such as may often be seen in old English houses, and perhaps often in the palaces of Italy, in which country they perhaps originated. This present cabinet was known to have been in the house as long ago as the reign of Queen Elizabeth, and how much longer neither tradition nor record told. Hammond particularly directed Middleton's attention to it.

"There is nothing in this house," said he, "better worth your attention than that cabinet. Consider its plan; it represents a stately mansion, with pillars, an entrance, with a lofty flight of steps, windows, and everything perfect. Examine it well."

There was such an emphasis in the old man's way of speaking that Middleton turned suddenly round from all that he had been looking at, and fixed his whole attention on the cabinet; and strangely enough, it seemed to be the representative, in small, of something that he had seen in a dream. To say the truth, if some cunning workman had been employed to copy his idea of the old family mansion, on a scale of half an inch to a yard, and in ebony and ivory instead of stone, he could not have produced a closer imitation. Everything was there.

"This is miraculous!" exclaimed he. "I do not understand it."

"Your friend seems to be curious in these matters," said Mr. Eldredge graciously. "Perhaps he is of some trade that makes this sort of manufacture particularly interesting to him. You are quite at liberty, my friend, to open the cabinet and inspect it as minutely as you wish. It is an article that has a good deal to do with an obscure portion of our family history. Look, here is the key, and the mode of opening the outer door of the palace, as we may well call it." So saying, he threw open the outer door, and disclosed within the mimic likeness of a stately entrance hall, with a floor chequered of ebony and ivory. There were other doors that seemed to open into apartments in the interior of the palace; but when Mr. Eldredge threw them likewise wide, they proved to be drawers and secret receptacles, where papers, jewels, money, anything that it was desirable to store away secretly, might be kept.

"You said, sir," said Middleton, thoughtfully, "that your family history contained matter of interest in reference to this cabinet. Might I inquire what those legends are?"

"Why, yes," said Mr. Eldredge, musing a little. "I see no reason why I should have any idle concealment about the matter, especially to a foreigner and a man whom I am never likely to see again. You must know, then, my friend, that there was once a time when this cabinet was known to contain the fate of the estate and its possessors; and if it had held all that it was supposed to hold, I should not now be the lord of Pemberton Manor, nor the claimant of an ancient title. But my father, and his father before him, and his father besides, have held the estate and prospered on it; and I think we may fairly conclude now that the cabinet contains nothing except what we see."

And he rapidly again threw open one after another all the numerous drawers and receptacles of the cabinet.

"It is an interesting object," said Middleton, after looking very closely and with great attention at it, being pressed thereto, indeed, by the owner's good-natured satisfaction in possessing this rare article of vertu. "It is admirable work," repeated he, drawing back. "That mosaic floor, especially, is done with an art and skill that I never saw equalled."

There was something strange and altered in Middleton's tones, that attracted the notice of Mr. Eldredge. Looking at him, he saw that he had grown pale, and had a rather bewildered air.

"Is your friend ill?" said he. "He has not our English ruggedness of look. He would have done better to take a sip of the cool tankard, and a slice of the cold beef. He finds no such food and drink as that in his own country, I warrant."

"His color has come back," responded Hammond, briefly. "He does not need any refreshment, I think, except, perhaps, the open air."

In fact, Middleton, recovering himself, apologized to Mr. Hammond. [Eldredge?]; and as they had now seen nearly the whole of the house, the two visitants took their leave, with many kindly offers on Mr. Eldredge's part to permit the young man to view the cabinet whenever he wished. As they went out of the house (it was by another door than that which gave them entrance), Hammond laid his hand on Middleton's shoulder and pointed to a stone on the threshold, on which he was about to set his foot. "Take care!" said he. "It is the Bloody Footstep."

Middleton looked down and saw something, indeed, very like the shape of a footprint, with a hue very like that of blood. It was a twilight sort of a place, beneath a porch, which was much overshadowed by trees and shrubbery. It might have been blood; but he rather thought, in his wicked skepticism, that it was a natural, reddish stain in the stone. He measured his own foot, however, in the Bloody Footstep.

May 10th, Monday.—This is the present aspect of the story: Middleton is the descendant of a family long settled in the United States; his ancestor having emigrated to New England with the Pilgrims; or, perhaps, at a still earlier date, to Virginia with Raleigh's colonists. There had been a family dissension,—a bitter hostility between two brothers in England; on account, probably, of a love affair, the two both being attached to the same lady. By the influence of the family on both sides, the young lady had formed an engagement with the elder brother, although her affections had settled on the younger. The marriage was about to take place when the younger brother and the bride both disappeared, and were never heard of with any certainty afterwards; but it was believed at the time that he had been killed, and in proof of it a bloody footstep remained on the threshold of the ancestral mansion. There were rumors, afterwards, traditionally continued to the present day, that the younger brother and the bride were seen, and together, in England; and that some voyager across the sea had found them living together, husband and wife, on the other side of the Atlantic. But the elder brother became a moody and reserved man, never married, and left the inheritance to the children of a third brother, who then became the representative of the family in England; and the better authenticated story was that the second brother had really been slain, and that the young lady (for all the parties may have been Catholic) had gone to the Continent and taken the veil there. Such was the family history as known or surmised in England, and in the neighborhood of the manor-house, where the Bloody Footstep still remained on the threshold; and the posterity of the third brother still held the estate, and perhaps were claimants of an ancient baronage, long in abeyance.

162

Now, on the other side of the Atlantic, the second brother and the young lady had really been married, and became the parents of a posterity, still extant, of which the Middleton of the romance is the surviving male. Perhaps he had changed his name, being so much tortured with the evil and wrong that had sprung up in his family, so remorseful, so outraged, that he wished to disconnect himself with all the past, and begin life quite anew in a new world. But both he and his wife, though happy in one another, had been remorsefully and sadly so; and, with such feelings, they had never again communicated with their respective families, nor had given their children the means of doing so. There must, I think, have been something nearly approaching to guilt on the second brother's part, and the bride should have broken a solemnly plighted troth to the elder brother, breaking away from him when almost his wife. The elder brother had been known to have been wounded at the time of the second brother's disappearance; and it had been the surmise that he had received this hurt in the personal conflict in which the latter was slain. But in truth the second brother had stabbed him in the emergency of being discovered in the act of escaping with the bride; and this was what weighed upon his conscience throughout life in America. The American family had prolonged itself through various fortunes, and all the ups and downs incident to our institutions, until the present day. They had some old family documents, which had been rather carelessly kept; but the present representative, being an educated man, had looked over them, and found one which interested him strongly. It was—what was it?—perhaps a copy of a letter written by his ancestor on his deathbed, telling his real name, and relating the above incidents. These incidents had come down in a vague wild way, traditionally, in the American family, forming a wondrous and incredible legend, which Middleton had often laughed at, yet been greatly interested in; and the discovery of this document seemed to give a certain aspect of veracity and reality to the tradition. Perhaps, however, the document only related to the change of name, and made reference to certain evidences by which, if any descendant of the family should deem it expedient, he might prove his hereditary identity. The legend must be accounted for by having been gathered from the talk of the first ancestor and his wife. There must be in existence, in the early records of the colony, an authenticated statement of this change of name, and satisfactory proofs that the American family, long known as Middleton, were really a branch of the English family of Eldredge, or whatever. And in the legend, though not in the written document, there must be an account of a certain magnificent, almost palatial residence, which Middleton shall presume to be the ancestral house; and in this palace there shall be said to be a certain secret chamber, or receptacle, where is reposited a document that shall complete the evidence of the genealogical descent.

Middleton is still a young man, but already a distinguished one in his own country; he has entered early into politics, been sent to Congress, but having met with some disappointments in his ambitious hopes, and being disgusted with the fierceness of political contests in our country, he has come abroad for recreation and rest. His imagination has dwelt much, in his boyhood, on the legendary story of his family; and the discovery of the document has revived these dreams. He determines to search out the family mansion; and thus he arrives, bringing half of a story, being the only part known in America, to join it on to the other half, which is the only part known in England. In an introduction I must do the best I can to state his side of the matter to the reader, he having communicated it to me in a friendly way, at the Consulate; as many people have communicated quite as wild pretensions to English genealogies.

He comes to the midland counties of England, where he conceives his claims to lie, and seeks for his ancestral home; but there are difficulties in the way of finding it, the estates having passed into the female line, though still remaining in the blood. By and by, however, he comes to an old town where there is one of the charitable institutions bearing the name of his family, by whose beneficence it had indeed been founded, in Queen Elizabeth's time. He of course becomes interested in this Hospital; he finds it still going on, precisely as it did in the old days; and all the character and life of the establishment must be picturesquely described. Here he gets acquainted with an old man, an inmate of the Hospital, who (if the uncontrollable fatality of the story will permit) must have an active influence on the ensuing events. I suppose him to have been an American, but to have fled his country and taken refuge in England; he shall have been a man of the Nicholas Biddle stamp, a mighty speculator, the ruin of whose schemes had crushed hundreds of people, and Middleton's father among the rest. Here he had quitted the activity of his mind, as well as he could, becoming a local antiquary, etc., and he has made himself acquainted with the family history of the Eldredges, knowing more about it than the members of the family themselves do. He had known in America (from Middleton's father, who was his friend) the legends preserved in this branch of the family, and perhaps had been struck by the way in which they fit into the English legends; at any rate, this strikes him when Middleton tells him his story and shows him the document respecting the change of name. After various conversations together (in which, however, the old man keeps the secret of his own identity, and indeed acts as mysteriously as possible) they go together to visit the ancestral mansion. Perhaps it should not be in their first visit that the cabinet, representing the stately mansion, shall be seen. But the Bloody Footstep may; which shall interest Middleton much, both because Hammond has told him the English tradition respecting it, and because too the legends of the American family made some obscure allusions to his ancestor having left blood—a bloody footstep—on the ancestral threshold. This is the point to which the story has now been sketched out. Middleton finds a commonplace old English country gentleman in possession of the estate, where his forefathers had lived in peace for many generations; but there must be circumstances contrived which shall cause Middleton's conduct to be attended by no end of turmoil and trouble. The old Hospitaller, I suppose, must be the malicious agent in this; and his malice must be motived in some satisfactory way. The more serious question, what shall be the nature of this tragic trouble, and how can it be brought about?

May 11th, Tuesday.—How much better would it have been if this secret, which seemed so golden, had remained in the obscurity in which two hundred years had buried it! That deep, old, grass-grown grave being opened, out from it streamed into the sunshine the old fatalities, the old crimes, the old misfortunes, the sorrows, that seemed to have departed from the family forever. But it was too late now to close it up; he must follow out the thread that led him on,—the thread of fate, if you choose to call it so; but rather the impulse of an evil will, a stubborn self-interest, a desire for certain objects of ambition which were preferred to what yet were recognized as real goods. Thus reasoned, thus raved, Eldredge, as he considered the things that he had done, and still intended to do; nor did these perceptions make the slightest difference in his plans, nor in the activity with which he set about their performance. For this purpose he sent for his lawyer, and consulted him on the feasibility of the design which he had already communicated to him respecting Middleton. But the man of law shook his head, and, though deferentially, declined to have any active concern with the matter that threatened to lead him beyond the bounds which he allowed himself, into a seductive but perilous region.

"My dear sir," said he, with some earnestness, "you had much better content yourself with such assistance as I can professionally and consistently give you. Believe [me], I am willing to do a lawyer's utmost, and to do more would be as unsafe for the client as for the legal adviser."

Thus left without an agent and an instrument, this unfortunate man had to meditate on what means he would use to gain his ends through his own unassisted efforts. In the struggle with himself through which he had passed, he had exhausted pretty much all the feelings that he had to bestow on this matter; and now he was ready to take hold of almost any temptation that might present itself, so long as it showed a good prospect of success and a plausible chance of impunity. While he was thus musing, he heard a female voice chanting some song, like a bird's among the pleasant foliage of the trees, and soon he saw at the end of a wood-walk Alice, with her basket on her arm, passing on toward the village. She looked towards him as she passed, but made no pause nor yet hastened her steps; not seeming to think it worth her while to be influenced by him. He hurried forward and overtook her.

So there was this poor old gentleman, his comfort utterly overthrown, decking his white hair and wrinkled brow with the semblance of a coronet, and only hoping that the reality might crown and bless him before he was laid in the ancestral tomb. It was a real calamity; though by no means the greatest that had been fished up out of the pit of domestic discord that had been opened anew by the advent of the American; and by the use which had been made of it by the cantankerous old man of the Hospital. Middleton, as he looked at these evil consequences, sometimes regretted that he had not listened to those forebodings which had warned him back on the eve of his enterprise; yet such was the strange entanglement and interest which had wound about him, that often he rejoiced that for once he was engaged in something that absorbed him fully, and the zeal for the development of which made him careless for the result in respect to its good or evil, but only desirous that it show itself. As for Alice, she seemed to skim lightly through all these matters, whether as a spirit of good or ill he could not satisfactorily judge. He could not think her wicked; yet her actions seemed unaccountable on the plea that she was otherwise. It was another characteristic thread in the wild web of madness that had spun itself about all the prominent characters of our story. And when Middleton thought of these things, he felt as if it might be his duty (supposing he had the power) to shovel the earth again into the pit that he had been the means of opening; but also felt that, whether duty or not, he would never perform it.

For, you see, on the American's arrival he had found the estate in the hands of one of the descendants; but some disclosures consequent on his arrival had thrown it into the hands of another; or, at all events, had seemed to make it apparent that justice required that it should be so disposed of. No sooner was the discovery made than the possessor put on a coronet; the new heir had commenced legal proceedings; the sons of the respective branches had come to blows and blood; and the devil knows what other devilish consequences had ensued. Besides this, there was much falling in love at cross-purposes, and a general animosity of every body against everybody else, in proportion to the closeness of the natural ties and their obligation to love one another.

The moral, if any moral were to be gathered from these petty and wretched circumstances, was, "Let the past alone: do not seek to renew it; press on to higher and better things,—at all events, to other things; and be assured that the right way can never be that which leads you back to the identical shapes that you long ago left behind. Onward, onward, onward!"

"What have you to do here?" said Alice. "Your lot is in another land. You have seen the birthplace of your forefathers, and have gratified your natural yearning for it; now return, and cast in your lot with your own people, let it be what it will. I fully believe that it is such a lot as the world has never yet seen, and that the faults, the weaknesses, the errors, of your countrymen will vanish away like morning mists before the rising sun. You can do nothing better than to go back."

"This is strange advice, Alice," said Middleton, gazing at her and smiling. "Go back, with such a fair prospect before me; that were strange indeed! It is enough to keep me here, that here only I shall see you,—enough to make me rejoice to have come, that I have found you here."

"Do not speak in this foolish way," cried Alice, panting. "I am giving you the best advice, and speaking in the wisest way I am capable of,— speaking on good grounds too,—and you turn me aside with a silly compliment. I tell you that this is no comedy in which we are performers, but a deep, sad tragedy; and that it depends most upon you whether or no it shall be pressed to a catastrophe. Think well of it."

"I have thought, Alice," responded the young man, "and I must let things take their course; if, indeed, it depends at all upon me, which I see no present reason to suppose. Yet I wish you would explain to me what you mean."

To take up the story from the point where we left it: by the aid of the American's revelations, some light is thrown upon points of family history, which induce the English possessor of the estate to suppose that the time has come for asserting his claim to a title which has long been in abeyance. He therefore sets about it, and engages in great expenses, besides contracting the enmity of many persons, with whose interests he interferes. A further complication is brought about by the secret interference of the old Hospitaller, and Alice goes singing and dancing through the whole, in a way that makes her seem like a beautiful devil, though finally it will be recognized that she is an angel of light. Middleton, half bewildered, can scarcely tell how much of this is due to his own agency; how much is independent of him and would have happened had he stayed on his own side of the water. By and by a further and unexpected development presents the singular fact that he himself is the heir to whatever claims there are, whether of property or rank,—all centring in him as the representative of the eldest brother. On this discovery there ensues a tragedy in the death of the present possessor of the estate, who has staked everything upon the issue; and Middleton, standing amid the ruin and desolation of which he has been the innocent cause, resigns all the claims which he might now assert, and retires, arm in arm with Alice, who has encouraged him to take this course, and to act up to his character. The estate takes a passage into the female line, and the old name becomes extinct, nor does Middleton seek to continue it by resuming it in place of the one long ago assumed by his ancestor. Thus he and his wife become the Adam and Eve of a new epoch, and the fitting missionaries of a new social faith, of which there must be continual hints through the book.

A knot of characters may be introduced as gathering around Middleton, comprising expatriated Americans of all sorts: the wandering printer who came to me so often at the Consulate, who said he was a native of Philadelphia, and could not go home in the thirty years that he had been trying to do so, for lack of the money to pay his passage; the large banker; the consul of Leeds; the woman asserting her claims to half Liverpool; the gifted literary lady, maddened by Shakespeare, etc., etc. The Yankee who had been driven insane by the Queen's notice, slight as it was, of the photographs of his two children which he had sent her. I have not yet struck the true key-note of this Romance, and until I do, and unless I do, I shall write nothing but tediousness and nonsense. I do not wish it to be a picture of life, but a Romance, grim, grotesque, quaint, of which the Hospital might be the fitting scene. It might have so much of the hues of life that the reader should sometimes think it was intended for a picture, yet the atmosphere should be such as to excuse all wildness. In the Introduction, I might disclaim all intention to draw a real picture, but say that the continual meetings I had with Americans bent on such errands had suggested this wild story. The descriptions of scenery, etc., and of the Hospital, might be correct, but there should be a tinge of the grotesque given to all the characters and events.

The tragic and the gentler pathetic need not be excluded by the tone and treatment. If I could but write one central scene in this vein, all the rest of the Romance would readily arrange itself around that nucleus. The begging-girl would be another American character; the actress too; the caravan people. It must be humorous work, or nothing.

III.

May 12th, Wednesday.—Middleton found his abode here becoming daily more interesting; and he sometimes thought that it was the sympathies with the place and people, buried under the supergrowth of so many ages, but now coming forth with the life and vigor of a fountain, that, long hidden beneath earth and ruins, gushes out singing into the sunshine, as soon as these are removed. He wandered about the neighborhood with insatiable interest; sometimes, and often, lying on a hill-side and gazing at the gray tower of the church; sometimes coming into the village clustered round that same church, and looking at the old timber and plaster houses, the same, except that the thatch had probably been often renewed, that they used to be in his ancestor's days. In those old cottages still dwelt the families, the ———s, the Prices, the Hopnorts, the Copleys, that had dwelt there when America was a scattered progeny of infant colonies; and in the churchyard were the graves of all the generations since—including the dust of those who had seen his ancestor's face before his departure.

The graves, outside the church walls indeed, bore no marks of this antiquity; for it seems not to have been an early practice in England to put stones over such graves; and where it has been done, the climate causes the inscriptions soon to become obliterated and unintelligible. But, within the church, there were rich words of the personages and times with whom Middleton's musings held so much converse.

But one of his greatest employments and pastimes was to ramble through the grounds of Smithell's, making himself as well acquainted with its wood paths, its glens, its woods, its venerable trees, as if he had been bred up there from infancy. Some of those old oaks his ancestor might have been acquainted with, while they were already sturdy and well-grown trees; might have climbed them in boyhood; might have mused beneath them as a lover; might have flung himself at full length on the turf beneath them, in the bitter anguish that must have preceded his departure forever from the home of his forefathers. In order to secure an uninterrupted enjoyment of his rambles here, Middleton had secured the good-will of the game-keepers and other underlings whom he was likely to meet about the grounds, by giving them a shilling or a half-crown; and he was now free to wander where he would, with only the advice rather than the caution, to keep out of the way of their old master,—for there might be trouble, if he should meet a stranger on the grounds, in any of his tantrums. But, in fact, Mr. Eldredge was not much in the habit of walking about the grounds; and there were hours of every day, during which it was altogether improbable that he would have emerged from his own apartments in the manor-house. These were the hours, therefore, when Middleton most frequented the estate; although, to say the truth, he would gladly have so timed his visits as to meet and form an acquaintance with the lonely lord of this beautiful property, his own kinsman, though with so many ages of dark oblivion between. For Middleton had not that feeling of infinite distance in the relationship, which he would have had if his branch of the family had continued in England, and had not intermarried with the other branch, through such a long waste of years; he rather felt as if he were the original emigrant who, long resident on a foreign shore, had now returned, with a heart brimful of tenderness, to revisit the scenes of his youth, and renew his tender relations with those who shared his own blood.

There was not, however, much in what he heard of the character of the present possessor of the estate—or indeed in the strong family characteristic that had become hereditary—to encourage him to attempt any advances. It is very probable that the religion of Mr. Eldredge, as a Catholic, may have excited a prejudice against him, as it certainly had insulated the family, in a great degree, from the sympathies of the neighborhood. Mr. Eldredge, moreover, had resided long on the Continent; long in Italy; and had come back with habits that little accorded with those of the gentry of the neighborhood; so that, in fact, he was almost as much of a stranger, and perhaps quite as little of a real Englishman, as Middleton himself. Be that as it might, Middleton, when he sought to learn something about him, heard the strangest stories of his habits of life, of his temper, and of his employments, from the people with whom he conversed. The old legend, turning upon the monomania of the family, was revived in full force in reference to this poor gentleman; and many a time Middleton's interlocutors shook their wise heads, saying with a knowing look and under their breath that the old gentleman was looking for the track of the Bloody Footstep. They fabled—or said, for it might not have been a false story—that every descendant of this house had a certain portion of his life, during which he sought the track of that footstep which was left on the threshold of the mansion; that he sought it far and wide, over every foot of the estate; not only on the estate, but throughout the neighborhood; not only in the neighborhood but all over England; not only throughout England but all about the world. It was the belief of the neighborhood—at least of some old men and women in it—that the long period of Mr. Eldredge's absence from England had been spent in the search for some trace of those departing footsteps that had never returned. It is very possible—probable, indeed—that there may have been some ground for this remarkable legend; not that it is to be credited that the family of Eldredge, being reckoned among sane men, would seriously have sought, years and generations after the fact, for the first track of those bloody footsteps which the first rain of drippy England must have washed away; to say nothing of the leaves that had fallen and the growth and decay of so many seasons, that covered all traces of them since. But nothing is more probable than that the continual recurrence to the family genealogy, which had been necessitated by the matter of the dormant peerage, had caused the Eldredges, from father to son, to keep alive an interest in that ancestor who had disappeared, and who had been supposed to carry some of the most important family papers with him. But yet it gave Middleton a strange thrill of pleasure, that had something fearful in it, to think that all through these ages he had been waited for, sought for, anxiously expected, as it were; it seemed as if the very ghosts of his kindred, a long shadowy line, held forth their dim arms to welcome him; a line stretching back to the ghosts of those who had flourished in the old, old times; the doubletted and beruffled knightly shades of Queen Elizabeth's time; a long line, stretching

172

from the mediaeval ages, and their duskiness, downward, downward, with only one vacant space, that of him who had left the Bloody Footstep. There was an inexpressible pleasure (airy and evanescent, gone in a moment if he dwelt upon it too thoughtfully, but very sweet) to Middleton's imagination, in this idea. When he reflected, however, that his revelations, if they had any effect at all, might serve only to quench the hopes of these long expectants, it of course made him hesitate to declare himself.

One afternoon, when he was in the midst of musings such as this, he saw at a distance through the park, in the direction of the manor-house, a person who seemed to be walking slowly and seeking for something upon the ground. He was a long way off when Middleton first perceived him; and there were two clumps of trees and underbrush, with interspersed tracts of sunny lawn, between them. The person, whoever he was, kept on, and plunged into the first clump of shrubbery, still keeping his eyes on the ground, as if intensely searching for something. When he emerged from the concealment of the first clump of shrubbery, Middleton saw that he was a tall, thin person, in a dark dress; and this was the chief observation that the distance enabled him to make, as the figure kept slowly onward, in a somewhat wavering line, and plunged into the second clump of shrubbery. From that, too, he emerged; and soon appeared to be a thin elderly figure, of a dark man with gray hair, bent, as it seemed to Middleton, with infirmity, for his figure still stooped even in the intervals when he did not appear to be tracking the ground. But Middleton could not but be surprised at the singular appearance the figure had of setting its foot, at every step, just where a previous footstep had been made, as if he wanted to measure his whole pathway in the track of somebody who had recently gone over the ground in advance of him. Middleton was sitting at the foot of an oak; and he began to feel some awkwardness in the consideration of what he would do if Mr. Eldredge—for he could not doubt that it was he—were to be led just to this spot, in pursuit of his singular occupation. And even so it proved.

Middleton could not feel it manly to fly and hide himself, like a guilty thing; and indeed the hospitality of the English country gentleman in many cases gives the neighborhood and the stranger a certain degree of freedom in the use of the broad expanse of ground in which they and their forefathers have loved to sequester their residences. The figure kept on, showing more and more distinctly the tall, meagre, not unvenerable features of a gentleman in the decline of life, apparently in ill-health; with a dark face, that might once have been full of energy, but now seemed enfeebled by time, passion, and perhaps sorrow. But it was strange to see the earnestness with which he looked on the ground, and the accuracy with which he at last set his foot, apparently adjusting it exactly to some footprint before him; and Middleton doubted not that, having studied and restudied the family records and the judicial examinations which described exactly the track that was seen the day after the memorable disappearance of his ancestor, Mr. Eldredge was now, in some freak, or for some purpose best known to himself, practically following it out. And follow it out he did, until at last he lifted up his eyes, muttering to himself: "At this point the footsteps wholly disappear."

Lifting his eyes, as we have said, while thus regretfully and despairingly muttering these words, he saw Middleton against the oak, within three paces of him.

May 13th, Thursday.—Mr. Eldredge (for it was he) first kept his eyes fixed full on Middleton's face, with an expression as if he saw him not; but gradually—slowly, at first—he seemed to become aware of his presence; then, with a sudden flush, he took in the idea that he was encountered by a stranger in his secret mood. A flush of anger or shame, perhaps both, reddened over his face; his eyes gleamed; and he spoke hastily and roughly.

"Who are you?" he said. "How come you here? I allow no intruders in my park. Begone, fellow!"

"Really, sir, I did not mean to intrude upon you," said Middleton blandly. "I am aware that I owe you an apology; but the beauties of your park must plead my excuse; and the constant kindness of [the] English gentleman, which admits a stranger to the privilege of enjoying so much of the beauty in which he himself dwells as the stranger's taste permits him to enjoy."

"An artist, perhaps," said Mr. Eldredge, somewhat less uncourteously. "I am told that they love to come here and sketch those old oaks and their vistas, and the old mansion yonder. But you are an obtrusive set, you artists, and think that a pencil and a sheet of paper may be your passport anywhere. You are mistaken, sir. My park is not open to strangers."

"I am sorry, then, to have intruded upon you," said Middleton, still in good humor; for in truth he felt a sort of kindness, a sentiment, ridiculous as it may appear, of kindred towards the old gentleman, and besides was not unwilling in any way to prolong a conversation in which he found a singular interest. "I am sorry, especially as I have not even the excuse you kindly suggest for me. I am not an artist, only an American, who have strayed hither to enjoy this gentle, cultivated, tamed nature which I find in English parks, so contrasting with the wild, rugged nature of my native land. I beg your pardon, and will retire."

"An American," repeated Mr. Eldredge, looking curiously at him. "Ah, you are wild men in that country, I suppose, and cannot conceive that an English gentleman encloses his grounds—or that his ancestors have done so before him—for his own pleasure and convenience, and does not calculate on having it infringed upon by everybody, like your own forests, as you say. It is a curious country, that of yours: and in Italy I have seen curious people from it."

"True, sir," said Middleton, smiling. "We send queer specimens abroad; but Englishmen should consider that we spring from them, and that we present after all only a picture of their own characteristics, a little varied by climate and in situation."

Mr. Eldredge looked at him with a certain kind of interest, and it seemed to Middleton that he was not unwilling to continue the conversation, if a fair way to do so could only be afforded to him. A secluded man often grasps at any opportunity of communicating with his kind, when it is casually offered to him, and for the nonce is surprisingly familiar, running out towards his chance-companion with the gush of a dammed-up torrent, suddenly unlocked. As Middleton made a motion to retire, he put out his hand with an air of authority to restrain him.

"Stay," said he. "Now that you are here, the mischief is done, and you cannot repair it by hastening away. You have interrupted me in my mood of thought, and must pay the penalty by suggesting other thoughts. I am a lonely man here, having spent most of my life abroad, and am separated from my neighbors by various circumstances. You seem to be an intelligent man. I should like to ask you a few questions about your country."

He looked at Middleton as he spoke, and seemed to be considering in what rank of life he should place him; his dress being such as suited a humble rank. He seemed not to have come to any very certain decision on this point.

"I remember," said he, "you have no distinctions of rank in your country; a convenient thing enough, in some respects. When there are no gentlemen, all are gentlemen. So let it be. You speak of being Englishmen; and it has often occurred to me that Englishmen have left this country and been much missed and sought after, who might perhaps be sought there successfully."

"It is certainly so, Mr. Eldredge," said Middleton, lifting his eyes to his face as he spoke, and then turning them aside. "Many footsteps, the track of which is lost in England, might be found reappearing on the other side of the Atlantic; ay, though it be hundreds of years since the track was lost here."

Middleton, though he had refrained from looking full at Mr. Eldredge as he spoke, was conscious that he gave a great start; and he remained silent for a moment or two, and when he spoke there was the tremor in his voice of a nerve that had been struck and still vibrated.

"That is a singular idea of yours," he at length said; "not singular in itself, but strangely coincident with something that happened to be occupying my mind. Have you ever heard any such instances as you speak of?"

"Yes," replied Middleton, "I have had pointed out to me the rightful heir to a Scottish earldom, in the person of an American farmer, in his shirt-sleeves. There are many Americans who believe themselves to hold similar claims. And I have known one family, at least, who had in their possession, and had had for two centuries, a secret that might have been worth wealth and honors if known in England. Indeed, being kindred as we are, it cannot but be the case."

Mr. Eldredge appeared to be much struck by these last words, and gazed wistfully, almost wildly, at Middleton, as if debating with himself whether to say more. He made a step or two aside; then returned abruptly, and spoke.

"Can you tell me the name of the family in which this secret was kept?" said he; "and the nature of the secret?"

"The nature of the secret," said Middleton, smiling, "was not likely to be extended to any one out of the family. The name borne by the family was Middleton. There is no member of it, so far as I am aware, at this moment remaining in America."

"And has the secret died with them?" asked Mr. Eldredge.

"They communicated it to none," said Middleton.

"It is a pity! It was a villainous wrong," said Mr. Eldredge. "And so, it may be, some ancient line, in the old country, is defrauded of its rights for want of what might have been obtained from this Yankee, whose democracy has demoralized them to the perception of what is due to the antiquity of descent, and of the bounden duty that there is, in all ranks, to keep up the honor of a family that has had potence enough to preserve itself in distinction for a thousand years."

"Yes," said Middleton, quietly, "we have sympathy with what is strong and vivacious to-day; none with what was so yesterday."

The remark seemed not to please Mr. Eldredge; he frowned, and muttered something to himself; but recovering himself, addressed Middleton with more courtesy than at the commencement of their interview; and, with this graciousness, his face and manner grew very agreeable, almost fascinating: he [was] still haughty, however.

"Well, sir," said he, "I am not sorry to have met you. I am a solitary man, as I have said, and a little communication with a stranger is a refreshment, which I enjoy seldom enough to be sensible of it. Pray, are you staying hereabouts?"

Middleton signified to him that he might probably spend some little time in the village.

"Then, during your stay," maid Mr. Eldredge, "make free use of the walks in these grounds; and though it is not probable that you will meet me in them again, you need apprehend no second questioning of your right to be here. My house has many points of curiosity that may be of interest to a stranger from a new country. Perhaps you have heard of some of them."

"I have heard some wild legend about a Bloody Footstep," answered Middleton; "indeed, I think I remember hearing something about it in my own country; and having a fanciful sort of interest in such things, I took advantage of the hospitable custom which opens the doors of curious old houses to strangers, to go to see it. It seemed to me, I confess, only a natural stain in the old stone that forms the doorstep."

"There, sir," said Mr. Eldredge, "let me say that you came to a very foolish conclusion; and so, good-by, sir."

And without further ceremony, he cast an angry glance at Middleton, who perceived that the old gentleman reckoned the Bloody Footstep among his ancestral honors, and would probably have parted with his claim to the peerage almost as soon as have given up the legend.

Present aspect of the story: Middleton on his arrival becomes acquainted with the old Hospitaller, and is familiarized at the Hospital. He pays a visit in his company to the manor-house, but merely glimpses at its remarkable things, at this visit, among others at the old cabinet, which does not, at first view, strike him very strongly. But, on musing about his visit afterwards, he finds the recollection of the cabinet strangely identifying itself with his previous imaginary picture of the palatial mansion; so that at last he begins to conceive the mistake he has made. At this first [visit], he does not have a personal interview with the possessor of the estate; but, as the Hospitaller and himself go from room to room, he finds that the owner is preceding them, shyly flitting like a ghost, so as to avoid them. Then there is a chapter about the character of the Eldredge of the day, a Catholic, a morbid, shy man, representing all the peculiarities of an old family, and generally thought to be insane. And then comes the interview between him and Middleton, where the latter excites such an interest that he dwells upon the old man's mind, and the latter probably takes pains to obtain further intercourse with him, and perhaps invites him to dinner, and [to] spend a night in his house. If so, this second meeting must lead to the examination of the cabinet, and the discovery of some family documents in it. Perhaps the cabinet may be in Middleton's sleeping-chamber, and he examines it by himself, before going to bed; and finds out a secret which will perplex him how to deal with it.

May 14th, Friday.—We have spoken several times already of a young girl, who was seen at this period about the little antiquated village of Smithells; a girl in manners and in aspect unlike those of the cottages amid which she dwelt. Middleton had now so often met her, and in solitary places, that an acquaintance had inevitably established itself between them. He had ascertained that she had lodgings at a farm-house near by, and that she was connected in some way with the old Hospitaller, whose acquaintance had proved of such interest to him; but more than this he could not learn either from her or others. But he was greatly attracted and interested by the free spirit and fearlessness of this young woman; nor could he conceive where, in staid and formal England, she had grown up to be such as she was, so without manner, so without art, yet so capable of doing and thinking for herself. She had no reserve, apparently, yet never seemed to sin against decorum; it never appeared to restrain her that anything she might wish to do was contrary to custom; she had nothing of what could be called shyness in her intercourse with him; and yet he was conscious of an unapproachableness in Alice. Often, in the old man's presence, she mingled in the conversation that went on between him and Middleton, and with an acuteness that betokened a sphere of thought much beyond what could be customary with young English maidens; and Middleton was often reminded of the theories of those in our own country, who believe that the amelioration of society depends greatly on the part that women shall hereafter take, according to their individual capacity, in all the various pursuits of life. These deeper thoughts, these higher qualities, surprised him as they showed themselves, whenever occasion called them forth, under the light, gay, and frivolous exterior which she had at first seemed to present. Middleton often amused himself with surmises in what rank of life Alice could have been bred, being so free of all conventional rule, yet so nice and delicate in her perception of the true proprieties that she never shocked him.

One morning, when they had met in one of Middleton's rambles about the neighborhood, they began to talk of America; and Middleton described to Alice the stir that was being made in behalf of women's rights; and he said that whatever cause was generous and disinterested always, in that country, derived much of its power from the sympathy of women, and that the advocates of every such cause were in favor of yielding the whole field of human effort to be shared with women.

"I have been surprised," said he, "in the little I have seen and heard of Englishwomen, to discover what a difference there is between them and my own countrywomen."

"I have heard," said Alice, with a smile, "that your countrywomen are a far more delicate and fragile race than Englishwomen; pale, feeble hot-house plants, unfit for the wear and tear of life, without energy of character, or any slightest degree of physical strength to base it upon. If, now, you had these large-framed Englishwomen, you might, I should imagine, with better hopes, set about changing the system of society, so as to allow them to struggle in the strife of politics, or any other strife, hand to hand, or side by side, with men."

"If any countryman of mine has said this of our women," exclaimed Middleton, indignantly, "he is a slanderous villain, unworthy to have been borne by an American mother; if an Englishman has said it—as I know many of them have and do—let it pass as one of the many prejudices only half believed, with which they strive to console themselves for the inevitable sense that the American race is destined to higher purposes than their own. But pardon me; I forgot that I was speaking to an Englishwoman, for indeed you do not remind me of them. But, I assure you, the world has not seen such women as make up, I had almost said the mass of womanhood in my own country; slight in aspect, slender in frame, as you suggest, but yet capable of bringing forth stalwart men; they themselves being of inexhaustible courage, patience, energy; soft and tender, deep of heart, but high of purpose. Gentle, refined, but bold in every good cause."

"Oh, you have said quite enough," replied Alice, who had seemed ready to laugh outright, during this encomium. "I think I see one of those paragons now, in a Bloomer, I think you call it, swaggering along with a Bowie knife at her girdle, smoking a cigar, no doubt, and tippling sherry-cobblers and mint-juleps. It must be a pleasant life."

"I should think you, at least, might form a more just idea of what women become," said Middleton, considerably piqued, "in a country where the roles of conventionalism are somewhat relaxed; where woman, whatever you may think, is far more profoundly educated than in England, where a few ill-taught accomplishments, a little geography, a catechism of science, make up the sum, under the superintendence of a governess; the mind being kept entirely inert as to any capacity for thought. They are cowards, except within certain rules and forms; they spend a life of old proprieties, and die, and if their souls do not die with them, it is Heaven's mercy."

Alice did not appear in the least moved to anger, though considerably to mirth, by this description of the character of English females. She laughed as she replied, "I see there is little danger of your leaving your heart in England." She added more seriously, "And permit me to say, I trust, Mr. Middleton, that you remain as much American in other respects as in your preference of your own race of women. The American who comes hither and persuades himself that he is one with Englishmen, it seems to me, makes a great mistake; at least, if he is correct in such an idea he is not worthy of his own country, and the high development that awaits it. There is much that is seductive in our life, but I think it is not upon the higher impulses of our nature that such seductions act. I should think ill of the American who, for any causes of ambition,—any hope of wealth or rank,—or even for the sake of any of those old, delightful ideas of the past, the associations of ancestry, the loveliness of an age-long home,—the old poetry and romance that haunt these ancient villages and estates of England,—would give up the chance of acting upon the unmoulded future of America."

"And you, an Englishwoman, speak thus!" exclaimed Middleton. "You perhaps speak truly; and it may be that your words go to a point where they are especially applicable at this moment. But where have you learned these ideas? And how is it that you know how to awake these sympathies, that have slept perhaps too long?"

"Think only if what I have said be the truth," replied Alice. "It is no matter who or what I am that speak it."

"Do you speak," asked Middleton, from a sudden impulse, "with any secret knowledge affecting a matter now in my mind?"

Alice shook her head, as she turned away; but Middleton could not determine whether the gesture was meant as a negative to his question, or merely as declining to answer it. She left him; and he found himself strangely disturbed with thoughts of his own country, of the life that he ought to be leading there, the struggles in which he ought to be taking part; and, with these motives in his impressible mind, the motives that had hitherto kept him in England seemed unworthy to influence him.

May 15th, Saturday.—It was not long after Middleton's meeting with Mr. Eldredge in the park of Smithell's, that he received—what it is precisely the most common thing to receive—an invitation to dine at the manor-house and spend the night. The note was written with much appearance of cordiality, as well as in a respectful style; and Middleton could not but perceive that Mr. Eldredge must have been making some inquiries as to his social status, in order to feel him justified in putting him on this footing of equality. He had no hesitation in accepting the invitation, and on the appointed day was received in the old house of his forefathers as a guest. The owner met him, not quite on the frank and friendly footing expressed in his note, but still with a perfect and polished courtesy, which however could not hide from the sensitive Middleton a certain coldness, a something that seemed to him Italian rather than English; a symbol of a condition of things between them, undecided, suspicious, doubtful very likely. Middleton's own manner corresponded to that of his host, and they made few advances towards more intimate acquaintance. Middleton was however recompensed for his host's unapproachableness by the society of his daughter, a young lady born indeed in Italy, but who had been educated in a Catholic family in England; so that here was another relation—the first female one—to whoa he had been introduced. She was a quiet, shy, undemonstrative young woman, with a fine bloom and other charms which she kept as much in the background as possible, with maiden reserve. (There is a Catholic priest at table.)

Mr. Eldredge talked chiefly, during dinner, of art, with which his long residence in Italy had made him thoroughly acquainted, and for which he seemed to have a genuine taste and enjoyment. It was a subject on which Middleton knew little; but he felt the interest in it which appears to be not uncharacteristic of Americans, among the earliest of their developments of cultivation; nor had he failed to use such few opportunities as the English public or private galleries offered him to acquire the rudiments of a taste. He was surprised at the depth of some of Mr. Eldredge's remarks on the topics thus brought up, and at the sensibility which appeared to be disclosed by his delicate appreciation of some of the excellencies of those great masters who wrote their epics, their tender sonnets, or their simple ballads, upon canvas; and Middleton conceived a respect for him which he had not hitherto felt, and which possibly Mr. Eldredge did not quite deserve. Taste seems to be a department of moral sense; and yet it is so little identical with it, and so little implies conscience, that some of the worst men in the world have been the most refined.

After Miss Eldredge had retired, the host appeared to desire to make the dinner a little more social than it had hitherto been; he called for a peculiar species of wine from Southern Italy, which he said was the most delicious production of the grape, and had very seldom, if ever before, been imported pure into England. A delicious perfume came from the cradled bottle, and bore an ethereal, evanescent testimony to the truth of what he said: and the taste, though too delicate for wine quaffed in England, was nevertheless delicious, when minutely dwelt upon.

"It gives me pleasure to drink your health, Mr. Middleton," said the host. "We might well meet as friends in England, for I am hardly more an Englishman than yourself; bred up, as I have been, in Italy, and coming back hither at my age, unaccustomed to the manners of the country, with few friends, and insulated from society by a faith which makes most people regard me as an enemy. I seldom welcome people here, Mr. Middleton; but you are welcome."

"I thank you, Mr. Eldredge, and may fairly say that the circumstances to which you allude make me accept your hospitality with a warmer feeling than I otherwise might. Strangers, meeting in a strange land, have a sort of tie in their foreignness to those around them, though there be no positive relation between themselves."

"We are friends, then?" said Mr. Eldredge, looking keenly at Middleton, as if to discover exactly how much was meant by the compact. He continued, "You know, I suppose, Mr. Middleton, the situation in which I find myself on returning to my hereditary estate; which has devolved to me somewhat unexpectedly by the death of a younger man than myself. There is an old flaw here, as perhaps you have been told, which keeps me out of a property long kept in the guardianship of the crown, and of a barony, one of the oldest in England. There is an idea—a tradition—a legend, founded, however, on evidence of some weight, that there is still in existence the possibility of finding the proof which we need, to confirm our cause."

"I am most happy to hear it, Mr. Eldredge," said Middleton.

"But," continued his host, "I am bound to remember and to consider that for several generations there seems to have been the same idea, and the same expectation; whereas nothing has ever come of it. Now, among other suppositions—perhaps wild ones—it has occurred to me that this testimony, the desirable proof, may exist on your side of the Atlantic; for it has long enough been sought here in vain."

"As I said in our meeting in your park, Mr. Eldredge," replied Middleton, "such a suggestion may very possibly be true; yet let me point out that the long lapse of years, and the continual melting and dissolving of family institutions—the consequent scattering of family documents, and the annihilation of traditions from memory, all conspire against its probability."

"And yet, Mr. Middleton," said his host, "when we talked together at our first singular interview, you made use of an expression—of one remarkable phrase—which dwelt upon my memory and now recurs to it."

"And what was that, Mr. Eldredge?" asked Middleton.

"You spoke," replied his host, "of the Bloody Footstep reappearing on the threshold of the old palace of S———. Now where, let me ask you, did you ever hear this strange name, which you then spoke, and which I have since spoken?"

"From my father's lips, when a child, in America," responded Middleton.

"It is very strange," said Mr. Eldredge, in a hasty, dissatisfied tone. "I do not see my way through this."

May 16th, Sunday.—Middleton had been put into a chamber in the oldest part of the house, the furniture of which was of antique splendor, well befitting to have come down for ages, well befitting the hospitality shown to noble and even royal guests. It was the same room in which, at his first visit to the house, Middleton's attention had been drawn to the cabinet, which he had subsequently remembered as the palatial residence in which he had harbored so many dreams. It still stood in the chamber, making the principal object in it, indeed; and when Middleton was left alone, he contemplated it not without a certain awe, which at the same time he felt to be ridiculous. He advanced towards it, and stood contemplating the mimic facade, wondering at the singular fact of this piece of furniture having been preserved in traditionary history, when so much had been forgotten,—when even the features and architectural characteristics of the mansion in which it was merely a piece of furniture had been forgotten. And, as he gazed at it, he half thought himself an actor in a fairy portal [tale?]; and would not have been surprised—at least, he would have taken it with the composure of a dream—if the mimic portal had unclosed, and a form of pigmy majesty had appeared within, beckoning him to enter and find the revelation of what had so long perplexed him. The key of the cabinet was in the lock, and knowing that it was not now the receptacle of anything in the shape of family papers, he threw it open; and there appeared the mosaic floor, the representation of a stately, pillared hall, with the doors on either side opening, as would seem, into various apartments. And here should have stood the visionary figures of his ancestry, waiting to welcome the descendant of their race, who had so long delayed his coming. After looking and musing a considerable time,—even till the old clock from the turret of the house told twelve, he turned away with a sigh, and went to bed. The wind moaned through the ancestral trees; the old house creaked as with ghostly footsteps; the curtains of his bed seemed to waver. He was now at home; yes, he had found his home, and was sheltered at last under the ancestral roof after all those long, long wanderings,—after the little log-built hut of the early settlement, after the straight roof of the American house, after all the many roofs of two hundred years, here he was at last under the one which he had left, on that fatal night, when the Bloody Footstep was so mysteriously impressed on the threshold. As he drew nearer and nearer towards sleep, it seemed more and more to him as if he were the very individual—the self-same one throughout the whole—who had done, seen, suffered, all these long toils and vicissitudes, and were now come back to rest, and found his weariness so great that there could be no rest.

Nevertheless, he did sleep; and it may be that his dreams went on, and grew vivid, and perhaps became truer in proportion to their vividness. When he awoke he had a perception, an intuition, that he had been dreaming about the cabinet, which, in his sleeping imagination, had again assumed the magnitude and proportions of a stately mansion, even as he had seen it afar from the other side of the Atlantic. Some dim associations remained lingering behind, the dying shadows of very vivid ones which had just filled his mind; but as he looked at the cabinet, there was some idea that still seemed to come so near his consciousness that, every moment, he felt on the point of grasping it. During the process of dressing, he still kept his eyes turned involuntarily towards the cabinet, and at last he approached it, and looked within the mimic portal, still endeavoring to recollect what it was that he had heard or dreamed about it,—what half obliterated remembrance from childhood, what fragmentary last night's dream it was, that thus haunted him. It must have been some association of one or the other nature that led him to press his finger on one particular square of the mosaic pavement; and as he did so, the thin plate of polished marble slipt aside. It disclosed, indeed, no hollow receptacle, but only another leaf of marble, in the midst of which appeared to be a key-hole: to this Middleton applied the little antique key to which we have several times alluded, and found it fit precisely. The instant it was turned, the whole mimic floor of the hall rose, by the action of a secret spring, and discovered a shallow recess beneath. Middleton looked eagerly in, and saw that it contained documents, with antique seals of wax appended; he took but one glance at them, and closed the receptacle as it was before.

Why did he do so? He felt that there would be a meanness and wrong in inspecting these family papers, coming to the knowledge of them, as he had, through the opportunities offered by the hospitality of the owner of the estate; nor, on the other hand, did he feel such confidence in his host, as to make him willing to trust these papers in his hands, with any certainty that they would be put to an honorable use. The case was one demanding consideration, and he put a strong curb upon his impatient curiosity, conscious that, at all events, his first impulsive feeling was that he ought not to examine these papers without the presence of his host or some other authorized witness. Had he exercised any casuistry about the point, however, he might have argued that these papers, according to all appearance, dated from a period to which his own hereditary claims ascended, and to circumstances in which his own rightful interest was as strong as that of Mr. Eldredge. But he had acted on his first impulse, closed the secret receptacle, and hastening his toilet descended from his room; and, it being still too early for breakfast, resolved to ramble about the immediate vicinity of the house. As he passed the little chapel, he heard within the voice of the priest performing mass, and felt how strange was this sign of mediaeval religion and foreign manners in homely England.

As the story looks now: Eldredge, bred, and perhaps born, in Italy, and a Catholic, with views to the church before he inherited the estate, has not the English moral sense and simple honor; can scarcely be called an Englishman at all. Dark suspicions of past crime, and of the possibility of future crime, may be thrown around him; an atmosphere of doubt shall envelop him, though, as regards manners, he may be highly refined. Middleton shall find in the house a priest; and at his first visit he shall have seen a small chapel, adorned with the richness, as to marbles, pictures, and frescoes, of those that we see in the churches at Rome; and here the Catholic forms of worship shall be kept up. Eldredge shall have had an Italian mother, and shall have the personal characteristics of an Italian. There shall be something sinister about him, the more apparent when Middleton's visit draws to a conclusion; and the latter shall feel convinced that they part in enmity, so far as Eldredge is concerned. He shall not speak of his discovery in the cabinet.

May 17th, Monday.—Unquestionably, the appointment of Middleton as minister to one of the minor Continental courts must take place in the interval between Eldredge's meeting him in the park, and his inviting him to his house. After Middleton's appointment, the two encounter each other at the Mayor's dinner in St. Mary's Hall, and Eldredge, startled at meeting the vagrant, as he deemed him, under such a character, remembers the hints of some secret knowledge of the family history, which Middleton had thrown out. He endeavors, both in person and by the priest, to make out what Middleton really is, and what he knows, and what he intends; but Middleton is on his guard, yet cannot help arousing Eldredge's suspicions that he has views upon the estate and title. It is possible, too, that Middleton may have come to the knowledge—may have had some knowledge—of some shameful or criminal fact connected with Mr. Eldredge's life on the Continent; the old Hospitaller, possibly, may have told him this, from some secret malignity hereafter to be accounted for. Supposing Eldredge to attempt his murder, by poison for instance, bringing back into modern life his old hereditary Italian plots; and into English life a sort of crime which does not belong to it,— which did not, at least, although at this very period there have been fresh and numerous instances of it. There might be a scene in which Middleton and Eldredge come to a fierce and bitter explanation; for in Eldredge's character there must be the English surly boldness as well as the Italian subtlety; and here, Middleton shall tell him what he knows of his past character and life, and also what he knows of his own hereditary claims. Eldredge might have committed a murder in Italy; might have been a patriot and betrayed his friends to death for a bribe, bearing another name than his own in Italy; indeed, he might have joined them only as an informer. All this he had tried to sink, when he came to England in the character of a gentleman of ancient name and large estate. But this infamy of his previous character must be foreboded from the first by the manner in which Eldredge is introduced; and it must make his evil designs on Middleton appear natural and probable. It may be, that Middleton has learned Eldredge's previous character through some Italian patriot who had taken refuge in America, and there become intimate with him; and it should be a piece of secret history, not known to the world in general, so that Middleton might seem to Eldredge the sole depositary of the secret then in England. He feels a necessity of getting rid of him; and thenceforth Middleton's path lies always among pitfalls; indeed, the first attempt should follow promptly and immediately on his rupture with Eldredge. The utmost pains must be taken with this incident to give it an air of reality; or else it must be quite removed out of the sphere of reality by an intensified atmosphere of romance. I think the old Hospitaller must interfere to prevent the success of this attempt, perhaps through the means of Alice.

The result of Eldredge's criminal and treacherous designs is, somehow or other, that he comes to his death; and Middleton and Alice are left to administer on the remains of the story; perhaps, the Mayor being his friend, he may be brought into play here. The foreign ecclesiastic shall likewise come forward, and he shall prove to be a man of subtile policy perhaps, yet a man of religion and honor; with a Jesuit's principles, but a Jesuit's devotion and self-sacrifice. The old Hospitaller must die in his bed, or some other how; or perhaps not—we shall see. He may just as well be left in the Hospital. Eldredge's attempt on Middleton must be in some way peculiar to Italy, and which he shall have learned there; and, by the way, at his dinner-table there shall be a Venice glass, one of the kind that were supposed to be shattered when poison was put into them. When Eldredge produces his rare wine, he shall pour it into this, with a jesting allusion to the legend. Perhaps the mode of Eldredge's attempt on Middleton's life shall be a reproduction of the attempt made two hundred years before; and Middleton's knowledge of that incident shall be the means of his salvation. That would be a good idea; in fact, I think it must be done so and no otherwise. It is not to be forgotten that there is a taint of insanity in Eldredge's blood, accounting for much that is wild and absurd, at the same time that it must be subtile, in his conduct; one of those perplexing mad people, whose lunacy you are continually mistaking for wickedness or vice versa. This shall be the priest's explanation and apology for him, after his death. I wish I could get hold of the Newgate Calendar, the older volumes, or any other book of murders—the Causes Celebres, for instance. The legendary murder, or attempt at it, will bring its own imaginative probability with it, when repeated by Eldredge; and at the same time it will have a dreamlike effect; so that Middleton shall hardly know whether he is awake or not. This incident is very essential towards bringing together the past time and the present, and the two ends of the story.

May 18th, Tuesday.—All down through the ages since Edward had disappeared from home, leaving that bloody footstep on the threshold, there had been legends and strange stories of the murder and the manner of it. These legends differed very much among themselves. According to some, his brother had awaited him there, and stabbed him on the threshold. According to others, he had been murdered in his chamber, and dragged out. A third story told, that he was escaping with his lady love, when they were overtaken on the threshold, and the young man slain. It was impossible at this distance of time to ascertain which of these legends was the true one, or whether either of them had any portion of truth, further than that the young man had actually disappeared from that night, and that it never was certainly known to the public that any intelligence had ever afterwards been received from him. Now, Middleton may have communicated to Eldredge the truth in regard to the matter; as, for instance, that he had stabbed him with a certain dagger that was still kept among the curiosities of the manor-house. Of course, that will not do. It must be some very ingenious and artificially natural thing, an artistic affair in its way, that should strike the fancy of such a man as Eldredge, and appear to him altogether fit, mutatis mutandis, to be applied to his own requirements and purposes. I do not at present see in the least how this is to be wrought out. There shall be everything to make Eldredge look with the utmost horror and alarm at any chance that he may be superseded and ousted from his possession of the estate; for he shall only recently have established his claim to it, tracing out his pedigree, when the family was supposed to be extinct. And he is come to these comfortable quarters after a life of poverty, uncertainty, difficulty, hanging loose on society; and therefore he shall be willing to risk soul and body both, rather than return to his former state. Perhaps his daughter shall be introduced as a young Italian girl, to whom Middleton shall decide to leave the estate.

On the failure of his design, Eldredge may commit suicide, and be found dead in the wood; at any rate, some suitable end shall be contrived, adapted to his wants. This character must not be so represented as to shut him out completely from the reader's sympathies; he shall have taste, sentiment, even a capacity for affection, nor, I think, ought he to have any hatred or bitter feeling against the man whom he resolves to murder. In the closing scenes, when he thinks the fate of Middleton approaching, there might even be a certain tenderness towards him, a desire to make the last drops of life delightful; if well done, this would produce a certain sort of horror, that I do not remember to have seen effected in literature. Possibly the ancient emigrant might be supposed to have fallen into an ancient mine, down a precipice, into some pitfall; no, not so. Into a river; into a moat. As Middleton's pretensions to birth are not publicly known, there will be no reason why, at his sudden death, suspicion should fix on Eldredge as the murderer; and it shall be his object so to contrive his death as that it shall appear the result of accident. Having failed in effecting Middleton's death by this excellent way, he shall perhaps think that he cannot do better them to make his own exit in precisely the same manner. It might be easy, and as delightful as any death could be; no ugliness in it, no blood; for the Bloody Footstep of old times might be the result of the failure of the old plot, not of its success. Poison seems to be the only elegant method; but poison is vulgar, and in many respects unfit for my purpose. It won't do. Whatever it may be, it must not come upon the reader as a sudden and new thing, but as one that might have been foreseen from afar, though he shall not actually have foreseen it until it is about to happen. It must be prevented through the agency of Alice. Alice may have been an artist in Rome, and there have known Eldredge and his daughter, and thus she may have become their guest in England; or he may be patronizing her now—at all events she shall be the friend of the daughter, and shall have a just appreciation of the father's character. It shall be partly due to her high counsel that Middleton foregoes his claim to the estate, and prefers the life of an American, with its lofty possibilities for himself and his race, to the position of an Englishman of property and title; and she, for her part, shall choose the condition and prospects of woman in America, to the emptiness of the life of a woman of rank in England. So they shall depart, lofty and poor, out of the home which might be their own, if they would stoop to make it so. Possibly the daughter of Eldredge may be a girl not yet in her teens, for whom Alice has the affection of an elder sister.

It should be a very carefully and highly wrought scene, occurring just before Eldredge's actual attempt on Middleton's life, in which all the brilliancy of his character—which shall before have gleamed upon the reader—shall come out, with pathos, with wit, with insight, with knowledge of life. Middleton shall be inspired by this, and shall vie with him in exhilaration of spirits; but the ecclesiastic shall look on with singular attention, and some appearance of alarm; and the suspicion of Alice shall likewise be aroused. The old Hospitaller may have gained his situation partly by proving himself a man of the neighborhood, by right of descent; so that he, too, shall have a hereditary claim to be in the Romance.

Eldredge's own position as a foreigner in the midst of English home life, insulated and dreary, shall represent to Middleton, in some degree, what his own would be, were he to accept the estate. But Middleton shall not come to the decision to resign it, without having to repress a deep yearning for that sense of long, long rest in an age-consecrated home, which he had felt so deeply to be the happy lot of Englishmen. But this ought to be rejected, as not belonging to his country, nor to the age, nor any longer possible.

May 19th, Wednesday.—The connection of the old Hospitaller with the story is not at all clear. He is an American by birth, but deriving his English origin from the neighborhood of the Hospital, where he has finally established himself. Some one of his ancestors may have been somehow connected with the ancient portion of the story. He has been a friend of Middleton's father, who reposed entire confidence in him, trusting him with all his fortune, which the Hospitaller risked in his enormous speculations, and lost it all. His fame had been great in the financial world. There were circumstances that made it dangerous for his whereabouts to be known, and so he had come hither and found refuge in this institution, where Middleton finds him, but does not know who he is. In the vacancy of a mind formerly so active, he has taken to the study of local antiquities; and from his former intimacy with Middleton's father, he has a knowledge of the American part of the story, which he connects with the English portion, disclosed by his researches here; so that he is quite aware that Middleton has claims to the estate, which might be urged successfully against the present possessor. He is kindly disposed towards the son of his friend, whom he had so greatly injured; but he is now very old, and ———. Middleton has been directed to this old man, by a friend in America, as one likely to afford him all possible assistance in his researches; and so he seeks him out and forms an acquaintance with him, which the old man encourages to a certain extent, taking an evident interest in him, but does not disclose himself; nor does Middleton suspect him to be an American. The characteristic life of the Hospital is brought out, and the individual character of this old man, vegetating here after an active career, melancholy and miserable; sometimes torpid with the slow approach of utmost age; sometimes feeble, peevish, wavering; sometimes shining out with a wisdom resulting from originally bright faculties, ripened by experience. The character must not be allowed to get vague, but, with gleams of romance, must yet be kept homely and natural by little touches of his daily life.

As for Alice, I see no necessity for her being anywise related to or connected with the old Hospitaller. As originally conceived, I think she may be an artist—a sculptress—whom Eldredge had known in Rome. No; she might be a granddaughter of the old Hospitaller, born and bred in America, but who had resided two or three years in Rome in the study of her art, and have there acquired a knowledge of the Eldredges and have become fond of the little Italian girl his daughter. She has lodgings in the village, and of course is often at the Hospital, and often at the Hall; she makes busts and little statues, and is free, wild, tender, proud, domestic, strange, natural, artistic; and has at bottom the characteristics of the American woman, with the principles of the strong-minded sect; and Middleton shall be continually puzzled at meeting such a phenomenon in England. By and by, the internal influence [evidence?] of her sentiments (though there shall be nothing to confirm it in her manner) shall lead him to charge her with being an American.

Now, as to the arrangement of the Romance;—it begins as an integral and essential part, with my introduction, giving a pleasant and familiar summary of my life in the Consulate at Liverpool; the strange species of Americans, with strange purposes, in England, whom I used to meet there; and, especially, how my countrymen used to be put out of their senses by the idea of inheritances of English property. Then I shall particularly instance one gentleman who called on me on first coming over; a description of him must be given, with touches that shall puzzle the reader to decide whether it is not an actual portrait. And then this Romance shall be offered, half seriously, as the account of the fortunes that he met with in his search for his hereditary home. Enough of his ancestral story may be given to explain what is to follow in the Romance; or perhaps this may be left to the scenes of his intercourse with the old Hospitaller.

The Romance proper opens with Middleton's arrival at what he has reason to think is the neighborhood of his ancestral home, and here he makes application to the old Hospitaller. Middleton shall be described as approaching the Hospital, which shall be pretty literally copied after Leicester's, although the surrounding village must be on a much smaller scale of course. Much elaborateness may be given to this portion of the book. Middleton shall have assumed a plain dress, and shall seek to make no acquaintances except that of the old Hospitaller; the acquaintance of Alice naturally following. The old Hospitaller and he go together to the old Hall, where, as they pass through the rooms, they find that the proprietor is flitting like a ghost before them from chamber to chamber; they catch his reflection in a glass, etc., etc. When these have been wrought up sufficiently, shall come the scene in the wood, where Eldredge is seen yielding to the superstition that he has inherited, respecting the old secret of the family, on the discovery of which depends the enforcement of his claim to a title. All this while, Middleton has appeared in the character of a man of no note; and now, through some political change, not necessarily told, he receives a packet addressed to him as an ambassador, and containing a notice of his appointment to that dignity. A paragraph in the "Times" confirms the fact, and makes it known in the neighborhood. Middleton immediately becomes an object of attention; the gentry call upon him; the Mayor of the neighboring county-town invites him to dinner, which shall be described with all its antique formalities. Here he meets Eldredge, who is surprised, remembering the encounter in the wood; but passes it all off, like a man of the world, makes his acquaintance, and invites him to the Hall. Perhaps he may make a visit of some time here, and become intimate, to a certain degree, with all parties; and here things shall ripen themselves for Eldredge's attempt upon his life.

THE END

About Author

Nathaniel Hawthorne (**Hathorne**; July 4, 1804 – May 19, 1864) was an American novelist, dark romantic, and short story writer. His works often focus on history, morality, and religion.

He was born in 1804 in Salem, Massachusetts, to Nathaniel Hathorne and the former Elizabeth Clarke Manning. His ancestors include John Hathorne, the only judge involved in the Salem witch trials who never repented of his actions. He entered Bowdoin College in 1821, was elected to Phi Beta Kappa in 1824, and graduated in 1825. He published his first work in 1828, the novel Fanshawe; he later tried to suppress it, feeling that it was not equal to the standard of his later work. He published several short stories in periodicals, which he collected in 1837 as Twice-Told Tales. The next year, he became engaged to Sophia Peabody. He worked at the Boston Custom House and joined Brook Farm, a transcendentalist community, before marrying Peabody in 1842. The couple moved to The Old Manse in Concord, Massachusetts, later moving to Salem, the Berkshires, then to The Wayside in Concord. The Scarlet Letter was published in 1850, followed by a succession of other novels. A political appointment as consul took Hawthorne and family to Europe before their return to Concord in 1860. Hawthorne died on May 19, 1864, and was survived by his wife and their three children.

Much of Hawthorne's writing centers on New England, many works featuring moral metaphors with an anti-Puritan inspiration. His fiction works are considered part of the Romantic movement and, more specifically, dark romanticism. His themes often center on the inherent evil and sin of humanity, and his works often have moral messages and deep psychological complexity. His published works include novels, short stories, and a biography of his college friend Franklin Pierce, the 14th President of the United States.

Biography

Early life

Nathaniel Hawthorne was born on July 4, 1804, in Salem, Massachusetts;

his birthplace is preserved and open to the public. William Hathorne was the author's great-great-great-grandfather. He was a Puritan and was the first of the family to emigrate from England, settling in Dorchester, Massachusetts, before moving to Salem. There he became an important member of the Massachusetts Bay Colony and held many political positions, including magistrate and judge, becoming infamous for his harsh sentencing. William's son and the author's great-great-grandfather John Hathorne was one of the judges who oversaw the Salem witch trials. Hawthorne probably added the "w" to his surname in his early twenties, shortly after graduating from college, in an effort to dissociate himself from his notorious forebears. Hawthorne's father Nathaniel Hathorne Sr. was a sea captain who died in 1808 of yellow fever in Suriname; he had been a member of the East India Marine Society. After his death, his widow moved with young Nathaniel and two daughters to live with relatives named the Mannings in Salem, where they lived for 10 years. Young Hawthorne was hit on the leg while playing "bat and ball" on November 10, 1813, and he became lame and bedridden for a year, though several physicians could find nothing wrong with him.

In the summer of 1816, the family lived as boarders with farmers before moving to a home recently built specifically for them by Hawthorne's uncles Richard and Robert Manning in Raymond, Maine, near Sebago Lake. Years later, Hawthorne looked back at his time in Maine fondly: "Those were delightful days, for that part of the country was wild then, with only scattered clearings, and nine tenths of it primeval woods." In 1819, he was sent back to Salem for school and soon complained of homesickness and being too far from his mother and sisters. He distributed seven issues of The Spectator to his family in August and September 1820 for the sake of having fun. The homemade newspaper was written by hand and included essays, poems, and news featuring the young author's adolescent humor.

Hawthorne's uncle Robert Manning insisted that the boy attend college, despite Hawthorne's protests. With the financial support of his uncle, Hawthorne was sent to Bowdoin College in 1821, partly because of family connections in the area, and also because of its relatively inexpensive tuition rate. Hawthorne met future president Franklin Pierce on the way to

Bowdoin, at the stage stop in Portland, and the two became fast friends. Once at the school, he also met future poet Henry Wadsworth Longfellow, future congressman Jonathan Cilley, and future naval reformer Horatio Bridge. He graduated with the class of 1825, and later described his college experience to Richard Henry Stoddard:

> I was educated (as the phrase is) at Bowdoin College. I was an idle student, negligent of college rules and the Procrustean details of academic life, rather choosing to nurse my own fancies than to dig into Greek roots and be numbered among the learned Thebans.

Early career

In 1836, Hawthorne served as the editor of the American Magazine of Useful and Entertaining Knowledge. At the time, he boarded with poet Thomas Green Fessenden on Hancock Street in Beacon Hill in Boston. He was offered an appointment as weigher and gauger at the Boston Custom House at a salary of $1,500 a year, which he accepted on January 17, 1839. During his time there, he rented a room from George Stillman Hillard, business partner of Charles Sumner. Hawthorne wrote in the comparative obscurity of what he called his "owl's nest" in the family home. As he looked back on this period of his life, he wrote: "I have not lived, but only dreamed about living." He contributed short stories to various magazines and annuals, including "Young Goodman Brown" and "The Minister's Black Veil", though none drew major attention to him. Horatio Bridge offered to cover the risk of collecting these stories in the spring of 1837 into the volume Twice-Told Tales, which made Hawthorne known locally.

Marriage and family

While at Bowdoin, Hawthorne wagered a bottle of Madeira wine with his friend Jonathan Cilley that Cilley would get married before Hawthorne did. By 1836, he had won the bet, but he did not remain a bachelor for life. He had public flirtations with Mary Silsbee and Elizabeth Peabody, then he began pursuing Peabody's sister, illustrator and transcendentalist Sophia Peabody. He joined the transcendentalist Utopian community at Brook Farm in 1841, not because he agreed with the experiment but because it helped him save money to marry Sophia. He paid a $1,000 deposit and was put in charge of shoveling the hill of manure referred to as "the Gold Mine". He left later that year, though his Brook Farm adventure became an inspiration for his novel The Blithedale Romance. Hawthorne married Sophia Peabody on July 9, 1842, at a ceremony in the Peabody parlor on West Street in Boston. The couple moved to The Old Manse in Concord, Massachusetts, where they lived for three years. His neighbor Ralph Waldo Emerson invited him into his social circle, but Hawthorne was almost pathologically shy and stayed silent at gatherings. At the Old Manse, Hawthorne wrote most of the tales collected in Mosses from an Old Manse.

Like Hawthorne, Sophia was a reclusive person. Throughout her early life, she had frequent migraines and underwent several experimental medical treatments. She was mostly bedridden until her sister introduced her to Hawthorne, after which her headaches seem to have abated. The Hawthornes enjoyed a long and happy marriage. He referred to her as his "Dove" and wrote that she "is, in the strictest sense, my sole companion; and I need no other—there is no vacancy in my mind, any more than in my heart ... Thank God that I suffice for her boundless heart!" Sophia greatly admired her husband's work. She wrote in one of her journals:

> I am always so dazzled and bewildered with the richness, the depth, the ... jewels of beauty in his productions that I am always looking forward to a second reading where I can ponder and muse and fully take in the miraculous wealth of thoughts.

Poet Ellery Channing came to the Old Manse for help on the first anniversary of the Hawthornes' marriage. A local teenager named Martha Hunt had drowned herself in the river and Hawthorne's boat Pond Lily was needed to find her body. Hawthorne helped recover the corpse, which he described as "a spectacle of such perfect horror ... She was the very image of death-agony". The incident later inspired a scene in his novel The Blithedale Romance.

The Hawthornes had three children. Their first was daughter Una, born March 3, 1844; her name was a reference to The Faerie Queene, to the displeasure of family members. Hawthorne wrote to a friend, "I find it a very sober and serious kind of happiness that springs from the birth of a child ... There is no escaping it any longer. I have business on earth now, and must look about me for the means of doing it." In October 1845, the Hawthornes moved to Salem. In 1846, their son Julian was born. Hawthorne wrote to his sister Louisa on June 22, 1846: "A small troglodyte made his appearance here at ten minutes to six o'clock this morning, who claimed to be your nephew." Daughter Rose was born in May 1851, and Hawthorne called her his "autumnal flower".

Middle years

In April 1846, Hawthorne was officially appointed the Surveyor for the District of Salem and Beverly and Inspector of the Revenue for the Port of Salem at an annual salary of $1,200. He had difficulty writing during this period, as he admitted to Longfellow:

> I am trying to resume my pen ... Whenever I sit alone, or walk alone, I find myself dreaming about stories, as of old; but these forenoons in the Custom House undo all that the afternoons and evenings have done. I should be happier if I could write.

This employment, like his earlier appointment to the custom house in Boston, was vulnerable to the politics of the spoils system. Hawthorne was a Democrat and lost this job due to the change of administration in Washington after the presidential election of 1848. He wrote a letter of protest to the Boston Daily Advertiser which was attacked by the Whigs and supported by the Democrats, making Hawthorne's dismissal a much-talked about event in New England. He was deeply affected by the death of his mother in late July, calling it "the darkest hour I ever lived". He was appointed the corresponding secretary of the Salem Lyceum in 1848. Guests who came to speak that season included Emerson, Thoreau, Louis Agassiz, and Theodore Parker.

Hawthorne returned to writing and published The Scarlet Letter in mid-March 1850, including a preface that refers to his three-year tenure in the Custom House and makes several allusions to local politicians—who did not appreciate their treatment. It was one of the first mass-produced books in America, selling 2,500 volumes within ten days and earning Hawthorne $1,500 over 14 years. The book was pirated by booksellers in London and became a best-seller in the United States; it initiated his most lucrative period as a writer. Hawthorne's friend Edwin Percy Whipple objected to the novel's "morbid intensity" and its dense psychological details, writing that the book "is therefore apt to become, like Hawthorne, too painfully anatomical in his exhibition of them", though 20th-century writer D. H. Lawrence said that there could be no more perfect work of the American imagination than The Scarlet Letter.

Hawthorne and his family moved to a small red farmhouse near Lenox, Massachusetts, at the end of March 1850. He became friends with Herman Melville beginning on August 5, 1850, when the authors met at a picnic hosted by a mutual friend. Melville had just read Hawthorne's short story collection Mosses from an Old Manse, and his unsigned review of the collection was printed in The Literary World on August 17 and August 24 titled "Hawthorne and His Mosses". Melville wrote that these stories revealed a dark side to Hawthorne, "shrouded in blackness, ten times black". He was composing his novel Moby-Dick at the time, and dedicated the work in 1851 to Hawthorne: "In token of my admiration for his genius, this book is inscribed to Nathaniel Hawthorne."

Hawthorne's time in the Berkshires was very productive. While there, he wrote The House of the Seven Gables (1851), which poet and critic James Russell Lowell said was better than The Scarlet Letter and called "the most valuable contribution to New England history that has been made." He also wrote The Blithedale Romance (1852), his only work written in the first person. He also published A Wonder-Book for Girls and Boys in 1851, a collection of short stories retelling myths which he had been thinking about writing since 1846. Nevertheless, poet Ellery Channing reported that Hawthorne "has suffered much living in this place". The family enjoyed the scenery of the Berkshires, although Hawthorne did not enjoy the winters in their small house. They left on November 21, 1851. Hawthorne noted, "I am sick to death of Berkshire ... I have felt languid and dispirited, during almost my whole residence."

The Wayside and Europe

In May 1852, the Hawthornes returned to Concord where they lived until July 1853. In February, they bought The Hillside, a home previously inhabited by Amos Bronson Alcott and his family, and renamed it The Wayside. Their neighbors in Concord included Emerson and Henry David Thoreau. That year, Hawthorne wrote The Life of Franklin Pierce, the campaign biography of his friend which depicted him as "a man of peaceful pursuits". Horace Mann said, "If he makes out Pierce to be a great man or a brave man, it will be the greatest work of fiction he ever wrote." In the biography, Hawthorne depicts Pierce as a statesman and soldier who had accomplished no great feats because of his need to make "little noise" and so "withdrew into the background". He also left out Pierce's drinking habits, despite rumors of his alcoholism, and emphasized Pierce's belief that slavery could not "be remedied by human contrivances" but would, over time, "vanish like a dream".

With Pierce's election as President, Hawthorne was rewarded in 1853 with the position of United States consul in Liverpool shortly after the publication of Tanglewood Tales. The role was considered the most lucrative foreign service position at the time, described by Hawthorne's wife as "second in dignity to the Embassy in London". His appointment ended in 1857 at the close of the Pierce administration, and the Hawthorne family toured France and Italy. During his time in Italy, the previously clean-shaven Hawthorne grew a bushy mustache.

The family returned to The Wayside in 1860, and that year saw the publication of The Marble Faun, his first new book in seven years. Hawthorne admitted that he had aged considerably, referring to himself as "wrinkled with time and trouble".

Later years and death

At the outset of the American Civil War, Hawthorne traveled with William D. Ticknor to Washington, D.C., where he met Abraham Lincoln and other notable figures. He wrote about his experiences in the essay "Chiefly About War Matters" in 1862.

Failing health prevented him from completing several more romance novels. Hawthorne was suffering from pain in his stomach and insisted on a recuperative trip with his friend Franklin Pierce, though his neighbor Bronson Alcott was concerned that Hawthorne was too ill. While on a tour of the White Mountains, he died in his sleep on May 19, 1864, in Plymouth, New Hampshire. Pierce sent a telegram to Elizabeth Peabody asking her to inform Mrs. Hawthorne in person. Mrs. Hawthorne was too saddened by the news to handle the funeral arrangements herself. Hawthorne's son Julian was a freshman at Harvard College, and he learned of his father's death the next day; coincidentally, he was initiated into the Delta Kappa Epsilon fraternity on the same day by being blindfolded and placed in a coffin. Longfellow wrote a tribute poem to Hawthorne published in 1866 called "The Bells of Lynn". Hawthorne was buried on what is now known as "Authors' Ridge" in Sleepy Hollow Cemetery, Concord, Massachusetts. Pallbearers included Longfellow, Emerson, Alcott, Oliver Wendell Holmes Sr., James Thomas Fields, and Edwin Percy Whipple. Emerson wrote of the funeral: "I thought there was a tragic element in the event, that might be more fully rendered—in the painful solitude of the man, which, I suppose, could no longer be endured, & he died of it."

His wife Sophia and daughter Una were originally buried in England. However, in June 2006, they were reinterred in plots adjacent to Hawthorne.

Writings

Hawthorne had a particularly close relationship with his publishers William Ticknor and James Thomas Fields. Hawthorne once told Fields, "I care more for your good opinion than for that of a host of critics." In fact, it was Fields who convinced Hawthorne to turn The Scarlet Letter into a novel rather than a short story. Ticknor handled many of Hawthorne's personal matters, including the purchase of cigars, overseeing financial accounts, and even purchasing clothes. Ticknor died with Hawthorne at his side in Philadelphia in 1864; according to a friend, Hawthorne was left "apparently dazed".

Literary style and themes

Hawthorne's works belong to romanticism or, more specifically, dark romanticism, cautionary tales that suggest that guilt, sin, and evil are the most inherent natural qualities of humanity. Many of his works are inspired by Puritan New England, combining historical romance loaded with symbolism and deep psychological themes, bordering on surrealism. His depictions of the past are a version of historical fiction used only as a vehicle to express common themes of ancestral sin, guilt and retribution. His later writings also reflect his negative view of the Transcendentalism movement.

Hawthorne was predominantly a short story writer in his early career. Upon publishing Twice-Told Tales, however, he noted, "I do not think much of them," and he expected little response from the public. His four major romances were written between 1850 and 1860: The Scarlet Letter (1850), The House of the Seven Gables (1851), The Blithedale Romance (1852) and The Marble Faun (1860). Another novel-length romance, Fanshawe, was published anonymously in 1828. Hawthorne defined a romance as being radically different from a novel by not being concerned with the possible or probable course of ordinary experience. In the preface to The House of the Seven Gables, Hawthorne describes his romance-writing as using "atmospherical medium as to bring out or mellow the lights and deepen and enrich the shadows of the picture". The picture, Daniel Hoffman found, was one of "the primitive energies of fecundity and creation."

Critics have applied feminist perspectives and historicist approaches to Hawthorne's depictions of women. Feminist scholars are interested particularly in Hester Prynne: they recognize that while she herself could not be the "destined prophetess" of the future, the "angel and apostle of the coming revelation" must nevertheless "be a woman." Camille Paglia saw Hester as mystical, "a wandering goddess still bearing the mark of her Asiatic origins ... moving serenely in the magic circle of her sexual nature". Lauren Berlant termed Hester "the citizen as woman [personifying] love as a quality of the body that contains the purest light of nature," her resulting "traitorous political theory" a "Female Symbolic" literalization of futile Puritan metaphors. Historicists view Hester as a protofeminist and avatar of the self-reliance and responsibility that led to women's suffrage and reproductive emancipation. Anthony Splendora found her literary genealogy among other archetypally fallen but redeemed women, both historic and mythic. As examples, he offers Psyche of ancient legend; Heloise of twelfth-century France's tragedy involving world-renowned philosopher Peter Abelard; Anne Hutchinson (America's first heretic, circa 1636), and Hawthorne family friend Margaret Fuller. In Hester's first appearance, Hawthorne likens her, "infant at her bosom", to Mary, Mother of Jesus, "the image of Divine Maternity". In her study of Victorian literature, in which such "galvanic outcasts" as Hester feature prominently, Nina Auerbach went so far as to name Hester's fall and subsequent redemption, "the novel's one unequivocally religious activity". Regarding Hester as a deity figure, Meredith A. Powers found in Hester's characterization "the earliest in American fiction that the archetypal Goddess appears quite graphically," like a Goddess "not the wife of traditional marriage, permanently subject to a male overlord"; Powers noted "her syncretism, her flexibility, her inherent ability to alter and so avoid the defeat of secondary status in a goal-oriented civilization".

Aside from Hester Prynne, the model women of Hawthorne's other novels—from Ellen Langton of Fanshawe to Zenobia and Priscilla of The Blithedale Romance, Hilda and Miriam of The Marble Faun and Phoebe and Hepzibah of The House of the Seven Gables—are more fully realized than his male characters, who merely orbit them. This observation is equally true of his short-stories, in which central females serve as allegorical figures: Rappaccini's beautiful but life-altering, garden-bound, daughter; almost-perfect Georgiana of "The Birthmark"; the sinned-against (abandoned) Ester of "Ethan Brand"; and goodwife Faith Brown, linchpin of Young Goodman Brown's very belief in God. "My Faith is gone!" Brown exclaims in despair upon seeing his wife at the Witches' Sabbath. Perhaps the most sweeping statement of Hawthorne's impetus comes from Mark Van Doren: "Somewhere, if not in the New England of his time, Hawthorne unearthed the image of a goddess supreme in beauty and power."

Hawthorne also wrote nonfiction. In 2008, the Library of America selected Hawthorne's "A show of wax-figures" for inclusion in its two-century retrospective of American True Crime.

Criticism

In "Hawthorne and His Mosses", Herman Melville wrote a passionate argument for Hawthorne to be among the burgeoning American literary canon, "He is one of the new, and far better generation of your writers." In this review of Mosses from an Old Manse, Melville describes an affinity for Hawthorne that would only increase: "I feel that this Hawthorne has dropped germinous seeds into my soul. He expands and deepens down, the more I contemplate him; and further, and further, shoots his strong New-England roots into the hot soil of my Southern soul." Edgar Allan Poe wrote important reviews of both Twice-Told Tales and Mosses from an Old Manse. Poe's assessment was partly informed by his contempt of allegory and moral tales, and his chronic accusations of plagiarism, though he admitted,

> The style of Mr. Hawthorne is purity itself. His tone is singularly effective—wild, plaintive, thoughtful, and in full accordance with his themes ... We look upon him as one of the few men of indisputable genius to whom our country has as yet given birth.

Ralph Waldo Emerson wrote, "Nathaniel Hawthorne's reputation as a writer is a very pleasing fact, because his writing is not good for anything, and this is a tribute to the man." Henry James praised Hawthorne, saying, "The fine thing in Hawthorne is that he cared for the deeper psychology, and that, in his way, he tried to become familiar with it." Poet John Greenleaf Whittier wrote that he admired the "weird and subtle beauty" in Hawthorne's tales. Evert Augustus Duyckinck said of Hawthorne, "Of the American writers destined to live, he is the most original, the one least indebted to foreign models or literary precedents of any kind."

Contemporary response to Hawthorne's work praised his sentimentality and moral purity while more modern evaluations focus on the dark psychological complexity. Beginning in the 1950s, critics have focused on symbolism and didacticism.

The critic Harold Bloom opined that only Henry James and William Faulkner challenge Hawthorne's position as the greatest American novelist, although he admitted that he favored James as the greatest American novelist.

Bloom saw Hawthorne's greatest works to be principally The Scarlet Letter, followed by The Marble Faun and certain short stories, including "My Kinsman, Major Molineux", "Young Goodman Brown", "Wakefield", and "Feathertop". (Source: Wikipedia)

NOTABLE WORKS

NOVELS

Fanshawe (published anonymously, 1828)

The Scarlet Letter (1850)

The House of the Seven Gables (1851)

The Blithedale Romance (1852)

The Marble Faun: Or, The Romance of Monte Beni (1860) (as Transformation: Or, The Romance of Monte Beni, UK publication, same year)

The Dolliver Romance (1863) (unfinished)

Septimius Felton; or, the Elixir of Life (unfinished, published in the Atlantic Monthly, 1872)

Doctor Grimshawe's Secret: A Romance (unfinished, with preface and notes by Julian Hawthorne, 1882)

SHORT STORY COLLECTIONS

Twice-Told Tales (1837)

Grandfather's Chair (1840)

Mosses from an Old Manse (1846)

A Wonder-Book for Girls and Boys (1851)

The Snow-Image, and Other Twice-Told Tales (1852)

Tanglewood Tales (1853)

The Dolliver Romance and Other Pieces (1876)

The Great Stone Face and Other Tales of the White Mountains (1889)

SELECTED SHORT STORIES

"The Hollow of the Three Hills" (1830)

"Roger Malvin's Burial" (1832)

"My Kinsman, Major Molineux" (1832)

"The Minister's Black Veil" (1832)

"Young Goodman Brown" (1835)

"The Gray Champion" (1835)

"The White Old Maid" (1835)

"Wakefield" (1835)

"The Ambitious Guest" (1835)

"The Man of Adamant" (1837)

"The May-Pole of Merry Mount" (1837)

"The Great Carbuncle" (1837)

"Dr. Heidegger's Experiment" (1837)

"A Virtuoso's Collection" (May 1842)

"The Birth-Mark" (March 1843)

"The Celestial Railroad" (1843)

"Egotism; or, The Bosom-Serpent" (1843)

"Earth's Holocaust" (1844)

"Rappaccini's Daughter" (1844)

"P.'s Correspondence" (1845)

"The Artist of the Beautiful" (1846)

"Fire Worship" (1846)

"Ethan Brand" (1850)

"The Great Stone Face" (1850)

"Feathertop" (1852)

NONFICTION

Twenty Days with Julian & Little Bunny (written 1851, published 1904)

Our Old Home (1863)

Passages from the French and Italian Notebooks (1871)